Language Policy

Volume 18

Series Editor
Joseph Lo Bianco, University of Melbourne, Melbourne, Australia
Terrence G. Wiley, Arizona State University, Tempe, USA

Editorial Board
Claire Kramsch, University of California, Berkeley, USA
Georges Lüdi, University of Basel, Basel, Switzerland
Normand Labrie, University of Toronto, Toronto, Canada
Anne Pakir, National University of Singapore, Singapore
John Trim, Former Fellow, Selwyn College, Cambridge, UK
Guadalupe Valdes, Stanford University, Stanford, USA

The last half century has witnessed an explosive shift in language diversity not unlike the Biblical story of the Tower of Babel, but involving now a rapid spread of global languages and an associated threat to small languages. The diffusion of global languages, the stampede towards English, the counter-pressures in the form of ethnic efforts to reverse or slow the process, the continued determination of nation-states to assert national identity through language, and, in an opposite direction, the greater tolerance shown to multilingualism and the increasing concern for language rights, all these are working to make the study of the nature and possibilities of language policy and planning a field of swift growth.

The series will publish empirical studies of general language policy or of language education policy, or monographs dealing with the theory and general nature of the field. We welcome detailed accounts of language policy-making - who is involved, what is done, how it develops, why it is attempted. We will publish research dealing with the development of policy under different conditions and the effect of implementation. We will be interested in accounts of policy development by governments and governmental agencies, by large international companies, foundations, and organizations, as well as the efforts of groups attempting to resist or modify governmental policies. We will also consider empirical studies that are relevant to policy of a general nature, e.g. the local effects of the developing European policy of starting language teaching earlier, the numbers of hours of instruction needed to achieve competence, selection and training of language teachers, the language effects of the Internet. Other possible topics include the legal basis for language policy, the role of social identity in policy development, the influence of political ideology on language policy, the role of economic factors, policy as a reflection of social change.

The series is intended for scholars in the field of language policy and others interested in the topic, including sociolinguists, educational and applied linguists, language planners, language educators, sociologists, political scientists, and comparative educationalists.

More information about this series at http://www.springer.com/series/6209

David E. DeMatthews • Elena Izquierdo
Editors

Dual Language Education: Teaching and Leading in Two Languages

Editors
David E. DeMatthews
Department of Educational Leadership & Policy
University of Texas at Austin
Austin, TX, USA

Elena Izquierdo
Department of Teacher Education
University of Texas at El Paso
El Paso, TX, USA

ISSN 1571-5361 ISSN 2452-1027 (electronic)
Language Policy
ISBN 978-3-030-10830-4 ISBN 978-3-030-10831-1 (eBook)
https://doi.org/10.1007/978-3-030-10831-1

© The Editor(s) (if applicable) and The Author(s) 2019
This work is subject to copyright. All rights are reserved by the Publisher, whether the whole or part of the material is concerned, specifically the rights of translation, reprinting, reuse of illustrations, recitation, broadcasting, reproduction on microfilms or in any other physical way, and transmission or information storage and retrieval, electronic adaptation, computer software, or by similar or dissimilar methodology now known or hereafter developed.
The use of general descriptive names, registered names, trademarks, service marks, etc. in this publication does not imply, even in the absence of a specific statement, that such names are exempt from the relevant protective laws and regulations and therefore free for general use.
The publisher, the authors, and the editors are safe to assume that the advice and information in this book are believed to be true and accurate at the date of publication. Neither the publisher nor the authors or the editors give a warranty, express or implied, with respect to the material contained herein or for any errors or omissions that may have been made. The publisher remains neutral with regard to jurisdictional claims in published maps and institutional affiliations.

This Springer imprint is published by the registered company Springer Nature Switzerland AG.
The registered company address is: Gewerbestrasse 11, 6330 Cham, Switzerland

David E. DeMatthews: *I dedicate this book to all the district and school leaders, teachers, community activists, and families in the El Paso region. Their tireless efforts, sense of hope, and willingness to challenge themselves create new possibilities for the region's students. I am especially lucky to have benefited from countless hours of conversations with my graduate students who are knowledgeable about bilingual education and passionate about creating more equitable schools. Moreover, local principals and teachers in the community have provided me with rich understandings of dual-language education through sharing their rich stories, experiences, and expertise. Without these interactions, this book would not be possible. Lastly, I dedicate this book to Elena Izquierdo who has been my mentor, teacher, colleague, partner in research, advocate, and friend. Her tireless effort, depth of knowledge, and tenaciousness have inspired me to find practitioner-oriented relevance in all my endeavors as a researcher and scholar.*

Elena Izquierdo: *I dedicate this book to my parents – my father, an immigrant from Mexico, and my mother, a first-generation Mexican American – who throughout my life showed me the importance of our rich cultural and linguistic assets, which are the tapestry of who we are and what matters. Collectively, our lived experiences guided and gave me purpose to persist in the advocacy of others who continue to face many of the sociocultural, linguistic, and academic challenges pervasive in schooling and addressed in this book. Just as important is the invaluable collaboration provided by district leaders, principals, teachers, and parents in this El Paso borderplex who gave their time and shared their stories. Lastly, I want to express my sincere gratitude to my esteemed colleague, David DeMatthews, whose tireless commitment to our research and work and incredible passion for social justice have made this book a reality.*

Preface

The demographics of public schools in the United States continue to change as the nation becomes more racially, culturally, and linguistically diverse. Unfortunately, many states, districts, and schools struggle to provide a high-quality education that meets the social, emotional, and academic needs of students, particularly students of color whose first language is not English. Racial, economic, and linguistic achievement gaps persist despite more than 50 years after the passage of the *Bilingual Education Act* of 1968. Students of color remain disproportionately identified into special education and removed from classrooms and neighborhood schools. Administrators and teachers have sometimes labeled students of color as "testing liabilities," deemed them "deficient" and "in need of intervention." They are frequently pushed into lower academic tracks, provided narrower and less culturally relevant curricula, and sometimes exit school altogether. Low-income parents of color and parents in immigrant communities are often looked down upon by educators and viewed as disinterested in their child's education or unable to successfully fulfill the duties of a parent (Valencia & Black, 2002).

Racist discourses in American society suggest that students of color who struggle or fail in school do so because of their internal deficits which are manifested through their limited intellectual abilities, lack of motivation, immoral behavior, problematic culture, and deficient family and community experiences (Valencia, 2010). Many scholars, both presently and in the past century, explain this phenomenon through sociological and Marxist critiques of public schools. Schools are social institutions that elevate the norms and values of dominant groups at the expense of non-dominant groups (Anyon, 1980; Bowles & Gintis, 2011). The dominant group has been White, male, middle-class, and monolingual English speakers. Variance from the dominant group is considered problematic and in need of an "intervention" or "remedy." From this perspective, any language other than English is viewed as a problem, especially in low-income Spanish-speaking immigrant communities (Ruiz, 1984).

Racism and discrimination directed toward non-dominant groups in the United States are arguably less overt and subtler but still deeply ingrained in the institutions, practices, and taken-for-granted assumptions. Principals, teachers, and staff may not recognize that they view students whose first language is not English through a deficit lens, but their daily routines, practices, and skillsets (or lack thereof) may unknowingly reproduce a schooling experience that disadvantages racially and linguistically diverse students of color. Moreover, many university teacher and principal preparation programs are ill-prepared to educate a majority White and monolingual English-speaking teacher workforce to understand the unique and important cultural and linguistic assets many students of color and of diverse linguistic backgrounds bring to school each day. This is a missed opportunity, because as a result of a narrow and a critical teacher and principal preparation curriculum, these educators and leaders are likely to judge their students' standardized test scores or other traditional schooling indicators as the child and family's failure rather than on their own (DeMatthews, 2018; Valencia, 2010). They cannot see how increasing student achievement and family engagement needs to be addressed by rethinking school structures and instructional practices, developing new forms of professional development that promote cultural responsiveness, adopting curriculum and instruction aligned to students' needs and interests, and establishing a more welcoming, inclusive, and inquiry-oriented school culture. The limited foresight of traditionally prepared educators and school leaders and the many other challenges that face public schools are complex, multifaceted, and not easily resolved. However, now more than ever, educators and school leaders need to recognize their students' assets, learn to teach and lead in new and more adaptive ways, and foster a school-community environment that is inclusive and focused on truly improving the lives of their students.

While civil rights activists, critical educators, politicians and scholars of color, and other community-based advocates have long argued for schooling to recognize the unique assets of racially and linguistically diverse students, the demographics of today's schools necessitate a shift in public education more than ever. The percentage of public school students identified as "English Language Learners" (ELLs) makes up approximately 4.6 million or 9.4 percent of total student enrollment nationwide (National Center for Education Statistics (NCES), 2016). The population of ELLs is growing nationally in 35 of the 50 states over the past 10 years. California (22.4%), Nevada (17%), Texas (15.5%), and Illinois (10.3%) student populations are well above the national average. Spanish is the most commonly reported home language of ELLs as more than 3.7 million or 77.1% of ELLs speak the language at home (NCES, 2016). In the 2014–2015 school year, about 3.7 million ELLs were Hispanic. Arabic, Chinese, and Vietnamese were the next most common languages.

Students who are identified as ELLs are enrolled in language assistant programs to help them attain "English proficiency" and meet the state-level academic achievement standards commonly measured through standardized tests. Education language policies and the implementation of these policies are not always reflective of educational research recommendations or student needs but instead the social and political perspectives related to race, class, and immigration status. For example, in Arizona, Proposition 203, or the "English for the Children," passed in 2000 led to the dismantling of research-based bilingual education programs and to an English immersion model that has not achieved academic results or reflected a genuine belief that all students have assets, including their family's language (Gándara & Orfield, 2012). States, districts, and schools often fail to equitably distribute learning opportunities and meaningful school resources to schools within majority Latinx communities. In Texas, districts with large populations of ELLs have been disproportionately impacted by recessionary budget cuts (Alemán, 2007; Knight & DeMatthews, 2017). Curriculum, instructional practices, and social interactions between schools and students and families frequently fail to value and incorporate Latinx immigrant communities' input, culture, history, and linguistic assets (Gandara & Contreras, 2009; Valenzuela, 1999). The lack of inclusiveness in curricula, teaching practices, and school-family interactions is concerning, especially considering how researchers have identified multiple forms of capital that Latinx students acquire from their families and communities that can be used to increase student achievement (Araujo & de la Piedra, 2013; Delgado Bernal, 2002; Yosso, 2005). Consequently, Latinx students, including those who are classified as ELLs, tend to perform poorly on standardized tests and are less likely to graduate, go to college, and gain access to professional jobs in comparison to their White and monolingual English-speaking peers (López & McEneaney, 2012).

Dual Language Education: Teaching and Leading in Two Languages provides a comprehensive and interdisciplinary examination of dual-language education for Latinx ELLs in the United States, with a particular focus on the state of Texas. The book is broken into three parts. We use the term Latinx rather than Latino because it is gender-neutral.[1] Part I examines how Latinx ELLs have been historically underserved in public schools and how this has contributed to persistent educational inequities. Part II examines bilingualism, biliteracy, and dual-language education as an effective model for addressing the inequities identified in Part I. Part III examines research on dual-language education in a large urban school district, a high-performing elementary school that serves a high proportion of Mexican American students learning English and Spanish along the Texas-Mexico border, and best practices for principals, teachers, and preparation programs.

The contributors to this book include internationally recognized educational researchers and scholars, activists and professional developers, and leaders of nonprofit organizations and campaigns to improve public education in districts and schools that serve high proportions of Latinx students from immigrant families and communities. *Dual Language Education: Teaching and Leading in Two Languages* was developed to provide scholars, educators, policymakers, and graduate students with a comprehensive and interdisciplinary examination of the education of Latinx students learning English and Spanish simultaneously and the efficacy of dual-language education. The editors of this book, David DeMatthews and Elena Izquierdo, are faculty in a principal and teacher preparation programs at the University of Texas at Austin and the University of Texas at El Paso. Both work as educational consultants and researchers in several districts serving high proportions of Latinx ELLs. Before developing this book, we found that a broad range of

---

[1] Some authors in this book utilize Latina/Latino instead of Latinx.

interested stakeholders failed to grasp the complexity of dual-language education. Superintendents, school board members, and graduate students have asked for a resource that could help them understand not only issues of practice associated with teaching or leadership but of the larger sociopolitical and legal factors that make developing, implementing, and maintaining dual-language education so challenging. Thus, the book has been developed and organized based on the following premises:

- The historical context, shortcomings, and disastrous effects of subtractive education models and deficit-oriented approaches to educating Latinx ELLs must be understood and challenged.
- Dual-language education is more than a program but instead a comprehensive school model that values families and communities and is focused on the development of students' unique cultural and linguistic assets.
- District- and school-level leadership and highly trained and culturally responsive teachers are prerequisites to creating inclusive, high-quality dual-language schools that meet the needs of all students. Educator and school leader pipelines need to be improved to supply the capacity needed to provide students from Latinx immigrant families and communities with the schools they need to be successful.

Labeling Students, Families, and Communities

No one word, classification, or category can accurately describe a group of students because each student, her or his family, and their lived experiences are unique and multifaceted. Contributors in this book describe Latinx students who are learning English using several terms, including English-language learners (ELLs), English learner students (ELs), bilingual students, dual-language learners (DLLs), and emergent bilinguals (EBs).[2] Many debate the underlying meanings and impact of any term used to classify students. However, the limited English proficiency (LEP) term is clearly deficit-oriented and disregards the importance of linguistic diversity and bilingualism. We reject any such classification or framing of any student group. We will not define children based on their standardized language proficiency scores. Some contributors use the term English-language learner or English learner student. Some critics argue that such terms assume a monolingual English-speaking student is the norm (see Palmer & Martínez, 2013). What we believe is most important, regardless of labels, is that researchers and educators value the cultural and linguistic assets of students, families, and communities. We also believe it is important that individuals recognize how Latinx students and other students of color have been undervalued, undereducated, and subjected to pervasive social inequalities.

---

[2] We refer to *emergent bilingual* to describe students who are engaged in learning Spanish and English.

Whenever we use a singular term to describe a group of students, we do violence to them because no term can reflect the unique identity of a student, family, or community. While we all use labels, categories, and classifications to succinctly communicate ideas and describe phenomenon in education and society, all the contributors in this book are committed to social justice and to valuing all students.

Summary of Chapters

Dual Language Education: Teaching and Leading in Two Languages offers a multidimensional analysis of dual-language education that considers academic, legal, political, sociocultural, and economic aspects of language policy and the work of pre-K-12 educators and leaders. The book offers an important focus on Latinx ELLs in the state of Texas and along the US-Mexico border while also highlighting research, challenges, perspectives, and best practices from other US states. Contributors explore the educational experiences and outcomes of Latinx ELLs, the politics and policies that impact how this student population is educated, models of dual-language education and best practices in teaching and leadership, and challenges confronted by students, families, leaders, and educators seeking to create more socially just schools. Examples of effective leadership and instructional practices are embedded within the book.

Part I examines how Latinx ELLs have been historically underserved in public schools and how this has contributed to numerous educational inequities. The chapters in this section cover language education policy, funding, special education, assessment, and curriculum with a focus on identifying the challenges to creating inclusive, high-quality, and equitable schools. In chapter, "Injustice and Redemption: The Education of Latinx Emergent Bilinguals," David E. DeMatthews and Elena Izquierdo introduce the volume, which includes a background to racial injustice in the state of Texas with a focus on Mexican American immigrant communities. The chapter also provides a discussion of Latinx students and their needs, a Latinx critical race theory framework to consider inequities confronting Latinx students in education, and a brief discussion of the efficacy of dual-language education.

In chapter, "Bilingual Education Policy in Texas: Promise and Lost Opportunities," David G. Hinojosa describes the federal laws and landmark court cases that have hindered and/or supported the education of Latinx ELLs, bilingual education, and dual-language education at the national level and in the state of Texas. The chapter makes connections to relevant cases and school funding policies in other states as a tool for comparison and to broaden the reader's understanding of law and policy related to the topic. This chapter also provides a history of legal disputes inside the state of Texas that is foundational for understanding why Latinx ELLs are so underserved by public schools, including the most recent Texas school finance case that highlighted significant funding inequities for districts serving high populations of Latinx ELLs.

In chapter, "Compounded Inequities: Tracking School Finance Equity for Districts Serving Low-Income Emergent Bilinguals," David S. Knight and Jesus E. Mendoza focus on school finance in the state of Texas. Districts confront different costs to produce the same level of educational opportunity because of differences in student population, geographical costs of living, and district size. School finance systems in many states fail to take these factors into account when distributing funds to school districts. Knight and Mendoza present the first longitudinal descriptive evidence of the extent to which state school finance systems compound inequities for districts serving high concentrations of both low-income students and ELLs. The chapter also assesses the extent to which high-ELL high-poverty districts are underfunded relative to otherwise similar districts in the same state and how these trends have changed leading up to and following the recession-era spending cuts. Findings suggest that prior to the recession, high-ELL districts received greater funding levels than otherwise similar low-ELL districts in the same state. However, recessionary spending cuts disproportionately impacted funding for ELLs. The remaining resource advantages for high-ELL districts are concentrated in low-poverty districts. These findings are consistent across measures of funding, expenditures, and staffing ratios.

In chapter, "Assessment and English Language Learners in Special Education," Edgar M. Torres Ovando, Danika L. S. Maddocks, and Angela Valenzuela examine assessment, special education, and ELLs in the state of Texas. While this chapter is not directly related to dual-language education, many Latinx ELLs are also students with disabilities and impacted by state assessment policies. We could not ignore the importance of assessment, special education, and ELLs in any discussion of dual-language education in US schools without recognizing this important but under-researched topic. This chapter provides an overview of key issues in the assessment of students with disabilities and ELLs as well as considerations for "fair assessments." First, the authors describe the special education population in the nation and Texas in terms of educational placement, assessment participation, educational outcomes, and misidentification of Latinx ELLs. Next, a historical overview of high-stakes assessments in Texas shows the participation and performance of students with disabilities on these assessments over time. Then, the chapter provides a critique of the current high-stakes assessment system and reviews research-based suggestions to improve the assessment of students with disabilities within the current framework, paying special attention to the negative impact these assessments have on ELL students. Finally, a proposal to adopt an authentic, performance-based assessment system for Texas is presented.

In chapter, "To Want the Unwanted: Latinx English Language Learners on the Border," Reynaldo Reyes III describes the impact of neoliberalism and high-stakes accountability on Latinx ELLs. One of the many consequences of the No Child Left Behind Act and other high-stakes accountability policies has been that some teachers and administrators have resorted to the systematic removal of vulnerable student groups, such as Latinx ELLs. This process has dehumanized students and dismissed aspects of their identity, such as language, and deemed them disposable in the pursuit of high test scores. Reyes III highlights how a critical pedagogy centered on a more just and humanizing education can empower educators of Latinx youth. Dual-language education is offered as a key component of a more just and humanizing education.

In Part II, "Bilingualism, Biliteracy, and Dual Language Education," chapters examine bilingualism, biliteracy, and dual-language education as an effective model for addressing the inequities identified in Part I. This collection of chapters examines foundational aspects of dual-language education, early childhood education and language development, the importance of biliteracy and translanguaging, and the need for schools and school leaders to build meaningful relationships with Latinx communities. In chapter, "Dual Language Education for All," Wayne P. Thomas and Virginia P. Collier provide an introductory overview and analysis of research on dual-language education models, to include 1-way, 2-way; 50-50, 90-10; 1 teacher, 2 teacher; and effective implementation associated with school leadership, instruction and assessment, and parent-community engagement. They provide additional insights from decades of studying dual-language education in Texas, North Carolina, and elsewhere in the United States. Thomas and Collier's chapter provides important foundational knowledge and an overview of how the effective implementation of dual-language education can have powerful effects on student achievement.

In chapter, "A More Comprehensive Perspective in Understanding the Development and Learning in Dual Language Learners," Eugene E. García examines early learning for Latinx ELLs and the significance of dual-language education learning opportunities as they are related to future academic achievement. This chapter highlights the importance of early childhood learning experiences, parent engagement, and school-family relationships. The chapter concludes with recommendations for district and school policies and models that can support early learning and address long-term racial and linguistic achievement gaps.

In chapter, "Biliteracy and Translanguaging in Dual-Language Bilingual Education," Susana Ibarra Johnson, Ofelia García, and Kate Seltzer focus on biliteracy and translanguaging. Using translanguaging as a resource has the potential to transform biliteracy instruction in dual-language bilingual education (DLBE). In a flexible model of biliteracy, the students' full repertoire of resources is used to interact with texts that are written in different named languages as they think, discuss, interact with, and produce written texts. Johnson, García, and Seltzer provide an example of this flexible model of biliteracy from a case study involving a third-grade dual-language bilingual teacher. The teacher designed a translanguaging space to create more holistic ways of doing biliteracy that allowed students to use their full linguistic repertoire for literacy performances. To do this, the teacher's *stance* about keeping the two languages in her DLBE class separate first had to change. She started consciously integrating what students were learning to do during English literacy and social studies instruction into her Spanish literacy instruction. She then designed a translanguaging instructional and assessment space she called *Los círculos*. In that classroom space, students take what they have learned across other content areas in instructional spaces dedicated to English and Spanish and do biliteracy juntos.

In chapter, "Preparing Leaders for Latina/o Academic and Language Success: Frameworks, Perspectives, and Strategies," Juan Manuel Niño and Enrique Alemán Jr. argue that school leaders need to address deficiencies in their leadership practice, especially with regard to their relationships and social interactions with Latinx students and families. Despite the increased enrollment of students of color in Texas schools, many school leaders still need to become more knowledgeable and pedagogically prepared to serve the needs of diverse students. This chapter highlights how school practices are not equitably serving all students and how state mandates often fail to incorporate an emphasis on diversity. In this chapter, the authors offer practical strategies and frameworks to facilitate a change process in schools and communities. School leaders can adopt these strategies and frameworks to foster a more socially just educational experience for students of color.

In Part III, "Leading the Way to Dual Language," chapters examine research on dual-language education in a large urban school district and a high-performing elementary school that serves a high proportion of ELLs along the Texas-Mexico border. These chapters also include best practices for principals and teachers. In chapter, "Dual Language for All: Central Office Leadership in the El Paso Independent School District," Elena Izquierdo, David E. DeMatthews, David Knight, and James Coviello describe how the El Paso Independent School District (EPISD) engaged in practices to address past injustices against Mexican and Mexican American students through the implementation of district-wide dual-language education for all ELLs. EPISD provided a strategic and important site for this study because the previous superintendent and administration were part of a large-scale cheating scandal that "disappeared" hundreds of Mexican and Mexican American students. This chapter highlights the important role of the district and superintendent in supporting equity-oriented school reforms such as dual-language education. The chapter also describes specific actions and values pertinent to leadership at the district level and provides insights into how superintendents can take advantage of political opportunities, frame educational injustices in ways that mobilize key stakeholders, and utilize networks and grassroots movements to achieve social justice ends.

In chapter, "Leading Dual Language: Twenty Years of Innovation in a Borderland Elementary School," Elena Izquierdo, David E. DeMatthews, Estefania Balderas, and Becca Gregory present a qualitative case study of authentic and social justice leadership of one exemplary bilingual principal working along the US-Mexico border. The principal at the center of this study nurtured, inspired, and motivated teachers and families to create innovative and inclusive school programs to meet the needs of all students, especially Mexican American ELLs. Two micro-cases are presented to examine the principal's role in founding a gifted and talented dual-language program for ELLs and a merger with a low-performing school. The study's key findings highlight how the principal developed strategic relationships to advocate for the needs of Latinx students and families. This chapter draws attention to areas where authentic and advocacy-oriented approaches to leadership can mitigate resistance from dominant groups. Implications for future research and principal preparation are discussed at the conclusion of the chapter.

In chapter, "A School Leadership Framework for Dual Language," David E. DeMatthews, Elena Izquierdo, and Stephen Kotok argue that calls for social justice are a key aspect of principal preparation but have failed to meaningfully incorporate content related to the efficacy of dual-language education. They draw upon scholarship focused on dual-language education, social justice leadership, and the Professional Standards for Educational Leadership (National Policy Board for Educational Administration, 2015) to describe how principals can create dual-language schools and lead in ways that support Latinx ELLs, their families, and immigrant communities.

In chapter, "The Challenges of Recruiting and Retaining Dual Language Teachers," Elizabeth Howard and Angela M. López-Velásquez examine dual-language education teacher recruitment and retention. This chapter provides a brief literature of key issues surrounding teacher recruitment and retention and includes findings from a qualitative research study focused on dual-language teacher recommendations for recruitment and retention. Teacher recommendations included strong university-district partnerships, proactive solutions to addressing certification challenges confronting Spanish-speaking teachers, and streamlining the certification process by incorporating it into preservice teacher education programs. Teachers in this study also emphasized the importance of workplace climate, administrative support, and opportunities to participate in meaningful professional development that is specific to dual-language education. Lastly, teachers emphasized the need to address the pressure of staff evaluations and high-stakes accountability, especially with relation to monolingual state assessments.

In chapter, "Implications for the Future," David E. DeMatthews and Elena Izquierdo review the purposes and goals of the book, point to key contributions of each chapter, and present important takeaways for social scientists as well as teachers, principals, superintendents, policymakers, and graduate students. The conclusion also makes broader connections between policies, laws, and practices in Texas to other states as well as highlights national themes, shifting demographics, and national political winds that impact Latinx ELLs and dual-language education.

Austin, TX, USA   David E. DeMatthews
El Paso, TX, USA   Elena Izquierdo

References

Alemán, E. (2007). Situating Texas school finance policy in a CRT framework: How "substantially equal" yields racial inequity. *Educational Administration Quarterly, 43*(5), 525–558.
Anyon, J. (1980). Social class and the hidden curriculum of work. *Journal of Education, 162*(1), 67–92.
Araujo, B., & de la Piedra, M. T. (2013). Violence on the US–Mexico border and the capital students use in response. *International Journal of Qualitative Studies in Education, 26*(3), 263–278.

Bowles, S., & Gintis, H. (2011). *Schooling in capitalist America: Educational reform and the contradictions of economic life*. New York, NY: Haymarket Books.

Bernal, D. D. (2002). Critical race theory, Latino critical theory, and critical raced-gendered epistemologies: Recognizing students of color as holders and creators of knowledge. *Qualitative Inquiry*, 8(1), 105–126.

DeMatthews, D. E. (2018). *Community engaged leadership for social justice. A critical approach in urban schools*. New York, NY: Routledge.

Gándara, P., & Orfield, G. (2012). Segregating Arizona's English learners: A return to the "Mexican room"? *Teachers College Record*, 114(9), 1–27.

Knight, D. S., & DeMatthews, D. E. (2017). *Assessing the educational opportunity of emergent bilingual students: Why are some state school finance systems more equitable than others?* Working Papers. 1. Retrieved from http://digitalcommons.utep.edu/cerps_wp/1

López, F., & McEneaney, E. (2012). State implementation of language acquisition policies and reading achievement among Hispanic students. *Educational Policy*, 26(3), 418–464.

National Center for Education Statistics. (2016). *Common Core of Data (CCD), "Local Education Agency Universe Survey," 2014–15. Digest of Education Statistics 2016*, table 204.20. Washington, DC: US Department of Education.

National Policy Board for Educational Administration. (2015). *Professional standards for educational leaders 2015*. Reston, VA: Author.

Palmer, D., & Martínez, R. A. (2013). Teacher agency in bilingual spaces: A fresh look at preparing teachers to educate Latinx bilingual children. *Review of Research in Education*, 37(1), 269–297. https://doi.org/10.3102/0091732X12463556

Ruiz, R. (1984). Orientations in language planning. *NABE Journal*, 8(2), 15–34.

Valencia, R. R. (2010). *Dismantling contemporary deficit thinking: Educational thought and practice*. New York, NY: Routledge.

Valencia, R. R., & Black, M. S. (2002). "Mexican Americans don't value education!" On the basis of the myth, mythmaking, and debunking. *Journal of Latinos and Education*, 1(2), 81–103.

Valenzuela, A. (1999). *Subtractive schooling: Issues of caring in education of US-Mexican youth*. Albany, NY: State University of New York Press.

Yosso, T. J. (2005). Whose culture has capital? A critical race theory discussion of community cultural wealth. *Race, Ethnicity and Education*, 8(1), 69–91.

Acknowledgments

David E. DeMatthews: This book has been inspired by the work and advocacy of its contributors as well as the authors, researchers, and activists referenced throughout the text. I am truly thankful for their efforts and insights into dual-language education and how to create more inclusive, culturally responsive, and socially just schools. Special thanks to the El Paso Independent School District (EPISD) for being a partner in teaching and research and to its principals and teachers who inspired us to develop this book. Juan Cabrera and Anabel Tanabe and many other current and former EPISD educators and leaders have provided us with time, resources, and opportunities to learn about dual-language education.

Elena Izquierdo: The development of this book would not have been possible without the dedication, enthusiasm, expertise, and collaboration of all of its contributors. Their professional, academic, and personal experiences have provided the context for prioritizing what matters in changing the discourse in politics and practices for marginalized populations. A special recognition goes to district leaders Ivonne Durant and Laila Ferris who gave of their time and who opened their doors to this invaluable district-university partnership, a collaboration that allowed for countless conversations, interviews, observations, and professional growth in their district. Their passion, dedication, tenacity, and knowledge provide a foundation for creating high-quality dual-language schools that value cultural and linguistic diversity and operationalize social justice.

Contents

Injustice and Redemption: The Education of Latinx Emergent Bilinguals.. 1
David E. DeMatthews and Elena Izquierdo

Part I Setting the "State": The Old and Subtractive Ways Haven't Worked

Bilingual Education Policy in Texas: Promise and Lost Opportunities.... 19
David G. Hinojosa

Compounded Inequities: Tracking School Finance Equity for Districts Serving Low-Income Emergent Bilingual Students........ 35
David S. Knight and Jesus E. Mendoza

Assessment and English Language Learners in Special Education... 57
Edgar M. Torres Ovando, Danika L. S. Maddocks, and Angela Valenzuela

To Want the Unwanted: Latinx English Language Learners on the Border... 77
Reynaldo Reyes III

Part II Bilingualism, Biliteracy, and Dual Language Education

Dual Language Education for All............................... 91
Wayne P. Thomas and Virginia P. Collier

A More Comprehensive Perspective in Understanding the Development and Learning in Dual Language Learners 107
Eugene E. García

Biliteracy and Translanguaging in Dual-Language Bilingual Education 119
Susana Ibarra Johnson, Ofelia García, and Kate Seltzer

Preparing Leaders for Latina/o Academic and Language Success: Frameworks, Perspectives and Strategies. 133
Juan Manuel Niño and Enrique Alemán Jr.

Part III   Leading the Way to Dual Language Education

Dual Language for All: Central Office Leadership in the El Paso Independent School District. 149
Elena Izquierdo, David E. DeMatthews, David S. Knight, and James Coviello

Leading Dual Language: Twenty Years of Innovation in a Borderland Elementary School 163
Elena Izquierdo, David E. DeMatthews, Estefania Balderas, and Becca Gregory

A School Leadership Framework for Dual Language. 181
David E. DeMatthews, Elena Izquierdo, and Stephen Kotok

The Challenges of Recruiting and Retaining Dual Language Teachers 195
Elizabeth Howard and Angela M. López-Velásquez

Implications for the Future 209
Elena Izquierdo and David E. DeMatthews

About the Editors and Contributors

Editors

David E. DeMatthews is an associate professor in the Department of Educational Leadership and Policy at the University of Texas at Austin. He has worked with urban districts as a high school teacher, middle school administrator, and district administrator. His research interests include K-12 school leadership, dual-language education, urban education, and social justice. His work has appeared in top-tier peer-reviewed research journals such as *Educational Administration Quarterly*, *Teachers College Record*, *Urban Education*, *Journal of School Leadership*, and *Leadership and Policy in Schools*, as well as in the mainstream media in *Education Week*, *USA Today*, *The Baltimore Sun*, *The Texas Tribune*, *Houston Chronicle*, and the *El Paso Times*. David has recently authored a book, *Community Engaged Leadership for Social Justice: A Critical Approach in Urban Schools*, with Routledge.

Elena Izquierdo is an associate professor of teacher education at the University of Texas at El Paso. Her research interests focus on biliteracy, dual language, and transforming schools/districts for English-language learner (ELL) success. She works with many teachers, principals, administrators, and school board members in shaping the schooling trajectory of ELLs. Her work has appeared in a number of edited volumes on dual-language education as well as in *Urban Education*, *Journal of Latinos and Education*, *The Educational Forum*, *Education Policy Analysis Archives*, *Journal of School Leadership*, and *Journal of Cases in Educational Leadership*. Elena has served as an expert witness in the Mexican American Legal Defense and Educational Fund (MALDEF) finance case for ELLs in the state of Texas and is a former principal of one of the nation's first dual-language schools and director of bilingual education in the District of Columbia Public Schools.

Contributors

Enrique Alemán Jr. is professor and chair in the Department of Educational Leadership and Policy Studies at the University of Texas at San Antonio. His research focuses on addressing the racialized and institutionalized inequities that have historically underserved students and communities of color, and his research agenda includes studying the impact of educational policies on Latina/Latino and Chicana/Chicano students and communities.

Estefania Balderas is a grant coordinator for Project LEAD at the University of Texas at El Paso (UTEP). She is completing a Master's in Curriculum and Instruction in Bilingual Education at UTEP in May 2018. She plans to work as a teacher in a local public school district implementing dual language and will begin a PhD in Teaching, Learning, and Culture with a focus on literacy and biliteracy in the near future.

Virginia P. Collier is professor emerita of bilingual/multicultural/English as a second language (ESL) education at George Mason University in Fairfax, Virginia, located in the metropolitan area of Washington, DC. She is best known for her work with senior researcher, Dr. Wayne Thomas, on school effectiveness for linguistically and culturally diverse students, working with many school districts in all regions of the United States over the past 28 years. Since 1988, Drs. Thomas and Collier have been regularly interviewed by the popular media, with 180 published newspaper articles and interviews on television and radio in the United States and abroad, reporting on their research findings. A popular speaker, Dr. Collier has given 221 keynote speeches and 437 invited and refereed presentations to international, national, state, and local conferences over the past 33 years. She and Dr. Thomas have also conducted educational leadership training for superintendents, principals, and education policymakers in 31 US states and 15 countries.

James Coviello is an assistant professor in the Department of Educational Leadership at Saint Joseph's University in Philadelphia, Pennsylvania. His research focuses on the interaction of leadership, decision-making, and policy implementation, particularly related to the superintendency. Before pursuing his doctorate, James was a classroom teacher for 10 years in New York and New Jersey.

Eugene E. García is presently professor emeritus at Arizona State University (ASU). From 2002 to 2006, he was the dean of the Mary Lou Fulton Teachers College on the Tempe campus of ASU. From 2006 to 2011, he was professor and vice-president for education partnerships at ASU. Before joining ASU, he served as professor and dean of the Graduate School of Education at the University of California, Berkeley, from 1995 to 2001. He has been a recipient of a National Kellogg Leadership Fellowship and received numerous academic and public honors. Dr. García is involved in various community activities and has served as an elected member of an urban school board. He served as a senior officer in the US Department of Education from 1993 to 1995. He has been honored by the American Educational Research Association (AERA), Society for Research in Child Development (SRCD), National Association for the Education of Young Children (NAEYC), Association for Supervision and Curriculum (ASCD), and American Association of Hispanics in Higher Education (AAHHE) for his research contributions, and in May 2011, he received an Honorary Doctorate of Letters from Erikson Institute, Chicago, in recognition of his contributions to the area of child development. Most recently, he was appointed to the Board on Children, Youth, and Families of the Institute of Medicine and the National Research Council.

Ofelia García is a professor in the urban education and Hispanic literatures and languages PhD programs at the Graduate Center, City University of New York (CUNY). García has published extensively on bilingualism and the education of bilingual children. Her work is grounded in her experience after leaving Cuba at the age of 11, teaching language minority students bilingually, and educating bilingual and English as a second-language teacher in New York City and internationally.

Becca Gregory is a PhD student in the Sociocultural Foundations of Education Program at the University of Texas at El Paso. Her research focuses on issues surrounding autism, special education, special education law and policy, social justice, and Latinx communities. She has presented her work at several national and international research conferences and has worked with various local Autism Advisory and Advocacy boards that focus on community involvement, education, and awareness.

David G. Hinojosa, JD is a leading litigator and advocate in the area of civil rights, with a focus on educational civil rights impact litigation and policy. He currently practices education law with Walsh Gallegos, P.C. in their New Mexico Office. Previously, Mr. Hinojosa served as a staff attorney, senior litigator, and for 3 years, as Southwest Regional Counsel, directing the office's litigation and policy work for the Mexican American Legal Defense and Educational Fund (MALDEF), the nation's premier Latino civil rights law firm. Mr. Hinojosa's litigation work included the representation of English learner (EL) students in language rights, school finance, and school desegregation cases. As the Intercultural Development Research Association's (IDRA's) first and former National Director of Policy, he supported the integration and coordination of national policy reform efforts impacting the education of all students, with special emphasis on students of color, low-income, EL, and recent immigrant populations. Mr. Hinojosa has published several book chapters, journal articles, and op-eds on educational opportunity policy and litigation in K-12 and higher education.

Elizabeth Howard is an associate professor of bilingual education in the Department of Curriculum and Instruction at the University of Connecticut (UConn). She is currently a co-investigator of Project WELLS (Writing for English Language

Learners), an exploratory study funded by the US Department of Education. Previously, she was a principal investigator of two federally funded studies – a vocabulary intervention for native Spanish-speaking adolescents and a longitudinal study focusing on the spelling development of Spanish/English bilingual children. She was also the co-director of a faculty learning community designed to build the capacity of teacher education faculty members to support preservice teachers' learning about emergent bilinguals. Prior to coming to UConn, she was a senior research associate with the Center for Applied Linguistics (CAL) in Washington, DC, where she directed a number of projects related to dual-language education and biliteracy development. In addition, she has worked as a bilingual elementary school teacher in California and Costa Rica and has also taught adult ESL and literacy courses as a Peace Corps volunteer in Costa Rica.

Susana Ibarra Johnson is an adjunct professor at the University of New Mexico in literacy and bilingual education. Her commitment to improving the education of bilingual students stems from her experience as a bilingual learner and teacher. For the past decade, she has been facilitating professional learning in bilingual education program implementation, critical literacy, and bilingual acquisition in New Mexico and nationally.

David S. Knight is an assistant professor at the University of Washington. His work focuses on equity in school finance and resource allocation, educator labor markets, and cost-effectiveness analysis. He received his PhD in Urban Education Policy and MA in Economics from the University of Southern California and Bachelor's Degrees in Economics and Anthropology from the University of Kansas.

Stephen Kotok is an assistant professor in the Department of Administrative and Instructional Leadership at St. John's University. His research focuses on how schools act as stratifying mechanisms or as levers of opportunity for low-income and minority students. Specifically, Kotok examines issues of school-level leadership such as school climate, school community, and detracking as well as policy-level equity issues such as school choice, resource allocation, and segregation. His recent work has appeared in the *American Journal of Education*, *Educational Policy*, and *The High School Journal*.

Angela M. López-Velásquez is an associate professor in the Department of Special Education at Southern Connecticut State University. Her research and teaching interests include literacy development of bilingual learners, preparation of teachers to work with bilingual learners, and the needs of bilingual learners with disabilities. Her most recent work has appeared in the *Bilingual Research Journal* and in *Reading and Writing*: An Interdisciplinary Journal.

Danika L. S. Maddocks is a doctoral student studying School Psychology at the University of Texas at Austin. Before beginning graduate school, Danika taught elementary school and middle school English in the San Francisco Bay Area. Her major research interests include the identification and support of students who are gifted or twice exceptional and the creation of classroom climates that are motivating and responsive to students' social-emotional needs.

Juan Manuel Niño, PhD is an associate professor in the Department of Educational Leadership and Policy Studies at the University of Texas at San Antonio. His research, which takes a critical perspective on the practice of education and leadership in multiple contexts, addresses issues of justice, equity, and excellence in education for diverse communities and the Latin@ experiences that influence identity and advocacy. Centering on the importance of research and practice, Dr. Niño co-coordinates the Urban School Leaders Collaborative programs that prepare aspiring school leaders for social justice.

Jesus E. Mendoza, MS is a research associate in the Center for Education Research and Policy Studies (CERPS) at the University of Texas at El Paso. His research at CERPS focuses on school finance.

Reynaldo Reyes III is associate professor of Bilingual, ESL, and Multicultural Education at the University of Texas at El Paso, El Paso, Texas.

Kate Seltzer is the current project director for City University of New York (CUNY), New York State Initiative on Emergent Bilinguals (NYSIEB). She holds a PhD in Urban Education from the CUNY Graduate Center. Kate has worked with teachers of emergent bilinguals as an instructor in the Bilingual/TESOL Department at CUNY and as a research assistant with the CUNY-NYSIEB project. She is coauthor of the recent book, *The Translanguaging Classroom: Leveraging Student Bilingualism for Learning*, with Ofelia García and Susana Ibarra Johnson. A former high school English Language arts teacher, her research interests include expanding traditionally English-medium spaces for bilingual students, particularly through shifts in curriculum and classroom design, and working with teachers to build on students' diverse language practices while also challenging their ideologies about these students and their ways of languaging.

Wayne P. Thomas is a specialist in program evaluation methodology and social science research methods who also has extensive experience in designing and developing computer software and databases for purposes of student testing, program evaluation, and educational data management. His research program and publications focus on the evaluation of at-risk student programs (especially programs for language minority students) and on educational technology applications. He is a former math/physics teacher, central-office school administrator, and school-based evaluation/research project manager who is now emeritus professor of Evaluation and Research Methods in the Graduate School of Education at George Mason University.

Edgar M. Torres Ovando is currently a doctoral student studying Education Policy and Planning in the Educational Policy and Leadership Department at the University of Texas at Austin. His research interests include assessments for English-language learners classified as special education students and Texas school finance policy and their impact on English-language learners. He holds a Bachelor of Arts Degree in History and Political Science and a Master of Education Degree in English as a Second Language from Texas A&M University-Kingsville. He has served as an elementary and middle school social studies and mathematics teacher and currently serves as the associate principal for Cedar Creek High School in Cedar Creek, Texas.

Angela Valenzuela is a professor in both the Educational Policy and Planning Program within the Department of Educational Administration at the University of Texas at Austin and holds a courtesy appointment in the Cultural Studies in Education Program within the Department of Curriculum and Instruction. She also serves as the director of the University of Texas Center for Education Policy. A Stanford University graduate, her previous teaching positions were in Sociology at Rice University in Houston, Texas (1990–1998), as well as a visiting scholar at the Center for Mexican American Studies at the University of Houston (1998–1999). She is also the author of *Subtractive Schooling: US-Mexican Youth and the Politics of Caring*. She also founded and operates an education blog titled *Educational Equity, Politics, and Policy in Texas*.

Injustice and Redemption: The Education of Latinx Emergent Bilinguals

David E. DeMatthews and Elena Izquierdo

Abstract This chapter introduces the volume by providing foundational knowledge related to bilingual education in the state of Texas with a focus on racial injustice in Mexican American immigrant communities. The chapter also provides a discussion of Latinx students and their academic needs, a Latinx critical race theory framework to consider inequities confronting Latinx children in public schools, and a brief overview of the efficacy of dual language education.

Keywords Dual language education · Latinx students · Immigrant communities · Latinx critical race theory · Critical race theory

Mexican and Mexican American students and other students of color across the state of Texas and nation have historically been forced to attend unequal schools that do not value their cultural and linguistic assets. The purpose of this chapter is threefold: (a) to provide foundational knowledge associated with the state of Texas and public education; (b) consider the unique assets and needs of Latinx students from immigrant communities and families; and (c) outline dual language as more than an effective educational approach, but also a holistic approach to addressing the persistent educational injustices that exist in many public schools. We begin with a brief historical overview of how the state of Texas has maintained unequal schools and limited the learning opportunities of students of color, with a particular focus on Latinx students, families, and communities. Next, we discuss the group of students at the center of this book, Latinx students who are learning English and, hopefully, continuing to learn and utilize Spanish in schools, at home, and in their

D. E. DeMatthews (✉)
Department of Educational Leadership and Policy, University of Texas at Austin, Austin, TX, USA
e-mail: ddematthews@austin.utexas.edu

E. Izquierdo
Department of Teacher Education, University of Texas at El Paso, El Paso, TX, USA
e-mail: ielena@utep.edu

communities. In this chapter, we use the term emergent bilingual to describe this group of students. Then, we concisely present critical race theory (CRT) and Latinx critical race theory (LatCrit), because both provide insights into understanding the challenges confronting Latinx students, families, and communities and how these challenges can be addressed in public education. Finally, we conclude with a discussion on the efficacy of dual language education for all students.

1 Texas-Style Injustice

In 1954, the United States Supreme Court rendered their decision in the landmark case, *Brown v Board of Education of Topeka*. Thurgood Marshall, a lawyer leading the National Association for the Advancement of Colored People's (NAACP) Legal Defense and Educational Fund argued to the Court that state-imposed segregation "was inherently discriminatory and therefore a denial of the Equal Protection Clause of the Fourteenth Amendment" (Patterson, 2001, p. 53). Chief Justice Warren read aloud the Court's unanimous decision, which rejected the "separate but equal" doctrine and noted the following: "To separate them [students of color] from others of similar age and qualifications solely because of their race generates a feeling of inferiority as to their status in the community that may affect their hearts and minds in a way unlikely ever to be undone" (*Brown v Board of Education of Topeka*, 1954). After the decision, several states and cities advanced integration while others made piecemeal attempts or tenaciously and violently resisted integration.

In 1971, plaintiff parents in El Paso, Texas filed a class action suit known as *Alvarado v. El Paso Independent School District* (EPISD) (1976). The suit alleged that EPISD operated a dual, segregated, and unequal school system for children of Mexican decent. Evidence of immigration patterns, residential segregation, school construction and attendance boundaries, bus routes, and school infrastructure were introduced to the court and reviewed as part of the decision. In 1976, a U.S. District Court held that "the parents had successfully demonstrated that the school district had effectuated intentionally segregation policies against Mexican-Americans" (*Alvarado v. EPISD,* 1976). The court also noted that EPISD historically and intentionally maintained "inferior facilities for Mexican-American students," which included unequal funding, poor building maintenance, overcrowding, inadequate playground and sports facilities, poor lighting conditions, significant physical deterioration of facilities, and constructing new schools in predominantly White areas before correcting deterioration elsewhere. The court also found gerrymandering of attendance zones to maintain racial segregation.

More federal intervention was necessary across Texas in the years to come. In 1978, the case of *Castañeda v. Pickard* (1981) was tried in a U.S. District Court. Roy Castañeda, a father of two Mexican American children in the Rio Grande Valley, claimed that the Raymondville Independent School District segregated his children and failed to provide a sufficient bilingual education program to support his children's academic development. In 1981, the U.S. Court of Appeals ruled in favor of Castañeda and set standards for the development, implementation, and monitoring of bilingual education programs. Also, in 1981, a different federal court found "proof of pervasive, invidious discrimination against Mexican-Americans throughout the State of Texas" (*United States v. Texas*, 1981). The judge's opinion in the case described in detail how Mexican-American students were marginalized, undereducated, and uniformly exposed to disrespect for their language and cultural.

> State and local education officials justified this practice of segregation, on the grounds that Mexican-American children spoke little English and were often late arriving at school because their families engaged in migrant labor...No attempt was made to meet the special educational needs of these children, who had limited proficiency with the English language... On the contrary, the "Mexican schools" were invariably overcrowded, and were inferior in all respects to those open exclusively to Anglo students... Mexican-American children were prohibited from speaking their native language anywhere on school grounds. Those who violated the "No Spanish" rule were severely punished... Rather than attempting to provide adequate schooling for Mexican-American children, Texas educators viewed public education as simply a vehicle for "Americanizing" the "foreign element"...Both the language and cultural heritage of these children were uniformly treated with intolerance and disrespect... Official publications of the Texas State Department of Education, the predecessor of TEA, reflected a policy of Anglo racial domination over Mexican-American people, their language, and culture (*United States v. State of Texas*, 1981).

In 1982, the U.S. Supreme Court ruled on the *Plyler v. Doe* (1982) case. The case was related to a 1975 Texas legislative act that authorized local school districts to deny enrollment in public schools to immigrant students who were not "legally admitted" to the U.S. The Tyler Independent School District adopted a policy requiring immigrant students not "legally admitted" to the U.S. to pay tuition. The district also required documentation showing foreign-born students were legally admitted to the U.S. or confirmation from federal immigration authorities. A group of undocumented students from Mexico and their families brought a class action lawsuit to challenge the district's policy. The U.S. Supreme Court based its ruling on the Equal Protection Clause of the Fourteenth Amendment and held in favor of the students. The Court ruled that the district had no rational basis for denying children public education based on their immigration status. In Justice Brennan's majority opinion, he noted, that the Fourteenth Amendment was "not confined to the protection of citizens. It says: 'Nor shall any state deprive any person life, liberty, or property without due process of law; nor deny any person within its jurisdiction the equal protection of the laws'" (Plyler v. Doe, 1982). Brennan described the state's policy as one that:

> imposes a lifetime hardship on a discrete class of children not accountable for their disabling status. The stigma of illiteracy will mark them for the rest of their lives. By denying these children a basic education, we deny them the ability to live within the structure of our civic institutions, and foreclose any realistic possibility that they will contribute in even the smallest way to the progress of our Nation. (*Plyler v. Doe,* 1982).

The Supreme Court's decision highlighted the state of Texas' disregard for immigrant children and ensured undocumented students could receive a free public education.

Injustice and inequality have been stubborn and difficult to eradicate even after Supreme Court victories. In some ways Texas public schools have improved since the 1970s and 1980s, but it would be naïve to think the legacy of racism, inequality, and language-as-problem orientation has disappeared. In 2011, more than 600 school districts sued the state after a $5.4 billion dollar cut from the public education. A Travis County judge sided with plaintiff school districts who underscored how big disparities between property-wealthy and property-poor school districts in funding only grew larger with the cut and made providing a high-quality education increasingly difficult. However, the Texas Supreme Court upheld the state's cuts and funding system as constitutional, while acknowledging the funding system is "undeniably imperfect, with immense room for improvement" (*Morath v Texas Taxpayer and Student Fairness Coalition*, 2016). The historic failure of Texas to equitably fund its public schools is not just about poverty, but rather a long history of denying Mexican and Mexican American students the opportunities to attend high-quality schools (Alemán, 2007).

More recently, in 2012, EPISD superintendent Lorenzo Garcia pled guilty to two counts of conspiracy to commit mail fraud related to high-stakes test rigging. One significant aspect of the alleged cheating scandal was that a group of EPISD district administrators and principals inappropriately kept low-performing students out of classrooms by improperly promoting, holding back, or preventing them from arriving for the state's tests or enrolling in school altogether (Weaver & Tidwell, 2013). An independent evaluation of the cheating scandal found "systemic noncompliance with both District policy and state law at the campus level" (Weaver & Tidwell, 2013, p. 80).

The report concluded that numerous district officials either encouraged cheating or looked the other way. The report noted the following:

> It is important to remember that for a period of some five and a half years, the District was run by a criminal. Garcia insulated and surrounded himself with willing accomplices, and his influence and reach were vast. The District has since suffered from a culture that has put desires and egos of adults over the needs of students. The culture has manifested in many forms, including the intentional manipulation of recognized subpopulations to avoid consequences…Long after Garcia's arrest and departure on August 1, 2011, many of these practices continued unabated…In the rush to avoid accountability consequences for inadequate graduation rates, many District high schools became credit mills and, eventually diploma mills, as unearned credits resulted in the graduation of ill-prepared students. These students are the victims of the culture Garcia promulgated, and it is not a culture easily undone. (p. 2–3).

The majority of the students targeted where of Mexican decent and many were classified as "limited English proficient."

2 Reflecting on Injustice

Schools in El Paso, Texas, like many others across the Texas and nation, have historically failed to provide a high-quality public education to Mexican-American students, students learning English, and other racially and culturally diverse groups.

Mexican-American students, many of whom are learning English, continue to be marginalized, viewed as liabilities, and pushed out of school. Past and recent events are not surprising, but such problems can be remedied moving forward if educators, administrators and policymakers are willing to recognize that schools too often fail to value the unique cultural and linguistic assets of diverse students, and as a result, reproduce inequalities that exist within our society. Schools must be understood as social institutions that reflect the values, norms, and beliefs of society (DeMatthews, 2018). Schools often act as sorting mechanisms that sift children of color and students who are economically disadvantaged into under-resourced classrooms with underprepared teachers that lead to drop out and low-paying jobs. When principals and teachers enter schools each day, they do not shed their cultural baggage or beliefs. Their leadership and teaching practices, what they value or do not, and their beliefs about race, class, language, disability, and gender do not change when the school bell rings. The past informs the present, society infects belief systems and consciousness, and racism has been an ever-present part of society, daily experiences, and public schools.

Despite the history of racial discrimination, we believe deeply in the potential of public education. We know there are caring, dedicated, professional, and engaged teachers and school leaders that seek to create classrooms and schools that transform the lives of students and families. Therefore, while we are critical of the status quo in Texas and the U.S., we argue that hope can help focus the necessary energy and reflection needed to transform schools to better serve all students. While we recognize schools have fallen short of one of their intended purposes as the "great equalizer," we refuse to ignore their potential for transformational change. We believe that transformation includes dual language education. Dual language education, as we will discuss later in this chapter, is not only about bilingualism, biliteracy, or cognitive benefits of knowing two languages, but about valuing the unique cultural and linguistic assets of students, families, and communities. Dual language education is about preparing students to live as citizens in the twenty-first century and recognizing students are far more than test scores and deserve to be valued for who they are and what they bring to the classroom each day. Dual language education validates identities of Latinx children and families. In sum, we believe dual language education can disrupt the history of racism and discrimination in our society and bring about public schools that prepare children for an inclusive, innovative, and multicultural twenty-first century (DeMatthews & Izquierdo, 2018b).

Our optimism for dual language education and our desire to develop this book became a reality when EPISD began considering how to "right past wrongs" (a topic covered in chapter "Dual Language for All: Central Office Leadership in the El Paso Independent School District"). EPISD, with the support of local community activists and educators, viewed the district's majority Mexican-American population as an asset. The district also began to see the border region's linguistic diversity as a strength. In 2014, the EPISD's board unanimously voted to adopt dual language education for all students classified as "limited English proficient" (DeMatthews, Izquierdo, & Knight, 2017). We began working with the district and their teachers and principals. Some teachers had experience working in bilingual education and had state certifications. Some principals saw the value of dual language education. However, overwhelmingly, all stakeholders (district personnel, principals, instructional coaches, teachers, parents) lacked a basic understanding about dual language education, its core principles, or relevant information, research, and expertise with regards to creating dual language education in their schools. We scrapped together resources, drew upon our past research and expertise, and began working with the district, but we soon recognized a need to find collaborators and a more diverse group of experts.

The value of collaboration and an interdisciplinary focus is the foundation of this book. Some of the individuals who have participated in authoring chapters in this book have visited El Paso and talked to teachers and staff in EPISD with respects to dual language education as well as recognizing and valuing Mexican American students, families, and communities. Others have been lifelong activists, educators, researchers, students and engaged citizens who care deeply about ensuring Latinx students and all children receive a high-quality, inclusive, and culturally-responsive education. Each collaborator provides expertise and a critical discussion on a topic that is directly related to dual language education.

3 The Students at the Center of This Book

We cannot discuss dual language education without knowing more about the students that can directly benefit from it. The United States has long been a destination for immigrants seeking access to increased economic and social opportunities. As of 2014, approximately 42.4 million immigrants were living in the U.S., which makes up a total of about 13.3% of the nation's population (Camarota & Zeigler, 2016). At no other time in history have more immigrants lived in the U.S and these numbers are reflective in public school enrollments. Approximately 11 million students, making up almost a quarter of all public school enrollment, are from immigrant households. The immigrant population hails primarily from Latin America (51%), mostly from Mexico (26.5%), El Salvador (3.2%), and other nearby Spanish-speaking countries (Migration Policy Institute, 2018). About 26% of all preschool-age Latinx children are born in the U.S., but about 46% of this group has at least one immigrant parent (Ackerman & Tazi, 2015). Immigration and the diversification of U.S. public schools has typically not been viewed as positive by politicians, policy-makers, administrators, and educators. Millions of Latinx students have been under-served and suffered from the effects of racism and discrimination. Many come from families that have escaped poverty and violence in search of another life. These families are resilient, passionate about education and the opportunity of a new start in the U.S. and want only the best for their children. The 2016 election of President Donald Trump catalyzed a surge of anti-immigration rhetoric, with a concentrated and negative focus on immigrants from Latin America.

In order to develop schools that meet the diverse needs of Latinx students and other diverse groups, it is necessary to examine the role of language and culture in schools. Valuing language and culture is essential and cannot be ignored in any educational policies, reforms, or practices. In this book, authors primarily focus on Latinx children. Latinx (or Hispanic) is defined by the U.S. Office of Management and Budget as "a person of Cuban, Mexican, Puerto Rican, South or Central American, or other Spanish culture or origin regardless of race" (U.S. Census, 2018). Latinx children generally comprise two groups with respect to language acquisition: (1) children who are immigrants or have parents who are immigrants, and who speak little or no English when they enter school and (2) children who speak only English or emergent bilingual children fluent in English with varied levels of Spanish language proficiency (Lindholm-Leary & Block, 2010). Both groups appear different in early grades, but over time, appear more alike in terms of academic achievement, graduation rates, and achievement gaps when compared with White, monolingual English-speaking peers (Collier & Thomas, 2004). These students come from homes and often entire communities where English is not the primary language spoken.

Latinx immigrant students may require additional time and instruction to develop English skills and learn the state's curriculum standards, but they may also need additional support learning the culture of dominant society as well as emotional support to address trauma stemming from their immigration experiences (Gándara & Rumberger, 2009). Latinx immigrant families often live on a limited income. Parents are more likely to work low-wage jobs, live in poverty and overcrowded households, and lack health insurance. Approximately 21% of immigrants and their U.S. born children live in poverty (Camarota & Zeigler, 2016). Relatedly, Latinx immigrant children frequently live in racially segregated communities and attend racially-segregated schools, which often lack effective teachers and sufficient resources (Orfield & Lee, 2005). Latinx students may also have linguistic needs that schools are unprepared to meet. Toddlers often exhibit smaller cognitive gains and perform lower on pre-literacy and mathematics assessments than their White and monolingual English-speaking peers (Fuller et al., 2009). They tend to enter kindergarten with reading and mathematics achievement gaps (Han, Lee, & Waldfogel, 2012) and continue to struggle on the National Educational Assessment of Progress (NAEP) and on state accountability measures (López, Scanlan, & Gundrum, 2013). As Latinx students struggle in schools and fall behind, they are at risk of internalizing failure, developing low-self-esteem, and begin to sense a lack of belonging in school which contributes to dropout (McNeil, Coppola, Radigan, & Vasquez Heilig, 2008).

Schools have historically fallen short of effectively educating Latinx students and meaningfully engaging their families and communities as partners. Two general arguments are frequently used to explain underperformance: (1) less academically successful students have difficulties because of their English language proficiency levels or (2) less academically successful students possess different skillsets, resulting in a mismatch between the students' skills and the skills required by the school (Hoff, 2013). Latinx students and particularly Mexican-American students living in immigrant communities have been viewed through a deficit lens by educators and policymakers. Rather than recognizing the institutional structures and inequitable schooling arrangements that maintain uneven educational outcomes, deficit-thinkers link academic failure to a student's alleged cognitive abilities and motivations (Valencia, 2012). Latinx students can be viewed as un-educable because of racist and classist perceptions of their families and low-socioeconomic backgrounds.

The way the underperformance is understood by teachers, school leaders, and policymakers as well as how they frame and understand language has important implications for the educational policies and instructional practices that are advanced. Some claim that speaking a language other than English is a problem or believe that English proficiency should be a primary focus and prioritized among all other subjects and areas. As Richard Ruiz (1984) noted 35 years ago, a "language-as-problem" orientation exists in the U.S. reflected in how non-English language speakers have been viewed as at-risk and in need of intervention. From a language-as-problem orientation, English-only instruction, immersion, or transitional bilingual education is required to remediate students who lack English proficiency. The underlying theory of action is that cultural and linguistic assimilation will benefit students who lack English language proficiency. In other words, the quicker a child becomes proficient in English, the better off he or she will do in the long-run. Maintaining one's family language may be beneficial, but not necessarily emphasized or required. Longitudinal research fails to support the efficacy of English immersion (Slavin & Cheung, 2005).

The U.S. has a long history of viewing non-English speakers as a problem. Language diversity is often linked to social problems, which include poverty, limited social mobility, and lower student achievement. In the 1960s, programs were developed to "treat" students who did not speak English. The Bilingual Education Act of 1968 and subsequent state education policies initiated an assumption that non-English speaking students needed to overcome their limited English proficiency (Ruiz, 1984). The "language problem" was overcome by teaching English, even if it was at the expense of the student's first language or education. Subsequent court decisions and policies supported the language-as-problem orientation and continue to do so in many states, districts, and schools across the country.

4 Understanding Injustice and Repositioning Schools

Court decisions, cheating scandals, segregated and unequal schools, and chronic educational underperformance cannot be explained or understood without racism. In mainstream society and in schools, Mexican Americans (students, families, communities) and other Latinx groups are sometimes viewed as problematic, dangerous, lazy, inferior, disinterested and in need of fixing via educational and social policies (Valenzuela, 2010). These forms of individual prejudice support institutional and societal forms of racism with implications on public schools, the opportunities provided to Latinx students, and the educational and long-term outcomes that are likely for children as they transition out of school. Blatantly racist remarks have been increasingly rare in schools and in mainstream dialogue, although the

2016 election of President Donald Trump also came with a wave of racial violence across the nation. We believe it is necessary to engage in a discussion about the centrality of racism and discrimination, because part of the benefit of dual language education is the social justice outcomes that it can produce in schools.

Racism has been described in many ways. Marable's (1992) definition of racism takes the position that racism is about institutional power. It reflects a "system of ignorance, exploitation, and power used to oppress African-Americans, Latinos, Asians, Pacific Americans, American Indians and other people on the basis of ethnicity, culture, mannerisms, and color" (p. 5). Institutional racism reflects subtle forms of discrimination that privilege White, English speaking individuals over non-White and non-English speaking individuals. Institutional racism has been described as "the predication of decisions and policies on considerations of race for the purpose of subordinating a racial group and maintaining control over that group" (Ture & Hamilton, 1992, p. 10). Institutional racism has also been described as a "collective failure" to protect against discrimination that can be "seen or detected in processes, attitudes and behaviors which amount to discrimination through unwitting prejudice, ignorance, thoughtlessness and racist stereotyping which disadvantage ethnic people" (Macpherson, 1999, p. 28). These definitions help to explain discrimination against Latinx students and others from racially and culturally diverse backgrounds.

Critical race theory (CRT) and Latinx critical theory (LatCrit) also provide frameworks to understand racial injustice within schools, society, and social institutions. CRT emerged during the mid 1970s as Derrick Bell, Alan Freeman, Richard Delgado, and other legal scholars began to challenge traditional civil rights strategies and the slow pace of reform after the *Brown v. Board of Education* decision and other civil rights victories. By the 1990s, education scholars had adopted CRT as a framework for explaining why the nation's schools have not made more progress at addressing longstanding racial injustices. CRT was used to understand and challenge the ways race and racism impact schools, teaching practices, and educational discourses (Ladson-Billings, 1998) and open new avenues for improving education. Latinx scholars drew upon CRT to organize a new theoretical space for thinking about racism and discriminatory educational practices associated with race, culture, class, immigration status, and language (Delgado Bernal, 2001). CRT and LatCrit in education challenge dominant ideologies and their aligned practices, policies, and taken-for-granted assumptions that are rooted in White supremacy, which often underscores English-only paradigm and forced racial, cultural, and linguistic assimilation. As Solórzano and Yosso (2001) noted, "A CRT in education challenges the traditional claims that the educational system and its institutions make toward objectivity, meritocracy, color-blindness, race neutrality, and equal opportunity" (p. 472).

LatCrit challenges dominant ideologies and paradigms that identify Latinx children as "culturally deprived" and in need of intervention of "Americanizing" via assimilation. LatCrit is similar to CRT but differs with its attention to addressing "issues often ignored by critical race theorists such as language, immigration, ethnicity, culture, identity, phenotype, and sexuality" (Solórzano & Delgado Bernal,

2001, p. 311). To be clear, LatCrit is not in competition with CRT, but instead is a theory that "should operate as a close cousin – related to critical race theory in real and lasting ways, but not necessarily living under the same roof" (Valdes, 1996, p. 26–27). LatCrit theory has clarified the multiple identities of Latinx individuals and the intersectionality of racism, classism, and other forms of oppression.

CRT/LatCrit has five central tenets that support the critical analysis, naming, and addressing of issues that are specific to Mexican American students, Latinx students, and other culturally and linguistically diverse students. First, CRT starts from the premise that race and racism are endemic and permanent facets in American society, but also intersect with other forms of subordination such as gender, class, and linguistic background. LatCrit extends beyond race and class oppression alone to include gender, language, and immigration status (Solórzano & Delgado Bernal, 2001). Second, CRT/LatCrit rejects dominant claims of objectivity, meritocracy, color-blindness, neutrality, and equal opportunity because such claims camouflage self-interest and protect the privilege of dominant groups. Moreover, such terms fail to reflect the power and persistence of racism and fail to foster meaningful change in ways that disrupt the status quo (DeCuir & Dixson, 2004).

Third, CRT/LatCrit is committed to social justice which entails eliminating racism, sexism, poverty, and other marginalizing conditions as well as empowering underrepresented groups (Matsuda, 1991). The permanence of racism has played and will continue to play a dominant role in American society, in part because racist hierarchical structures in political, economic, and social domains continue to benefit White people (Bell, 1992). Fourth, CRT/LatCrit values experiential knowledge of people of color. Counter-storytelling is one tool used to expose and challenge dominant ideologies and discourses that perpetuate racial stereotypes, which can include personal stories, narratives, and various other forms of expression that give voice to marginalized groups (Solórzano & Yosso, 2001). Testimonios have been used by critical scholars to challenge racist nativist framing of Latinx immigrant families and highlight the ways in which Latinx people navigate, resist, survive, and succeed in spite of racial injustices (Huber, 2009). Moreover, Latinx communities have a long history of activism, community organizing, and resisting educational injustices which is often minimized in dominant narratives.

Finally, CRT/LatCrit rejects ahistorical perspectives and instead insists on understanding and analyzing race, racism, language, immigration status, and identity through multiple disciplines in both historical and contemporary context (Tate, 1997). An historical perspective of racial injustice underscores that the history of racism and its interconnection with U.S. jurisprudence continually reifies conceptions of race that privileges Whites at the expense of other minoritized groups (e.g., tracking, access to high-quality, rigorous curriculum as well as honors and gifted programs that support successful college transition) (Harris, 1995; Ladson-Billings & Tate, 1995). In Texas, despite numerous battles in courts and many civil rights victories, many schools in Latinx immigrant communities continue to be underfunded and non-responsive to their cultural and linguistic identities and needs. When viewing discrimination with knowledge of history, Bell's (1980) concept of "interest convergence" is revealed, which suggests that civil rights gains reflect superficial opportunities to provide basic rights to people of color because they converged with the self-interests of Whites. Accordingly, such gains are easily reversible when interests are no longer aligned.

5 Why Dual Language Education

Four factors have been found to be critical in effectively educating Latinx students who are also ELLs: a socioculturally supportive environment, development of the student's first language to a high cognitive level, uninterrupted cognitive development in the first language, and teaching English with cognitively complex tasks (Collier & Thomas, 2004). Dual language education, in its broadest sense, is the general education curriculum delivered through two languages, which fully includes all students, both emergent bilingual and English-proficient students, in the same classroom and provides academic instruction through two languages with the goals of bilingualism and biliteracy. Research focused on cognitive and academic functioning has documented the enhanced benefits of dual language education (Bialystok, 2007; Collier & Thomas, 2004). Emergent bilingual children instructed in English and their primary language have been found to achieve at or above their peers on standardized tests while emergent bilingual children in traditional English immersion programs lose or do not make progress in their family language (Genesee, Lindholm-Leary, Saunders, & Christian, 2005). In part, dual language is successful for all students, but particularly racially and linguistically diverse students, because developing one's family language promotes healthy multigenerational, multicultural, and multilinguistic communities and presents a counter-narrative to dominant racial ideologies that disregard Latinx families, cultures, and identities (Fránquiz, Salazar, & DeNicolo, 2011).

Dual language education in public schools tend to resemble two primary models: 50:50 and 90:10. In a 50:50 model, half the curriculum is provided in Spanish and half in English throughout all grades. In the 90:10 model, kindergarten students receive 90% of instruction in Spanish, with the percentage of Spanish dropping to 50% by fourth or fifth grade. High-quality dual language education often has three primary goals: (1) to support emergent bilingual children with learning English, succeed in schools, and continue language and academic development in their family's language; (2) to help English-proficient students learn a second language, including academic language; and (3) to promote linguistic, cultural, and racial/ethnic equity and social justice for all students, families, schools, and communities. Successful dual language education thereby values diversity and maintains a vision defined by acceptance.

Implementing dual language education is complex and requires committed principals and teachers. Principals, teachers, staff, families, and students must work together to create a school-community context that is inclusive and welcoming. Since most teacher preparation programs and in-service trainings neglect bilingual education topics and teaching practices, teachers need to be provided with tailored professional development as well as collaborative and flexible planning time (Goodwin, 2017). When implementing any new rigorous and multifaceted improvement effort, teachers need time and also need to maintain high expectations. A cultural shift is also necessary, because teachers and staff may need to be taught to see language diversity as an asset rather than a deficit. Lastly, teachers need time and resources to develop curricula and learning experiences that are developmentally appropriate and attentive to context (Schachter & Gass, 2013).

Dual language education is not resistant to problems in implementation and to being coopted for alternative interests. Policies associated with dual language instruction, accountability, testing, and teacher and leader evaluations often fail to promote a healthy and inclusive school environment. Palmer (2007) described an elementary school with a dual language immersion program or "strand," which meant that only a small segment of the school population received access to dual language while the overwhelming majority of the school was English-only and devoid of any Spanish language. The small segment of the school dedicated to dual language immersion was described as "small oases of Spanish in a vast desert of English-only" (p. 756). In this school context, dual language did not change the language-as-problem orientation beyond the small group of dual language classes, which in turn allowed the majority of teachers, staff, and students to continually view Spanish through a deficit lens. Parent groups from different social, cultural, linguistic, and economic backgrounds can also create complex and problematic power dynamics. For example, in a study of dual language implementation in a racially diverse Chicago-area school district, Dorner (2011) found that White and Black monolingual English-speaking parents were able to more successfully advocate for their students than Mexican American immigrants, which had implications for school and language policies.

Dual language offers tremendous promise for Latinx students and their families, but in order for dual language to live up to its fullest potential, schools need to be understanding of potential challenges and pitfalls. Schools can struggle to find necessary resources, assessment materials, and prepare staff to successfully implement dual language education. Deficit perspectives of Latinx families and students can inhibit meaningful school-community relationships and the creation of culturally relevant curriculum and instructional practices that empower Latinx students. School structures and policies need to be thoughtfully adapted or revised, including planning time, co-teaching and co-planning methods, professional development, and professional learning communities (DeMatthews & Izquierdo, 2016). Principals and teachers must work together to identify and solve difficult and shifting problems (DeMatthews & Izquierdo, 2018a). In sum, dual language education requires a significant school culture shift, a revamping of policies and practices, and a long-term commitment centered upon inquiry and collective action that involves all stakeholders.

6 Conclusion

Recreating public schools in ways that value Mexican, Mexican American, and other Latinx students and students of color will require tremendous effort, energy, and resources, but it must begin with a critique of public schools as they have existed and an honest recognition of the assets that all students, families, and communities bring to the table. This effort begins with understanding history and the present sociopolitical context of public education in Texas and across the nation. It also requires an understanding the diversity of unique needs and assets of Latinx students learning English and Spanish. However, information about student populations and a commitment to school improvement are insufficient alone. A critical framework that is insightful to thinking about how Latinx students have been marginalized is necessary to understand the complexities of public schools, school improvement processes, educational policies, and the ways in which all stakeholders can build solidarity and struggle together to improve educational experiences, opportunities, and outcomes. We offer CRT and LatCrit as critical frameworks to begin this thinking. With these understandings and frameworks in mind, dual language education provides an opportunity to radically recreate public schools in ways that will benefit all students and help contribute to the creation of a more equitable society.

References

Ackerman, D. J., & Tazi, Z. (2015). Enhancing young Hispanic dual language learners' achievement: Exploring strategies and addressing challenges. *ETS Research Report Series, 2015*, 1-39.

Alemán, E., Jr. (2007). Situating Texas school finance policy in a CRT framework: How "substantially equal" yields racial inequity. *Educational Administration Quarterly, 43*(5), 525–558.

Alvarado v. El Paso Independent School District, 426 F. Supp. 575. (1976).

Bell, D. A. (1980). Brown v. Board of Education and the interest convergence dilemma. *Harvard Law Review, 93*, 518–533.

Bell, D. A. (1992). *Faces at the bottom of the well: The permanence of racism*. New York, NY: Basic Books.

Bialystok, E. (2007). Cognitive effects of bilingualism: How linguistic experience leads to cognitive change. *International Journal of Bilingual Education and Bilingualism, 10*(3), 210–223. https://doi.org/10.2167/beb441.0

Brown v. Board of Education, 347 U.S. 483 (1954).

Camarota, S. A., & Zeigler, K. (2016). *Immigrants in the United States: A profile of the foreign-born using 2014 and 2015 census bureau data*. Washington, DC: Center for Immigration Studies. Retrieved from https://cis.org/sites/cis.org/files/immigrant-profile_0.pdf

Castañeda v. Pickard, 648 F.2d 989 (5th Cir. 1981).

Collier, V. P., & Thomas, W. P. (2004). The astounding effectiveness of dual language education for all. *NABE Journal of Research and Practice, 2*(1), 1–20.

DeCuir, J. T., & Dixson, A. D. (2004). "So when it comes out, they aren't that surprised that it is there": Using critical race theory as a tool of analysis of race and racism in education. *Educational Researcher, 33*(5), 26–31.

Delgado Bernal, D. (2001). Living and learning pedagogies of the home: The mestiza consciousness of Chicana students. *International Journal of Qualitative Studies in Education, 14*, 623–639.

DeMatthews, D. E. (2018). *Community engaged leadership for social justice: A critical approach in urban schools*. New York, NY: Routledge.

DeMatthews, D. E., & Izquierdo, E. (2016). School leadership for dual language education: A social justice approach. *The Educational Forum, 80*(3), 278–293.

DeMatthews, D. E., & Izquierdo, E. (2018a). Supporting Mexican American immigrant students on the border. A case study of culturally responsive leadership in a dual language elementary school. *Urban Education*. https://doi.org/10.1177/0042085918756715

DeMatthews, D. E., & Izquierdo, E. (2018b). The role of principals in developing dual language education: Implications for social justice leadership and preparation. *Journal of Latinos and Education, 17*(1), 53–70.

DeMatthews, D. E., Izquierdo, E., & Knight, D. (2017). Righting past wrongs: A superintendent's social justice leadership for dual language education along the US-Mexico border. *Education Policy Analysis Archives, 25*(1), 1–28.

Dorner, L. M. (2011). Contested communities in a debate over dual-language education: The import of "public" values on public policies. *Educational Policy, 25*(4), 577–613.

Fránquiz, M. E., Salazar, M. D. C., & DeNicolo, C. P. (2011). Challenging majoritarian tales: Portraits of bilingual teachers deconstructing deficit views of bilingual learners. *Bilingual Research Journal, 34*(3), 279–300. https://doi.org/10.1080/15235882.2011.625884

Fuller, B., Bridges, M., Bein, E., Jang, H., Jung, S., Rabe-Hesketh, S., ... Kuo, A. (2009). The health and cognitive growth of Latino toddlers: At risk or immigrant paradox? *Maternal and Child Health Journal, 13*(6), 755–768. https://doi.org/10.1007/s10995-009-0475-0

Gándara, P., & Rumberger, R. W. (2009). Immigration, language, and education: How does language policy structure opportunity. *Teachers College Record, 111*(3), 750–782.

Genesee, F., Lindholm-Leary, K., Saunders, W., & Christian, D. (2005). English language learners in US schools: An overview of research findings. *Journal of Education for Students Placed at Risk, 10*(4), 363–385. https://doi.org/10.1207/s15327671espr1004_2

Goodwin, A. L. (2017). Who is in the classroom now? Teacher preparation and the education of immigrant children. *Educational Studies, 53*(5), 433–449.

Han, W. J., Lee, R., & Waldfogel, J. (2012). School readiness among children of immigrants in the US: Evidence from a large national birth cohort study. *Children and Youth Services Review, 34*(4), 771–782. https://doi.org/10.1016/j.childyouth.2012.01.001

Harris, C. I. (1995). Whiteness as property. In K. Crenshaw, N. Gotanda, G. Peller, & K. Thomas (Eds.), *Critical race theory: The key writings that formed the movement* (pp. 357–383). New York, NY: The New Press.

Hoff, E. (2013). Interpreting the early language trajectories of children from low-SES and language minority homes: Implications for closing achievement gaps. *Developmental Psychology, 49*(1), 4–14.

Huber, L. P. (2009). Challenging racist nativist framing: Acknowledging the community cultural wealth of undocumented Chicana college students to reframe the immigration debate. *Harvard Educational Review, 79*(4), 704–730.

Ladson-Billings, G. (1998). Just what is critical race theory and what's it doing in a nice field like education? *International Journal of Qualitative Studies in Education, 11*(1), 7–24.

Ladson-Billings, G., & Tate, W. (1995). Toward a critical race theory of education. *Teachers College Record, 97*(1), 47–68.

Lindholm-Leary, K., & Block, N. (2010). Achievement in predominantly low SES/Hispanic dual language schools. *International Journal of Bilingual Education and Bilingualism, 13*(1), 43–60.

López, F., Scanlan, M., & Gundrum, B. (2013). Preparing teachers of English language learners: Empirical evidence and policy implications. *Education Policy Analysis Archives, 21*(20), 20. https://doi.org/10.14507/epaa.v21n20.2013

Macpherson, W. (1999). *The Stephen Lawrence inquiry: Report of an inquiry by Sir William Macpherson of Cluny.* London, UK: Stationary Office.
Matsuda, M. (1991). Voices of America: Accent, antidiscrimination law, and a jurisprudence for the last reconstruction. *Yale Law Journal, 100*, 1329–1407.
Marable, M. (1992). *The crisis of color and democracy: Essays on race, class, and power.* Monroe, ME: Common Courage.
McNeil, L. M., Coppola, E., Radigan, J., & Vasquez Heilig, J. (2008). Avoidable losses: High-stakes accountability and the dropout crisis. *Education Policy Analysis Archives, 16*(3), 3. https://doi.org/10.14507/epaa.v16n3.2008
Migration Policy Institute. (2018). *State immigration data profiles.* Washington, DC: Author. Retrieved from https://www.migrationpolicy.org/data/state-profiles/state/demographics/US
Morath v. The Texas Taxpayer & Student Fairness Coal., No. 14-0776, 2016 WL 2853868 (Tex. May 13, 2016).
Orfield, G., & Lee, C. (2005). *Why segregation matters: Poverty and educational inequality.* Cambridge, MA: The Civil Rights Project. Retrieved from https://escholarship.org/uc/item/4xr8z4wb
Palmer, D. (2007). A dual immersion strand programme in California: Carrying out the promise of dual language education in an English-dominant context. *International Journal of Bilingual Education and Bilingualism, 10*(6), 752–768.
Patterson, J. T. (2001). *Brown v. Board of Education: A civil rights milestone and its troubled legacy.* New York, NY: Oxford University Press.
Plyler v. Doe, 457 U.S. 202, 223 (1982).
Ruiz, R. (1984). Orientations in language planning. *NABE Journal, 8*(2), 15–34.
Schachter, J., & Gass, S. M. (2013). *Second language classroom research: Issues and opportunities.* New York, NY: Routledge.
Slavin, R. E., & Cheung, A. (2005). A synthesis of research on language of reading instruction for English language learners. *Review of Educational Research, 75*(2), 247–284.
Solórzano, D. G., & Bernal, D. D. (2001). Examining transformational resistance through a critical race and LatCrit theory framework: Chicana and Chicano students in an urban context. *Urban Education, 36*(3), 308–342.
Solórzano, D. G., & Yosso, T. J. (2001). Critical race and LatCrit theory and method: Counter-storytelling. *International Journal of Qualitative Studies in Education, 14*(4), 471–495.
Tate, W. F., IV. (1997). Chapter 4: Critical race theory and education: History, theory, and implications. *Review of Research in Education, 22*(1), 195–247.
Ture, K., & Hamilton, C. V. (1992). *Black power: The politics of liberation in America.* New York, NY: Vintage Books. (Original work published 1967).
United States v. Texas, 506 F. Supp. 405. (1981).
United States Census Bureau. (2018). *Hispanic origin.* Washington, DC: Author. Retrieved from https://www.census.gov/topics/population/hispanic-origin/about.html
Valdes, F. (1996). Foreword: Latina/o ethnicities, critical race theory and post-identity politics in postmodern legal culture: From practices to possibilities. *La Raza Law Journal, 9*, 1–31.
Valencia, R. R. (Ed.). (2012). *The evolution of deficit thinking: Educational thought and practice.* New York, NY: Routledge.
Valenzuela, A. (2010). *Subtractive schooling: US-Mexican youth and the politics of caring.* Albany, NY: SUNY Press.
Weaver & Tidwell. (2013, April 1). *Final report of investigation into alleged cheating scandal at El Paso Independent School District.* Retrieved from http://extras.mnginteractive.com/live/media/site525/2013/0401/20130401_045446_weaver_audit.pdf

# Part I
Setting the "State": The Old and Subtractive Ways Haven't Worked

Bilingual Education Policy in Texas: Promise and Lost Opportunities

David G. Hinojosa

Abstract Substantial research shows how bilingualism can result in cognitive, social, and academic benefits for the individual and for society. Nevertheless, many state and federal policies continue to reflect the influence of English-only, nationalistic proponents and the inadequate investment in education. This chapter recounts the struggles of bilingual education in the United States and in Texas through policy and litigation over the past fifty-plus years.

Keywords Bilingual education · English learners · Language rights · Civil rights · School finance · Educational opportunity · Education policy · Dual language

As state and national economies continue to expand into global markets each year, the need for a multilingual, multicultural workforce becomes even more important (Callahan & Gándara, 2014). Yet each year, English Learner students (ELs)[1] seemingly face ill-conceived policies, under-resourced schools, and litigation strategies seeking to strip them of their home language and culture. Consequently, not only are families deprived of cultural capital but so too is the United States denied a critical resource in present and future economies. This chapter focuses on critical policy-making and litigation events affecting ELs at the national level, with a special focus on Texas, dating back to the 1960s.

Historically, much tension has existed between communities, policymakers and state officials in defining the purpose and scope of language programs for ELs,

---

[1] "English learner" describes those students who have yet to be classified under a local, state or federal system as having achieved the level of required proficiency in the English language, respectively. The author recognizes that various terms have been used to describe this group of students, including "Emergent Bilinguals," "English Language Learners," "bilingual students," "language minorities," "English as a Second Language or ESL students," and "limited-English proficient students," among others.

D. G. Hinojosa (✉)
Walsch Gallegos, P.C., Albuquerque, NM, USA
e-mail: pil.david@gmail.com

including bilingual education.[2] Some officials advocate for asset-based, bilingual maintenance and dual language models, where students gain literacy in both their native language and the English language, thus promoting additive bilingualism (Solis, 2001). Research shows these programs to be the more successful language programs (DeMatthews & Izquierdo, 2017; Reardon, Umansky, Valentino, Khanna, & Wong, 2014; Collier & Thomas, 2004).

As the Annenberg Institute reported, however, "[t]he role of the EL[L] leaders in most states and districts is marginalized rather than elevated and is focused on compliance rather than asset and capacity building" (Tung, 2013, p. 2). Some policymakers and school administrators outright prohibit the use of either transitional or maintenance models and instead require the adoption of "subtractive" models, including structured English immersion or English as a Second Language (ESL) models (Valenzuela, 1999). While the courts occasionally step in to enforce the rights of ELs to sufficient language programs both at the national and state level, more recently courts have been reticent to opining on the quality of language programs offered by state and local education agencies. Consequently, it is incumbent upon researchers to conduct necessary and continuing research on the effectiveness of language programs and upon state and federal elected officials to provide the resources necessary to implement those programs.

1 Origins of Federal Bilingual Laws and Policies

According to González (2014), the "Tucson 66—A Symposium" served as the first real impetus toward federal bilingual education policy. The symposium, attended by educators, administrators and experts in the emerging field opened with a presentation by then-Texas State Representative Joe Bernal, who stated in part:

> I say we still have to look to a bilingual approach in teaching our Mexican-American (as well as others) children, especially in their formative elementary school years…because we know the importance of the mother tongue—both as a medium for concept development and as a means of building confidence in children whose English is non-functional (González, 2014, p. 31).

U.S. Senator Ralph Yarbrough (Tex.) followed this event with a series of public hearings on bilingual education held across the country in 1967 before the Special Subcommittee on Bilingual Education of the Committee on Labor and Public Welfare of the United States Senate (González, 2014). That same year, Yarbrough filed legislation that would provide funding for developing language programs for EL students, including the use of bilingual education and programs that accounted for the ancestral language and culture of Spanish-speaking students (Stewner-Manzanares, 1988).

---

[2] For purposes of this chapter, bilingual education includes both maintenance bilingual models, transitional bilingual models, as well as one-way and two-way dual language models. This does not include English as a second language models (ESL) because those do not focus on utilizing the EL student's non-English native language. However, in the context of funding, bilingual funding refers to funding for bilingual education and/or ESL, unless otherwise stated.

Along with 37 other bills, Congress rolled Yarbrough's bill into the Bilingual Education Act, Title VII of the Elementary and Secondary Education Act (ESEA) (Stewner-Manzanares, 1988). Enacted in 1968, the Act established policies allocating federal funds for innovative programs, including bilingual education programs (Crawford, 1997). While it did not require bilingual education, it was an important first step toward expanding bilingual education. In 1974, Congress amended the Act, calling for "the native language of the children of limited-English speaking ability... to the extent necessary to allow a child to progress effectively through the educational system" (Ramirez, Yuen, Ramey, & Pasta, 1991, p. 6). Thereafter, in 1978, Congress further amended the Act to expand the focus of language programs from speaking in English to reading, writing, speaking, and comprehending the English language.

Amendments to the Act in the 1980s signified a major philosophical shift away from instruction in the EL student's primary language to other methods, such as support for sheltered ESL programs where the child's native language was used only as necessary. Although federal funding for these alternative programs was originally capped at 10% of Title VII funds, in 1988 Congress increased the cap to 25%. The 1988 amendments also restricted funding to a maximum of 3 years in the program for ELs (Ramirez et al., 1991).

Congress enacted other amendments to the Act over the next decade, but a real turning point occurred in 2002 when the Bilingual Education Act was replaced with the English Language Acquisition Act as part of the No Child Left Behind Act (NCLB) (Crawford, 2002). Through this legislation, Congress moved from developing skills in both languages to emphasizing the development of English language skills. Although bilingual programs were not prohibited, these changes in federal legislation—coupled with a punitive accountability system that stressed performance on English-language exams—signaled a sea change that trickled down to the states.

2 Stepping Up Enforcement of EL Student Rights Under Title VI and the Equal Educational Opportunities Act (EEOA)

While the Bilingual Education Act is frequently cited as the seminal federal legislation that helped spearhead the development of bilingual education, Title VI of the Civil Rights Act of 1964 also heavily influenced both EL program policy and practice in the states and local school districts. Federal enforcement agencies have historically used Title VI, which forbids national origin discrimination, and its implementing regulations to investigate state and local education policies and practices that fail to support the learning and equitable treatment of ELs (U.S. Department of Justice [USDOJ], & U.S. Department of Education [DOED], 2015).

Pursuant to Title VI, the Office for Civil Rights issued a memorandum in 1970 to school districts receiving federal grants and enrolling at least 5% of EL students outlining their responsibilities to EL students. Among the responsibilities listed, the memo directed districts to: correct language gaps by opening special instructional programs to EL students; not assign EL students to special education classes based on their English proficiency; not ability group or otherwise track EL students into lesser programs and classes; communicate with non-English speaking families in their native language regarding school activities; and conduct self-assessments and submit corrective action plans to the US Department of Housing, Education, and Workforce (HEW) (González, 2014).[3] Thus, even before the *Lau* remedies were enacted (see below), the federal government was taking some action under Title VI to ensure that schools properly served EL students.

In 1974, the U.S. Supreme Court issued its opinion in *Lau v. Nichols*, a challenge to a school district's failure to modify its general education program for EL students. Across the U.S., school districts typically put the onus on school children and their families for learning English, instead of adapting instructional methods to the needs of EL students (Cárdenas, 1995). The Court held, however, that placing EL students in a sink-or-swim environment violates their rights to equal protection stating:

> there is no equality of treatment merely by providing students with the same facilities, textbooks, teachers, and curriculum; for students who do not understand English are effectively foreclosed from any meaningful education…. Imposition of a requirement that, before a child can effectively participate in the educational program, he must already have acquired those basic skills is to make a mockery of public education. We know that those who do not understand English are certain to find their classroom experiences wholly incomprehensible and in no way meaningful. (*Lau v. Nichols*, 1974, para. 15–16).

This was an emphatic victory for EL advocates. However, while the Court ordered the district to affirmatively address EL students' special language needs, the Court did not proscribe any specified language program.

In response to the *Lau* decision, the HEW issued a memorandum in 1975 to school districts outlining minimal remedies that school districts should consider enacting to counter the effects of violations similar to the equal protection violations found in *Lau*. Like in *Lau*, the HEW did not require the adoption of any specified model. However, the department did mandate that districts engage in comprehensive planning that required them to assess available resources to ensure the adoption and implementation of an appropriate language plan that addressed identification, assessment, achievement, and program offerings (Cárdenas, 1995).

In 1974, Congress enacted the Equal Educational Opportunities Act. Section 1703(f) of the Act requires that all state and local education agencies "take appropriate action to overcome language barriers that impeded equal participation by its students in its instructional program" (Equal Educational Opportunities Act, 1974). Congress did not specify what amounted to "appropriate action" but the Fifth Circuit's interpretation of the Act in *Castañeda v. Pickard* requires that school districts' selected programs comply with a three-part test: (1) adopt a language program based on a sound pedagogical theory; (2) implement the program with appropriate

---

[3] In 1979, the US Department of Education became a separate department and HEW was renamed as the Department of Health and Human Services.

resources and personnel required to implement the theory effectively; and (3) evaluate the program and make changes to ensure that students are actually overcoming their language barriers (*Castañeda v. Pickard*, 1981). The EEOA has been the source of varying enforcement at the federal level. The Department of Justice continues to investigate a range of complaints alleging violations of the rights of EL students under the EEOA, both at the administrative and litigation levels.

3 Bilingual Education in Texas

Texas has a sordid history of acknowledging the importance of being bilingual and literate in languages other than English. Texas had an English-only teaching law for approximately 65 years, which ended in 1969. School personnel across the Southwest often punished students for speaking Spanish in school (Texas Association for Bilingual Education [TABE], 2012). Discipline measures included: washing students' mouths with soap; hitting students with rulers on their knuckles; asking students to pronounce "sc/ch" words in front of the class until they cried and broke down; and not being able to ask to go to the bathroom because teachers didn't understand Spanish (Aparicio & Jose-Kampfner, 1995).

Through policy advocacy and litigation efforts, the tables turned in Texas. In 1969, the Texas Legislature passed House Bill 103, the state's first law that authorized, but did not require, school districts to provide bilingual instruction through Grade 6 (Midobouche & Benavides, 2008). Four years later, the state enacted the Bilingual Education and Training Act. Beginning with the 1974–75 school year, each school district with 20 or more students in the same grade who spoke the same language is required to offer bilingual education in grades K-3 (Gonzalez, 2014).

In 1981, a federal district court order required the Texas Legislature to enact further reforms to its bilingual/ESL education laws (*United States v Texas*, 1981). In this case filed by the Mexican American Legal Defense and Educational Fund (MALDEF) and the Multicultural Education, Training and Advocacy, Inc. (META) on behalf of the civil rights organizations LULAC and American GI Forum, the plaintiffs challenged both the intentional discrimination and segregation of Latino students in Texas and the failure of the state to ensure sufficient language programs for EL students. The court issued a scorching opinion of the state's language programs, requiring the state to remedy the ineffectiveness of the state-required one-hour of ESL instruction for grades 4–12 and the state's failure to appropriately monitor language programs across the state. The court issued an injunction requiring the state to remedy the deficiencies and ordered bilingual education throughout grades K-12.

During the state's appeal of the ruling, the legislature enacted Senate Bill 477, the 1981 Bilingual and Special Language Programs Act. Senate Bill 477 made significant reforms to Texas law, including: the expansion of bilingual education up to grade 6; standardized criteria for entering and exiting EL students from language programs; required onsite monitoring of language programs by the state; and the creation of Language Proficiency Assessment Committees (LPAC) that would monitor the progress for each EL student (*United States v. Texas*, 1982). On appeal, the Fifth Circuit noted these significant changes and vacated the court's injunction, including the requirement mandating bilingual education in secondary schools.

In 2003, the state curtailed its monitoring of language programs, going from cyclical onsite monitor to desk audits. Focusing on student achievement data aggregated at the school district level, the state assigned performance levels through its Performance-Based Monitoring Analysis System (PBMAS). Following a lengthy investigation, in 2006, MALDEF and META filed a motion seeking further relief under the *US v. Texas* lawsuit, challenging the lack of sufficient monitoring and supervision of language programs and the state's failure to adequately support secondary EL students (Mexican American Legal Defense and Educational Fund [MALDEF], n.d., para. 3). The parties tried the case in October and November 2006 and the court issued its ruling in favor of the state defendants on July 30, 2007. Due to critical legal and factual errors cited in the judge's ruling, LULAC and GI Forum asked the court to reconsider its ruling. In response, the court agreed and reversed its decision. In another scathing decision, the court cited the state for several infractions including: permitting the PBMAS to mask the failure of secondary programs by combining the dismal achievement data of secondary ESL programs with data from the more successful, more populous elementary bilingual programs; allowing state employees to serve as intervention monitors without having bilingual or ESL certifications, resulting in the "blind leading the blind;" and failing to ensure that secondary EL students were served with adequate language programs. (MALDEF, n.d., para. 3).

The state appealed the ruling. In 2010, the Fifth Circuit dealt a severe blow to the plaintiffs and the hundreds of thousands EL students by reversing the lower court ruling. Essentially, the Fifth Circuit held that the absence of longitudinal student achievement data, the newness of the PBMAS, and the lack of school districts as defendants in the lawsuit prevented the plaintiffs from prevailing. While the appellate court ignored the voluminous evidentiary record supporting the lower court's ruling, the Fifth Circuit did not dismiss the case as requested by the state. Instead, the court noted that "[EL] student performance is alarming" and directed the plaintiffs to add individual districts as defendants to better determine which entity, or both, should be held responsible for the failure (*United States v. Texas*, 2010).

In 2014, MALDEF and META renewed the EL student action by adding two school districts to the case, Southwest I.S.D. and Northeast I.S.D.—both in San Antonio. The plaintiff's amended class action lawsuit centered on three alleged violations of the EEOA: (1) continuing ineffective state monitoring and intervention of failing district and school programs; (2) the state's bare ESL supplemental certification test and procedures that fail to ensure teachers are properly trained and qualified to implement effective language programs; and (3) the provision of ineffective ESL pullout programs for secondary students (MALDEF, & Multicultural Education, Training and Advocacy, Inc.[META], n.d., para. 4). The case remains pending at the time of this chapter's publication.

4 Providing Adequate Resources for Bilingual Education in Texas

Strong, recent research shows that increased funding by the states has contributed to both improved student performance and lifetime outcomes, especially for underserved students (Jackson, Johnson, & Persico, 2016; Lafortune, Rothstein, & Whitmore Schanzenbach, 2016). Yet, Texas has historically funded its public schools based on available appropriations and politicking as opposed to actual student need. While much of the earlier school finance litigation in Texas focused on inequitable funding differences between property-poor and property-wealth school districts, claims filed by MALDEF in the last two cases focused heavily on the inadequate funding for EL students. However, the issue of school finance and EL student learning opportunities is hardly new.

In 1976, the Intercultural Development Research Association (IDRA) engaged in a bilingual education cost study using expert panel methodology to identify what practitioners in the field of bilingual education considered to be critical elements of effective bilingual education programs. These included: student assessment, program evaluation, supplemental curricular materials, staffing, staff development and parent involvement. In the IDRA bilingual cost model, only those costs unique to the implementation of the specialized program were considered. The bilingual cost levels varied slightly depending on the grade levels involved and the number of years a program had existed, with newer programs reflecting slightly higher costs for start-up. The study recommended a weight between 0.25 and 0.42, meaning that extra funding would be added on to the basic program allotment ranging from 25% to 42% more (Robledo Montecel & Cortez, 2008). The "weighted funding" differs from the "categorical" funding practice, the latter which allocated funding based on a fixed dollar amount for each student in the program. By tying bilingual funding to the basic program funding through a weight, researchers and advocates felt that when the basic program funding rose, so too would the funding for special programs like bilingual education.

Around the same time, the Governor's Office of Educational Research and Planning conducted an audit of exemplary school districts, resulting in a recommendation for a "beginning" bilingual weight of 0.15, increasing to 0.40 in 2 years. The Governor's bill was defeated. Instead, the legislature set the categorical allotment at $50 for each student in a bilingual program and $12.50 for each student in an ESL class (West Orange-Cove Consolidated Independent School District, 2004). In 1984, the legislature convened a school finance working group. After examining the essential services and programs required to assist EL students in meeting state expectations and standards, the group recommended a (0.4) weight for bilingual education. However, the legislature rejected the proposal and arbitrarily reduced the weight to (0.1) (West Orange-Cove CISD, 2004).

The issue of inadequate funding for special student populations, including EL students, played a prominent role in the 2004 state school finance case, *West Orange-Cove C.I.S.D. v. Neeley*. In their adequacy claim, the Edgewood ISD plaintiffs, a group of 22 property-poor Texas school districts represented by MALDEF and META, claimed that the growth of special populations and insufficient funding for EL and low-income students compounded educational challenges resulting from the low funding for property-poor school districts, thus rendering the system unconstitutionally inadequate. The Edgewood Plaintiffs also cited the state's increased rigor in curriculum and assessments. The evidence showed the changes resulted in low standardized test passage rates, low graduation rates and high dropout rates for EL students (Hinojosa, 2015).

The evidence also showed that in 2004, the state commissioned a cost-function study that analyzed student passage rates on the state assessment. The study concluded that it would take an additional $1248 to assist an EL student who failed to pass the state assessment, but the state failed to adjust the funding upward. Following a six-week trial, the court found the system unconstitutional. The court's ruling included dozens of findings on the state's failure to address the EL students' needs. (West Orange-Cove CISD, 2004).

Unfortunately, the victory was short-lived. The state filed an appeal with the Supreme Court of Texas. In 2005, the court reversed the adequacy ruling in favor of the plaintiffs, despite acknowledging strong evidence in the record:

> In the extensive record before us, there is much evidence, which the district court credited, that many schools and districts are struggling to teach an increasingly demanding curriculum to a population with a growing number of disadvantaged students, yet without additional funding needed to meet these challenges. There are wide gaps in performance among student groups differentiated by race, proficiency in English, and economic advantage. Non-completion and dropout rates are high, and the loss of students who are struggling may make performance measures applied to those who continue appear better than they should. The rate of students meeting college preparedness standards is very low. There is also evidence of high attrition and turnover among teachers statewide, due to increasing demands and stagnant compensation (*Neeley v. West Orange-Cove Consolidated Independent School District*, 2005, para. 123).

However, the court also held that evidence of Texas student scores on the National Assessment for Progress showed improvement relative to other states and scores on the state standardized tests showed some improvement, though that evidence did not necessarily reflect the performance of EL students (Hinojosa, 2015). The court did uphold a claim by one group of districts that the cap on property-taxes acted as a floor and a ceiling but with no ruling directing the legislature to improve funding for EL students, the legislature focused on compressing taxes and increasing funding of the basic allotment.

The issue, however, did not go away. When the state cut over $5 billion from public education in 2011 and increased the number of required high stakes exit exams from 5 to 15 while also increasing the rigor of testing, over half of the state's 1029 public school districts sued the state. The "Edgewood Plaintiffs," represented by MALDEF and META, included four parents and schoolchildren, as well as five property-poor school districts. These plaintiffs brought the first adequacy claim in Texas specifically on behalf of low income and EL students, arguing that the system for funding the education of these two student groups (as opposed to the system as a whole) was arbitrary and inadequate (Hinojosa, 2015).

Again, the Edgewood Plaintiffs marshaled forward substantial expert evidence showing the dismal performance of EL students across a variety of measures, including English proficiency tests and the correlated inadequate funding. Other districts across the state, rich and poor, similarly spoke of the increasing challenges and lost opportunities. Following a three-month trial, Travis County District Court Judge John K. Dietz issued his ruling from the bench in February 2013, holding the system unconstitutional and inadequate for EL students, among other rulings (Hinojosa & Walters, 2014).

In response, the state passed legislation that put some revenue back into the system (approximately $3.2 billion) and scaled back high stakes end-of-course exams from 15 to 5, among other reforms. The district court reopened the case to address the impact of the legislation. Following a two-week trial in 2014, Judge Dietz issued a blistering decision spelled out over 364 single-spaced pages of findings of fact and conclusions of law (*Texas Taxpayer & Student Fairness Coalition v. Williams*, 2014). The ruling included over 200 findings on EL education. In finding of fact number 344, Judge Dietz summed up the plight of EL students in Texas as follows:

> Like economically disadvantaged students, these students are capable of performing far better, but they, too, lack the necessary quality programs and interventions to help them achieve their full potential and to meet the State's standards. As shown below, the performance of EL[L] students is far below acceptable levels and demonstrates the failure of the school finance system to enable school districts to provide the opportunities EL[L] students need to acquire English proficiency and the essential knowledge and skills set forth in the State's curriculum. (*Texas Taxpayer & Student Fairness Coalition v. Williams*, 2014, p. 109).

Texas appealed to the Supreme Court of Texas, and again, the decision was reversed, changing the legal standard in the process to make it even more difficult for EL plaintiff children to prove a finding of inadequacy. In order to counter the extensive record of the state's failure, the court held that the constitutionally required "general diffusion of knowledge" is not intended to meet the needs for any particular group. The court went on to hold that the system as a "whole" must be inadequate and that any subgroup of students, including EL students, would have to demonstrate that an inadequate ruling be "truly exceptional" (*Morath, et al. v. The Texas Taxpayer and Student Fairness Coalition*, 2016).

These rulings are particularly troubling because ordinarily, disenfranchised groups tend to get as much or greater protection under the law, *not less* (Persily, 2014). Furthermore, courts ordinarily apply constitutional interpretations to the affected rights of the complainants because it does not matter whether other students in the system are unaffected. For example, in *Brown v. Board*, the U.S. Supreme Court did not hold that because White students could attend the Black schools but chose not to, the system "as a whole" was not unconstitutional.[4]

---

[4] This remarkable "as a whole" ruling was actually first proposed by counsel for the Calhoun County ISD group, the wealthy districts. During a conference with all parties following the second trial, Judge Dietz shared that given the strength of evidence presented in the case, he was inclined

Finally, despite the court previously holding in *West Orange-Cove* that an adequacy ruling depended on outputs and not inputs, the court changed the standard for EL and low-income students. The court stated that achievement gaps alone are not enough because other factors outside the school impact learning; the lack of resources alone does not lead to low student achievement; and the plaintiffs failed to prove that the gaps would be reduced significantly if more funding was provided (*Morath, et al. v. The Texas Taxpayer and Student Fairness Coalition*, 2016). These conclusions may not seem remarkable except for the fact that there was no evidentiary record supporting the existence of other factors impacting the learning of EL students that could not be overcome with appropriate programs and resources. And there was plenty of evidence showing that while money alone may not change the outcomes, it would create substantially greater research-based opportunities, such as smaller class size, full-day pre-K, and teacher mentoring opportunities, which together, would likely result in significantly reducing the achievement gaps (*Texas Taxpayer & Student Fairness Coalition v. Williams*, 2014).

5 Bilingual Education on the Horizon: Progress or Peril?

The outlook for bilingual education advocates seems to have not changed much over the last 60 years. Bilingual education laws passed at the national and state levels have helped provide the basis for bilingual education, and dual language programs have continued to proliferate across Texas and the country (Li, Steel, Slater, Bacon, & Miller, 2016). However, anti-bilingual education laws have been passed in other states, including California and Massachusetts (Cummins, 2000). Arizona policymakers have forced schools to segregate EL students into immersion programs, placing them at greater risk of school failure, negative academic self-concepts, and delaying graduation (Gándara & Orfield, 2012). The courts have done little to protect them (*Horne v. Flores*, 2009), but again, along with the dark spots there are bright spots.

Nationally, recent amendments to the administrative rules implementing the Head Start Act and the enactment of the most recent bipartisan iteration of the Elementary and Secondary Education Act, the Every Student Succeeds Act (ESSA), show some promising reforms for EL students. Under the new Head Start regulations, the revised standards reflect the research showing how bilingual children, including infants, toddlers and preschool children, develop through their home language and recognize bilingualism as an asset. The standards also include requirements to assess students in their home language and to develop and implement a comprehensive, coordinated approach to communicating with non-English speaking parents (U. S. Department of Health and Human Services [HHS], n.d.).

---

to hold the system was inadequate but only as to the EL and low-income students—where the evidence was strongest. Counsel for Calhoun County objected, stating—in the presence of state attorneys—that the court could not hold the system "partially unconstitutional" and that the whole system needed to be declared unconstitutional… or none of it. (Author notes).

Many of these reforms are consistent with the research cited in an in-depth report published by the National Academy of Sciences identifying several promising practices and policy reforms in early childhood and prekindergarten, among other areas (National Academies of Sciences, Engineering, and Medicine, 2017). Early verbal and nonverbal language development, strong relationships between early childhood educators and families, and positive adult-child interactions are all successful practices identified in the report and supported in public policy. Similarly, under ESSA, evidence-based prekindergarten programs may be expanded with the use of Title I funds, migrant funds, Native American funds and preschool grants. Essential practices identified in the National Academy report shown to support evidence-based preschool programs for EL students at the state level, include appropriately responding to each family's culture and language, effective family engagement, scaffolding techniques, qualified teachers and comprehensive curricula, developmentally sequenced and focused on specific content (National Academies of Sciences, Engineering, and Medicine, 2017).

ESSA has received much fanfare in ushering in a new era of accountability. While the long-term benefits of ESSA remain to be seen, there were some significant advances in the area of EL education. According to the Council of Chief State School Officers (CCSSO), the performance of EL students on proficiency exams and on academic performance measures as a disaggregated group will now be included as an indicator under Title I, as opposed to its former place in Title III, thus potentially bringing more attention to EL students (CCSSO, 2016). ESSA includes new reporting requirements for long-term EL students and EL students with disabilities, two of the most neglected groups of EL students (Pompa, 2015). Congress also created stricter timetables for identifying and beginning to serve EL students with language services and requires states to standardize entrance and exit criteria (CCSSO, 2016). States will now be required to assess potential EL students within 30 days of enrollment and will be required to create standards for exiting students. These measures should help ensure EL students receive language services earlier and are appropriately exited under uniform policies.

ESSA also includes controversial measures that could undermine EL progress. For example, states have the option of including former EL students for up to 4 years in the EL subgroup (Pompa, 2015). As IDRA explained, the inclusion of so many former EL students in the subgroup may mask the performance of students still classified as ELs (Robledo Montecel, 2015). ESSA also allows states to exclude the academic performance of recently arrived EL students on reading or language arts and math for the first year of testing, but growth in the second year would need to be included; and in the third year, assessment scores would need to be included in the accountability system (CCSSO, 2016). While some advocates have pushed for these measures because they believe it more appropriately aligns with EL students' language proficiency development, others remain leery as to whether attention will be taken away from the learning of recently arrived EL students in their first 2 years. If states can exclude the performance of certain categories of EL students, local educational officials may be less inclined to focus on the learning and growth of those students.

The US Department of Education and the Department of Justice also issued a strong, 40-page "Dear Colleague" letter to state and local education agencies on civil rights issues impacting EL students and parents of EL students (Lhamon & Gupta, 2015). This guidance addresses several critical areas, including the identification and assessment of EL students, access to core and advanced courses, segregating EL students, ensuring the effectiveness of language programs, and ensuring meaningful communication with non-English speaking parents. In addition, the US Department of Education released an extensive toolkit in 2016 to assist states and schools in meeting their civil rights obligations to EL students and providing ELs with the support they need.

On the programmatic and funding side in Texas, challenges remain. In recent years, Texas has seen a sharp growth in the number of school districts offering one-way and two-way dual language programs. However, a law passed over a decade ago allowing schools to exit students after only 2 years of service remains unchanged. Texas and 31 other states continue to experience shortages of certified bilingual and ESL teachers (Sanchez, 2017). Texas formerly supported teacher preparation programs for bilingual teacher aides with substantial funds but since the 2011 budget cuts, the state has failed to replace those funds despite efforts by the Texas Association for Bilingual Education and other members of the Texas Latino Education Coalition (TLEC) working with state representatives, including Representative Roberto Alonzo and Senator Jose Rodriguez.

Instead, several pieces of legislation sought to address the teacher shortage in negative ways. One example is House Bill 880 filed by Representative Ken King in the 85th Regular Session (2017). This bill would have allowed school districts to hire an ESL-only certified teacher to teach a bilingual education class without the appropriate bilingual certificate for 1 year if a bilingual certified teacher was not reasonably available to the district. After opposition by TLEC, HB 880 was left pending in the House Public Education Committee (King, 2017).

In the area of state bilingual funding, no progress was made. Bills that would either increase state funding or require cost studies did not move following significant support from TLEC and others. One bill, House Bill (HB 21), would have increased bilingual education by a fraction to (0.11), or approximately $50/year for each EL student. HB 21, however, failed to pass in the Senate. In the special session of 2017, the same bilingual education funding provision was attached to the major House school finance bill (HB 21, again), but in a last-minute negotiation with the Senate, the increase was left out.

Several researchers, parents and advocates continue to fight for comprehensive, sustainable and meaningful reforms. In the most recent Texas legislative session, IDRA presented testimony on behalf of TLEC on empirically-based policy reforms that could improve learning and opportunities for EL students. For example, citing in part IDRA's research and research by the Learning Policy Institute, TLEC (2017) recommended to the House Public Education Committee on HB 880 that instead of lowering or eliminating standards for certified bilingual educators, the State should enact policies that create stronger pathways and pipelines to bilingual teaching, including:

(a) Recruiting well-prepared bilingual-certified teachers who stay in teaching, and not through temporary faculty agencies.
(b) Supporting high quality mentoring of new bilingual-certified teachers.
(c) Creating, where necessary, and supporting high quality bilingual teacher education programs in high-need areas.
(d) Providing scholarships for entering bilingual-certified teachers, with special focus on high-need fields and locations.
(e) Providing resources to support recruitment incentives for experienced bilingual-certified teachers to teach in rural schools and other hard-to-staff schools and regions.
(f) Supporting increased teacher pay and benefits for bilingual-certified teachers.
(g) Supporting struggling bilingual teachers and school principals with strong, research-based professional development and mentoring.
(h) Requiring all teacher training programs (traditional and otherwise) to train teachers on cultural competency and inclusive communities.
(i) Studying teacher attrition rates and examining factors that could improve teacher retention of bilingual-certified teachers.

(Texas Latino Education Coalition [TLEC], 2017, p. 1–2).

Testimony by IDRA on school funding showed how increased funding for bilingual education could lead to several opportunities to learn, including accelerated learning and high quality tutoring, native language content-testing for placement of new immigrant EL students, professional development centered on language/content learning and cultural competency, coaching and mentoring, local monitoring to ensure biliteracy and biculturalism, smaller class size, and more bilingual books, supportive materials and technology. (IDRA, 2017).

6 Conclusion

EL students carry a special talent of fluency in another language. Substantial research shows how bilingualism can result in cognitive, social, and academic benefits for the individual and for society (Callahan & Gándara, 2014). By creating state and national policies that value EL students' multiculturalism and providing essential resources and tools for appropriate implementation of bilingual models, policymakers can help support educators and school leaders better prepare these students for success in life and the global economy. However, the counterweight of English-only, nationalistic proponents, inadequate investment overall in education, and poor implementation of bilingual education at the local level continue to heavily push back against more positive reforms. The federal government, although acknowledging some advances in Head Start policies supporting dual language policies, has largely failed to more aggressively support bilingual education on the programmatic side. At the state level, dual language programs continue to expand each year, yet inadequate funding and staffing remain key challenges to systemic success.

As the EL student population continues to increase, research on EL student program outcomes also continues to be produced. It is incumbent upon researchers to make this research understandable to policymakers and for policymakers to become aware of this research and apply it to policy. But until state and national leaders engage in comprehensive reforms to address the various components of successful bilingual programs, it seems like the State of Texas will repeat its one-step forward, one-step backward approach to bilingual education policy.

References

Aparicio, F. R., & Jose-Kampfner, C. (1995). Language, culture, and violence in the education crisis of US. Latino/as: Two course for intervention. *Michigan Journal of Community Service Learning, 6*, 95–104.

Callahan, R., & Gándara, P. (2014). Contextualizing bilingualism in the labor market: New destinations, established enclaves and the information age. In R. Callahan & P. Gándara (Eds.), *The bilingual advantage: Language, literacy and the US labor market* (pp. 3–15). Bristol, London: Channel View Publications.

Cárdenas, J. A. (1995). *Multicultural education: A generation of advocacy*. Needham Heights, MA: Simon & Schuster Custom Publishing.

Castañeda v. Pickard, 648 F.2d 989 (5th Cir. 1981).

Collier, V., & Thomas, W. (2004). The astounding effectiveness of dual language education for all. *NABE Journal of Research and Practice, 2*(1), 1–20.

Council of Chief State School Officers. (2016, March) *Major provisions of Every Student Succeeds Act (ESSA) related to the education of English learners*. Washington, DC: Author. Retrieved from https://www.ccsso.org/sites/default/files/2017-11/ccsso%20resource%20on%20els%20 and%20essa.pdf

Crawford, J. (1997). *Best evidence: Research foundations of the Bilingual Education Act*. NCBE Report. Retrieved from https://eric.ed.gov/?id=ED408858

Crawford, J. (2002). Obituary: The Bilingual Ed Act, 1968 to 2002. *Rethinking schools. Special collection on bilingual education*. Retrieved from http://www.rethinkingschools.org/special_reports/bilingual/Bil164.shtml

Cummins, J. (2000). Biliteracy, empowerment, and transformative pedagogy. In J. V. Tinajero & R. A. DeVillar (Eds.), *The power of two languages* (pp. 9–19). New York, NY: McGraw Hill.

DeMatthews, D., & Izquierdo, E. (2017). The importance of principals supporting dual language education: A social justice leadership framework. *Journal of Latinos and Education, 17*, 53–70. Retrieved from http://www.tandfonline.com/doi/full/10.1080/15348431.2017.1282365?scroll=top&needAccess=true

Equal Educational Opportunities Act. (1974). 2 Pub. L. No. 93–380, § 204(f), 88 Stat. 484, 515 (1974) (codified at 20 U.S.C. § 1703(f)).

Gándara, P., & Orfield, G. (2012). Segregating Arizona's English learners: A return to the "Mexican room"? *Teachers College Record, 114*(9), 1–27.

González, A. N. (2014). *Bilingual education: Learning while learning English*. Dallas, TX: AngelNoeGonzalez.com.

Hinojosa, D. (2015). Rodriguez v. San Antonio Independent School District: Forty years and counting. In C. J. Ogletree & K. J. Robinson (Eds.), *The enduring legacy of Rodriguez: Creating new pathways to equal educational opportunity* (pp. 23–44). Cambridge, MA: Harvard Edition Press.

Hinojosa, D., & Walters, K. (2014). How adequacy litigation fails to fulfill the promise of Brown [But how it can get us closer]. In K. L. Bowman (Ed.), *The pursuit of racial and ethnic equality in American public schools: Mendez, Brown, and beyond* (pp. 576–632). East Lansing, MI: Michigan State University Press.

Horne v. Flores, 557 U.S. 433 (2009).

Intercultural Development Research Association (IDRA). (2017). *Determining the true Costs of Educating Underserved Students – Cost Study of Bilingual/ESL and Compensatory Education*. Invited Testimony. Presented by David Hinojosa, J.D., IDRA National Director of Policy before the Texas House Public Education Committee. http://www.idra.org/resource-center/determining-true-costs-educating-underserved-students-cost-study-bilingualesl-compensatory-education/

Jackson, C. K., Johnson, R. C., & Persico, C. (2016). The effects of school spending on educational and academic outcomes: Evidence from school finance reforms. *Quarterly Journal of Economics, 131*(1), 157–218.

King, K. (2017). Bill: HB 880. 85th Regular Session. *Texas Legislature Online*. Retrieved from http://www.legis.state.tx.us/BillLookup/Text.aspx?LegSess=85R&Bill=HB880

Lafortune, J., Rothstein, J., & Whitmore Schanzenbach, D. (2016). School finance reform and the distribution of student achievement. NBER working paper No. 22011. *National Bureau of Economic Research*. Retrieved from http://www.nber.org/papers/w22011.pdf

Lau v. Nichols, 414 U.S. 563 (1974). Para. 15–16. Retrieved from http://caselaw.findlaw.com/us-supreme-court/414/563.html

Lhamon, C. E., & Gupta, V. (2015). *Dear colleague letter: English learner students and limited English proficient parents*. Washington, DC: U.S. Department of Justice: Civil Rights Division, and U.S. Department of Education: Office for Civil Rights. https://www2.ed.gov/about/offices/list/ocr/letters/colleague-el-201501.pdf

Li, J. J., Steele, J. L., Slater, R., Bacon, M., & Miller, T. (2016). *Implementing two-way dual-language immersion programs: Classroom insights from an urban district*. RAND Corporation. Retrieved from https://www.rand.org/pubs/research_briefs/RB9921.html

Mexican American Legal Defense and Educational Fund (MALDEF). (n.d.). *United States v. State of Texas*. Retrieved from http://maldef.org/education/litigation/us_v_texas/

Mexican American Legal Defense and Educational Fund (MALDEF), & Multicultural Education, Training and Advocacy, Inc. (META). (n.d.). *MALDEF and META file civil rights suit against the Texas Education Agency and two individual school districts*. Retrieved from http://www.maldef.org/news/releases/maldef_and_meta_file_civil_rights_suit_against_tx_education/

Midobouche, E., & Benavides, A. H. (2008). Title VII Elementary and Secondary Education Act: Subsequent amendments. In J. M. Gonzales (Ed.), *Encyclopedia of bilingual education* (pp. 840–862). Thousand Oaks, CA: SAGE.

Morath, et al. v. The Texas Taxpayer and Student Fairness Coalition, No. 14-0776 2016 WL 2853868 (Tex. 2016).

National Academies of Sciences, Engineering, and Medicine. (2017). *Promoting the educational success of children and youth learning English: Promising futures* (pp. 165–200). Washington, DC: The National Academies Press. https://doi.org/10.17226/24677

Neeley v. West Orange-Cove Consolidated Independent School District, 176 S.W.3d 740, 784 (Tex. 2005). Para. 123. Retrieved from http://caselaw.findlaw.com/tx-supreme-court/1153227.html

Persily, N. (2014). The meaning of equal protection: Then, now, and tomorrow. GPSOLO. *American Bar Association, 31*(6). Retrieved from https://www.americanbar.org/publications/gp_solo/2014/november_december/the_meaning_equal_protection_then_now_and_tomorrow.html

Pompa, D. (2015, December). *New education legislation includes important policies for English learners, potential pitfalls for their advocates*. Washington, DC: Migrant Policy Institute. Retrieved from http://www.migrationpolicy.org/news/new-education-legislation-includes-important-policies-english-learners-potential-pitfalls-their

Ramirez, J. D., Yuen, S. D., Ramey, D. R., & Pasta, D. J. (1991). *Final report: Longitudinal study of structured English immersion strategy, early-exit and late-exit transitional bilingual education programs for language-minority children*. San Mateo, CA: Aguirre International. Retrieved from http://files.eric.ed.gov/fulltext/ED330216.pdf

Reardon, S. F., Umansky, I., Valentino, R., Khanna, R., & Wong, C. (2014). *Differences among instructional models in English learners' academic and English proficiency trajectories: Findings from the SFUSD/Stanford research partnership*. Stanford, CA: Policy Analysis for California Education. Retrieved from www.edpolicyinca.org/sites/default/files/PACE%20slides%20feb2014.pdf

Robledo Montecel, M. (2015). The new Every Student Succeeds Act: Promise and progress or retreat and surrender. *Intercultural Development Research Association*. Retrieved from http://www.idra.org/images/stories/IDRA_Policy_Note_Every_Student_Succeeds_Act_2015.pdf

Robledo Montecel, M., & Cortez, A. (2008). Costs of bilingual education. In J. M. Gonzales (Ed.), *Encyclopedia of bilingual education* (pp. 180–183). Thousand Oaks, CA: Sage. https://doi.org/10.4135/9781412963985.n75

Sanchez, C. (2017, February 23). English language learners: How your state is doing. *National Public Radio Ed*. Retrieved from http://www.npr.org/sections/ed/2017/02/23/512451228/5-million-english-language-learners-a-vast-pool-of-talent-at-risk

Solis, A. (2001). Boosting our understanding of bilingual education: A refresher on philosophy and models. *Intercultural Development Research Association Newsletter*. Retrieved from http://www.idra.org/resource-center/boosting-our-understanding-of-bilingual-education/

Stewner-Manzanares, G. (1988). The Bilingual Education Act: Twenty years later. *The National Clearinghouse for Bilingual Education*, 1–10. Retrieved from https://ncela.ed.gov/files/rcd/BE021037/Fall88_6.pdf

Texas Association for Bilingual Education (TABE). (2012, December 19). *History of bilingual education in Texas*. YouTube. Retrieved from https://www.youtube.com/watch?v=AWbN_Y8aa5k

Texas Latino Education Coalition (TLEC). (2017, April 25). Texas Latino testimony opposing HB 880 (elimination of bilingual education certification). Retrieved from http://www.idra.org/wp-content/uploads/2017/04/TLEC-Testimony-Against-HB-880-04-25-17.pdf

Texas Taxpayer & Student Fairness Coalition v. Williams, Findings of Fact and Conclusions of Law, WL 4254969. (Tex. 2014). p. 109. Retrieved from http://www.lrl.state.tx.us/scanned/archive/2014/24917.pdf

Tung, R. (2013, Summer). Innovations in educational equity for English language learners. *Voices in Urban Education*, 2–5. Retrieved from http://vue.annenberginstitute.org/sites/default/files/issues/VUE37.pdf

U.S. Department of Health and Human Services (HHS). (n.d.). *Questions and answers (Q&A) on the release of the new Head Start program performance standards*. Administration for Children and Families. Head Start ECLKC. Washington, DC: Author. Retrieved from https://eclkc.ohs.acf.hhs.gov/sites/default/files/docs/pdf/hs-prog-pstandards-final-rule-qa.pdf

U.S. Department of Justice, and U.S. Department of Education. (2015). *English learners DCL*. Washington, DC: Author. Retrieved from https://www2.ed.gov/about/offices/list/ocr/letters/colleague-el-201501.pdf

United States v. State of Texas, 506 F. Supp. 405 (E.D. Tex. 1981).

United States v. Texas, 680 F.2d 356 ("LULAC I"). (5th Cir. 1982).

United States v. Texas, 601 F. 3d 354 ("LULAC II"). (5th Cir. 2010).

Valenzuela, A. (1999). *Subtractive schooling: U.S.-Mexican youth and the politics of caring*. Albany, NY: State University of New York Press.

West Orange-Cove Consolidated Independent School District v. Neeley, WL 5719215 (250th Dist. Ct., Austin 2004).

Compounded Inequities: Tracking School Finance Equity for Districts Serving Low-Income Emergent Bilingual Students

David S. Knight and Jesus E. Mendoza

Abstract School districts face different costs to produce the same level of educational opportunity because of differences in student populations, geographic variation in average wages, and district size. However, in many states, the school finance system fails to take these factors into account when distributing funds to school districts. Most prior analyses of state school finance systems focus on the relationship between district funding and the percent of low-income students in that district. Other studies explore funding for emergent bilinguals, who are typically classified as English language learners (ELLs) in state data systems. We present the first longitudinal descriptive evidence of the extent to which state school finance systems compound inequities for districts serving high concentrations of both low-income students and ELLs. We assess the extent to which high-ELL high-poverty districts are underfunded relative to otherwise similar districts in the same state and how these trends have changed leading up to and following the recession-era spending cuts. We find that prior to the recession, high-ELL districts received greater funding levels than otherwise similar low-ELL districts in the same state. However, recessionary spending cuts disproportionately impacted funding for ELLs. The remaining resource advantages for high-ELL districts are concentrated in low-poverty districts. We discuss implications for bilingual education and school finance policy.

Keywords Emergent bilinguals · English learners · School finance · Equity · Resource allocation · Great recession · School budgeting

The United States has one of the only education systems among advanced nations that provides less funding for schools serving higher-need students (Organization

---

D. S. Knight (✉)
University of Washington, Seattle, WA, USA
e-mail: dsknight84@gmail.com

J. E. Mendoza
Center for Education Research and Policy Studies, University of Texas at El Paso, El Paso, TX, USA
e-mail: MendozaJE@elpasotexas.gov

for Economic Development and Cooperation [OECD], 2016; Porter, 2013).[1] In contrast to all other developed countries, educational governance in the U.S. is controlled primarily at the state and local level, with the federal government contributing only about 10% of total funding. The decentralized structure – with heavy reliance on local property tax revenues for school funding – leads to resource disparities as school funding is a function of local property values and family income. In response to court mandates and legislative reforms over the past four decades, states target aid to high-poverty districts; however, state aid is often insufficient to alleviate the disparities that result from reliance on local property taxation. State legislatures maintain authority over both the level and distribution of funds across school districts and the degree of funding disparity varies substantially across states, with some states providing more equitable resource allocation than others. However, on average nationally, the highest-poverty and often the highest-need school districts receive less funding and have fewer resources than districts serving more privileged student populations (Baker, Farrie, Johnson, Luhm, & Sciarra, 2017).

School districts face different costs to produce the same level of educational opportunity because of differences in student background characteristics, geographic variation in average wages, and district size (Odden & Picus, 2014). For example, research shows that districts face higher costs to educate low-income and emergent bilingual students (Duncombe & Yinger, 2008; Parrish, 1994). Students in poverty may not have access to the same level of resources at home as do higher-income students, and schools often target special services such as after school tutoring or health related interventions to address these differences. For emergent bilingual students, additional costs pay for multilingual curricular materials, teacher professional development, and bilingual aides to help educators draw on the assets such students bring to schools including linguistic capital and cultural diversity (Gándara, Rumberger, Maxwell-Jolly, & Callahan, 2003; Jimenez-Castellanos & Topper, 2012). School districts classify emergent bilinguals as English language learners (ELLs). Students in poverty are identified based on their eligibility for free or reduced price meals (FRL), a federal program targeted to students at or below 185% of the federal poverty line. In many states, districts receive extra funds to cover the additional costs of serving ELLs and students eligible for FRL. In short, schools serving greater proportions of emergent bilinguals or students in poverty require additional funding to provide equitable learning opportunities, yet state school finance systems often fail to recognize these differences and fund districts accordingly.

Most prior analyses of state school finance systems focus on the relationship between district funding and the percent of low-income students in that district (Chingos & Blagg, 2017; Baker et al., 2017) or the percent of ELLs (Knight & DeMatthews, 2017; Rolle & Jimenez-Castellanos, 2014). More recent work focuses on the impact of the Great Recession on school resources (Chakrabarti & Setren, 2011; Baker, 2014; Knight, 2017; Knight & Strunk, 2016). Recessionary spending

---

[1] Among countries in the OECD, only the United States, Turkey, and Israel provide more teachers per student in schools serving more advantaged students (OECD, 2016; see also Porter, 2013).

cuts disproportionately reduced resources targeted to historically underserved students both across districts and within districts across schools. In this chapter, we present the first longitudinal descriptive evidence of the extent to which state school finance systems compound inequities for districts serving high concentrations of both low-income students and emergent bilinguals. We assess the extent to which high-ELL high-FRL districts are underfunded relative to otherwise similar districts in the same state and how these trends have changed leading up to and following the recession-era spending cuts. We focus on the following three research questions:

1. To what extent do districts receive additional funding to serve ELL students and how has that relationship changed since the Great Recession?
2. How does the proportion of students in poverty moderate the relationship between funding and the percent of ELLs in a district?
3. How do states differ in their provision of equitable funding for higher-need districts and what role do state funding mechanisms play in determining these differences?

We find that prior to the Great Recession funding cuts (2007–2008), high-ELL districts received approximately 12% more state and local funding than otherwise similar low-ELL districts. However, by 2012–2013, following substantial budget cuts in most states, the resource advantage in high-ELL districts decreased to 8%. In other words, recessionary spending cuts disproportionately impacted funding for emergent bilinguals. We also find that the remaining resource advantages for high-ELL districts are concentrated in low-poverty districts. Among districts serving lower-poverty student populations, high-ELL districts receive an additional 11% more funding over otherwise similar low-ELL districts. In contrast, among districts serving higher-poverty student populations, high-ELL districts receive an additional 7% more funding over otherwise similar low-ELL districts. These differences in funding result in real differences in staffing resources. We find that during the recessionary spending cuts, the number of students per teacher, counselor, and support staff all increased in high-ELL districts. Differences in resource levels have consequences for students. Recent research shows, for example, that a 10% increase in funding for all 12 years of K-12 schooling increases the likelihood of high school graduation by 11.5% and increases adult income by 12.3% (Jackson, Johnson, & Persico, 2015). Finally, our cross-state analyses identify wide differences in the extent to which states allocate resources equitably across districts. We find that larger student weights for ELL and FRL students may increase funding for those students, but there is a relatively weak relationship between the size of funding weights for special populations and the degree of funding equity for those students.

The balance of the chapter proceeds with a review of past studies focusing on (a) the impact of school funding for low-income students and emergent bilinguals; and (b) the degree to which higher-need districts receive more funding. Subsequent sections review the data and methods used in our analyses, findings, and recommendations for policy.

1 Review of Relevant Literature

Two areas of research are pertinent to the analysis described in this chapter. First, we synthesize research demonstrating the importance of school funding for higher-need students. Second, we review studies documenting inequitable funding for low-income students and emergent bilinguals.

1.1 The Impact of School Funding

Scholars have debated for decades whether increasing funding for schools improves outcomes (see Coleman et al., 1966; Hanushek, 1986, 1989, 1997; and Baker, 2012). Most of the prior studies are based on regression analysis using large-scale datasets. These studies allow researchers to compare short-term outcomes in school districts that have *otherwise similar* characteristics, but receive varying levels of funding.[2] If districts with more funding outperform otherwise similar districts with less funding, then one might conclude that providing extra resources improves outcomes. Many studies have identified a positive correlation between funding and outcomes through regression analyses; however, a roughly equal number (depending on how those studies are counted, Greenwald, Hedges, Laine, 1996) have found no systematic relationship. Because funding is not randomly distributed to school districts, determining the causal impact of school funding on outcomes is not possible through simple regression analysis of large-scale datasets. Moreover, because additional school resources may provide benefits to students that accrue over time, examining only short-term outcomes such as test scores may underestimate the true impact of school funding.

In recent years however, a new approach to measuring the impact of school funding on student outcomes emerged. Since the 1970s, school districts in almost every state have brought legal challenges alleging that their state school finance system does not provide an equitable or adequate level of school resources that meets state constitutionals mandates. Court decisions have often ruled in favor of plaintiffs, leading to immediate, long-lasting increases in school funding in those states. Researchers have used these "exogenous shocks" in school funding to carefully examine how outcomes changed over time for students living in those states, compared to other states that did not undergo a major school finance reform (Candelaria & Shores, 2017; Jackson, Johnson, & Perscico, 2015; Lafortune, Rothstein, & Schanzenbach, 2016). The findings from these studies are unequivocal: Greater funding in higher-need districts that is sustained over time improves students' test scores, graduation rates, and labor market earnings later in life.

---

[2] An educational production function refers to the broad set of analyses that estimate the amount of "output" produced in schools (i.e., test scores, graduation rates, or some other student outcome), based on a set of "inputs" such as funding, salaries, or teacher-student ratios.

1.2 The Distribution of School Funding

A number of studies and policy reports document inequitable funding across districts serving high and low-poverty student populations (Adamson & Darling-Hammond, 2012; Goldhaber & Callahan, 2001; Rolle & Liu, 2007; Knight, 2017). A yearly report from the Education Law Center identifies states that have the most inequitable funding systems, based on several measures including the relative funding between high- and low-poverty districts (Baker et al., 2017). The Education Trust also publishes reports documenting funding gaps between wealthy and poor districts nationally and between high- and low-minority districts (Ushomirsky & Williams, 2015). In both reports, Illinois, Nevada, New York, Pennsylvania, and Texas consistently rank among the bottom in measures of funding equity based on poverty rates. New Jersey, Minnesota, and Ohio are among the states most commonly identified as having equitable funding systems based on measures of student poverty.

Little prior research examines funding for emergent bilinguals (Gándara, Rumberger, Maxwell-Jolly, & Callahan, 2003). One study found that of the eight states with at least 10% of its student population classified as ELLs, five allocated less funding in high-ELL districts compared to low-ELL districts, two states spent approximately the same, and only Alaska allocated greater funding levels to districts serving more ELL students (Arroyo, 2008). Two other studies focused just on Texas found no significant relationship between state and local funding and the percent of students receiving bilingual education in Texas school districts (Rolle & Jimenez-Castellanos, 2014; Rolle, Torres & Eason, 2012). Finally, in prior work, we found that during the 2007–2008 school year, districts in the 95th percentile of percent ELL in their state received approximately 10% more funding on average nationally, compared to those in the 10th percentile, but this funding advantaged disappeared following the Great Recession funding cuts (Knight & DeMatthews, 2017).

Prior research on funding for ELLs does not consider the diversity within ELL student populations (Gándara & Rumberger, 2007, 2008, 2009; Rolle & Jimenez-Castellanos, 2014). Emergent bilinguals have a wide range of racial/ethnic identities, socioeconomic status, learning needs, and academic assets. In the most obvious case, districts serving high populations of ELLs may differ in the extent to which those students also come from high-poverty backgrounds. This chapter highlights the often-overlooked question of how funding for bilingual education differs in high- and low-poverty districts. In summary, despite the large number of studies demonstrating the negative relationship between district poverty rate and funding levels, fewer studies examine the funding equity for high-ELL districts and no study of which we are aware has considered how funding disparities may compound for districts serving high proportions of both ELL and low-income students.

2 Policy Context

2.1 High-Poverty High-ELL Districts

Table 1 demonstrates that districts serving high concentrations of ELL students differ considerably depending on district poverty rate. The table is limited to all school districts in the 25 states with the highest percent of ELL students. The first two columns compare low-poverty districts that are low-ELL (Column 1) and high-ELL (Column 2). In this table "low" and "high" indicate the bottom and top quartiles within each state. Most students attending low-ELL low-FRL districts live in suburban and rural neighborhoods and 88% are White. The majority of students in low-ELL high-FRL districts live in rural neighborhoods. Among high-ELL districts, there is a stark contrast in the percent of Asian and Hispanic students, depending on the poverty rate. As shown in Column 2, 14% of students identify as Asian in high-ELL districts that are low-poverty, compared to only 2% in high-ELL districts that are low-poverty. Hispanic students make up 28% of the student population in high-ELL low-poverty districts, and 62% in high-ELL high-poverty districts.

The fourth panel of Table 1 shows achievement scores based on standardized exams. These exam scores are nationally referenced and standardized so that the overall mean is 0 and negative values imply that the district is below the national average (Reardon et al., 2016). While low-ELL low-FRL districts are the highest achieving of the four groups, the ELL achievement gap is greater among districts serving low-income students, compared to districts serving higher-income students. The bottom panel shows funding and spending rates. These figures show that, consistent with prior literature, high-poverty districts generally receive less state and local funding than low-poverty districts. Similarly, high-ELL districts receive less funding and spend less per student than low-ELL districts, but funding gaps vary by district poverty rate. Based on unadjusted comparisons, the funding gap between low- and high-ELL districts is larger for low-poverty districts.

Comparisons in Table 1 do not take into account or adjust for local differences in cost that may be related to student demographics. For example, high-ELL high-FRL districts are more likely to be located in urban areas where the cost of wages is higher and educational dollar does not have as much buying power. Conversely, rural schools with sparse population density face higher costs for student transportation and through diseconomies of scale. The table also does not consider changes over time. In the section below, we describe how we adjust for local differences in cost and examine changes in funding rates over time. We first provide additional background on state funding mechanisms for higher need students.

Table 1 Summary statistics for low- and high-ELL and FRL districts and all other districts, 2012–2013

ELL	Low	High	Low	High	All other	
FRL	Low	Low	High	High	districts[a]	Total
Number of Students						
Urban	0	404,049	1969	2,992,755	6,615,983	10,014,756
Suburban	164,575	907,882	46,247	2,712,902	11,950,066	15,781,672
Rural	144,625	17,968	110,480	287,911	2,674,961	3,235,945
Total	309,200	1,329,899	158,696	5,993,568	21,241,010	29,032,373
Number of Districts						
Urban	0	34	2	114	310	460
Suburban	112	75	43	353	1999	2582
Rural	257	35	281	260	2227	3060
Total	369	144	326	727	4536	6102
District and student characteristics						
% ELL	0.04%	15.82%	0.01%	27.39%	4.75%	7.17%
% FRL	22.30%	23.84%	78.64%	81.38%	47.39%	51.03%
% Asian	1.0%	13.5%	0.3%	2.4%	2.2%	2.4%
% Black	1.4%	3.3%	10.2%	8.1%	6.3%	6.4%
% Hispanic	4.4%	28.0%	6.7%	61.7%	17.4%	21.6%
% Native American	1.6%	1.2%	21.7%	5.0%	2.9%	4.1%
% White	88.2%	48.6%	55.8%	20.6%	67.2%	61.8%
% multirace/other	3.4%	5.5%	5.3%	2.2%	3.9%	3.8%
Dist. Enroll.	838	9235	487	8244	4683	4758
Cost of Wage	1.38	1.64	1.26	1.42	1.37	1.38
Standardized exam scores						
Grade 3 ELA	0.602	0.380	−0.607	−1.322	−0.016	−0.161
Grade 3 Math	0.595	0.189	−0.478	−1.035	0.033	−0.088
District funding						
Total PPR	$14,724	$13,168	$12,752	$11,938	$12,508	$12,602
St./local PPR	$14,126	$12,485	$10,687	$10,216	$11,556	$11,527

Note: Low- and high-ELL districts refer to districts with fewer than 0.25% and greater than 9.05% ELL students, respectively. Low and high FRL districts refer to districts with fewer than 35.60% and greater than 67.80% FRL students, respectively. These figures correspond to the lowest and highest quartiles for 2012–2013. St./local PPR refers to state and local per-pupil revenues and per-pup. exp. refers to per-pupil expenditures

[a]All other districts refers to those that fall in the middle quartiles for % English language learner (ELL) or % of student eligible free/reduced price lunch (FRL). The table is limited to high-ELL states, defined as the 25 states with the highest percent of ELL students. These states include 91% of all ELLs nationally

2.2 State Funding for ELL and Low-Income Students

School districts in the U.S. receive funding from local property tax revenues, additional state aid, and directly from the federal government. On average, local and state funding sources account for about 45% of total funding each, while federal funding makes up the other 10%. All states have a school finance formula that determines the amount of aid each district will receive, which is typically based on district cost factors such as size and student population and the amount of local revenue generated through property taxation. State aid is used to provide additional funding for districts serving households with lower property values, which generate less local tax revenue. The purpose of this state aid is to ensure that all school districts receive an adequate level of funding. However, states vary widely in the extent to which aid is targeted to high-need districts and the mechanisms through which funds are allocated.

A total of 40 states have a specific mechanism within their school finance formula for targeting additional funds to high-ELL districts, whereas 35 states have a provision in their finance formula that increases funding for low-income students. States provide supplementary funding for bilingual education or other programs for ELLs through one of three mechanism: formula funding, categorical funding outside general formula funding, or through direct reimbursement. Funding formula mechanisms include student weights, where a student classified as ELL generate, for example, 10% additional funding, dollar amounts, where an ELL student generate a specific dollar amount of funding, and teacher allocations, in which additional teacher are allocated to districts based on the percent of ELL students (Odden & Picus, 2014). Categorical funding includes special grants that districts receive based on their student population. States use similar funding mechanisms to support low-income students.

Table 2 shows the different ELL and FRL funding mechanisms across states in 2015–2016, based on a policy scan that we conducted of the 25 states with the highest percent of ELL students. From the 25 states analyzed, 18 states use formula funding to send additional funds to districts serving greater concentrations of students in poverty and three states allocate funding for low-income students through categorical grants. In contrast, only 13 states use a formula to additionally fund ELL students and four rely on categorical funding. Only two states (Delaware and Rhode Island) of those analyzed in Table 2 lack any specific funding mechanism for poor students, whereas seven states do not have any funding mechanism for ELL students.

3 Data Sources and Methods for Adjusting Funding Rates for Local Costs

Analyses presented in this chapter are based on merged datasets that include the Local Education Finance Survey and Common Core of Data, the U.S. Census Bureau Small Area Income & Poverty Estimates, and the Educational Cost of Wage

Table 2 Funding mechanism by state for ELL and FRL student populations

	Number of districts	Number of students	Funding mechanism for ELL	Funding mechanism for FRL
Alaska	50	130,998	Formula (0.20)	No mechanism
Arizona	197	939,976	Formula (0.115)	No mechanism
Arkansas	236	475,003	Formula ($305/ELL, ~ 0.03)	Categorical ($526–$1576)
California	864	5,978,861	Formula (0.20)	Formula (0.20–0.50)
Colorado	175	850,957	Categorical	Formula (0.12–0.30, +$16/FRL)
Connecticut	166	517,812	Formula (0.15)	No mechanism
Delaware	16	111,667	No mechanism	1 instructor/250 unduplicated at-risk stu.
Florida	67	2,680,074	Formula (0.147)	No mechanism
Idaho	108	270,734	Categorical	No mechanism
Illinois	830	2,032,805	Reimbursement	Reimbursement ($355/FRL)
Kansas	275	483,289	Formula (0.395)	Formula (0.456)
Maryland	24	859,252	Formula (0.99)	Formula (0.97)
Massachusetts	289	889,911	Formula (0.07–0.34)	Categorical ($2767–$3422)
Minnesota	321	793,777	Formula ($700/ELL, ~ 0.06)	Formula (0.5–1.0)
Nevada	17	431,776	Formula (20:1)	No mechanism
New Mexico	87	327,127	Categorical	No mechanism
North Carolina	115	1,468,228	Formula (0.50)	Wealth and poverty-based adjustments
Oklahoma	512	667,802	Formula (0.25)	Formula (0.25)
Oregon	174	555,653	Formula (0.50)	Formula (0.25)
Rhode Island	36	136,401	No mechanism	Formula (0.40 of core instruction)
South Carolina	79	700,247	Formula (0.20)	Formula (0.20)
Texas	1018	4,886,471	Formula (0.10)	Formula (0.20)
Utah	40	528,364	Categorical	Categorical ($23,176,400 FY: 2015)
Virginia	132	1,264,880	Formula (58.8:1)	Formula (0.14–0.19)
Washington	274	1,050,308	Formula ($930/ELL, ~ 0.09)	Formula ($460/FRL)

Note: Districts in Minnesota with fewer than 20 ELLs receive a $14,000 block grant. Average district funding in Washington, Arkansas, and Minnesota is $10,382, $9126, and $12,003, so the dollar amounts equate to student weights for ELLs of approximately 0.090, 0.033, and 0.058, respectively. Student weights for ELLs in Massachusetts vary by grade level. The table includes the 25 states with the highest percent of ELLs. Delaware provides funding through academic excellence units that can be used to support low-income students. North Carolina provides districts with additional funding based on local property wealth and the percent of students in poverty (EdBuild, 2019; Millard, 2015).

Index (Taylor & Fowler, 2006). Our dataset includes all school districts nationally that educate students in any grades in K-12, and that reported finance and other data to the Department of Education National Center for Education Statistics (NCES), from school years 2007–2008 to 2012–2013 (about 96% of active districts in the U.S.). Districts report total enrollment and the number of students eligible for FRL, classified as ELL, and enrolled in special education. Our merged datasets also include information about the districts' local cost of wage index and population density (based on the NCES classifications of urban, urban fringe, suburban, rural-large town, and rural). In total, the sample includes 12,723 districts in 2012–2013, the most recent year of data used. For most of our analyses, we limited to the dataset to the 25 states with the highest overall percent of students classified as ELL, since funding disparities for ELL students in low-ELL states are more difficult to measure and may distort nationally averages. These 25 states educate approximately 91% of all ELLs nationally.

We compare funding, spending, and staffing levels across school districts that serve high and low proportions of ELL and FRL students. The goal of these analyses is to determine the extent to which states provide equitable funding and resources for these students. We create measures of funding progressiveness based on regressions that control for local differences in cost (the cost of wage, population density, the percent of students in special education, and district size). In other words, regressions allow us to compare districts within the same state that have similar cost factors, but differ in their percent of ELL or FRL students. The primary variables of interest are the percent of students classified as ELL and FRL. Our regression analyses weight districts by student enrollment so that larger districts contribute more to the results. We report both regression coefficients (Table 3) and, to clarify the results of these analyses, predicted values for the districts in each state with the highest and lowest percent of ELLs and FRL students (Tables 4 and 5). We compare resource levels across districts in the same state in the same year by including state and year fixed effects in the regressions. We include in our analytic sample only the 25 states with the highest percent of ELL students because in states that fall in the bottom half of percent ELL, fewer than 6% of students are classified as ELL. However, our results are similar when analyses include all states and when narrowing the sample to just Texas and just California – the two states educating the greatest number of emergent bilingual students (these results are available from the authors upon request).

4 Findings

Our results show that, consistent with prior studies, high-ELL districts received slightly more funding than otherwise similar low-ELL districts prior to the recession, but this funding advantage significantly decreased following the Great Recession funding cuts (from 14% down to 9%). However, we also find that funding for ELL students varies according to the degree of poverty in the school district. In particular, the funding advantage for high-ELL districts is significantly smaller

Table 3 Regression coefficients showing the relationship between district resources per student and the proportion of students in the district classified as English language learners and as low-income

	State and local funding per student		Expenditures per student		Average teacher salaries	
	Model 1	Model 2	Model 3	Model 4	Model 5	Model 6
Coefficients for the base school year (2008–2009)						
% ELL	3877***	6281***	4763***	9012***	3318+	16488***
	(619.85)	(1606.67)	(617.55)	(1654.37)	(2015.63)	(4928.86)
% FRL	−3658***	−3327***	−4283***	−4204***	−8992***	−7514**
	(773.97)	(761.98)	(735.79)	(745.29)	(2630.97)	(2586.42)
% ELL × % FRL		−3955+		−7372**		−22352**
		(2362.80)		(2480.15)		(7582.87)
Coefficients interacted with 2012–2013 school year						
% ELL	−1471**	−2111	−1919***	−1514	−8718**	−19147*
	(510.14)	(1530.28)	(452.62)	(1576.22)	(3080.61)	(8256.71)
% FRL	−1397***	−1585***	−1362***	−1613***	−6320***	−8330***
	(362.28)	(400.37)	(358.09)	(394.24)	(1412.56)	(1685.82)
% ELL × % FRL		1481.00		497.00		18214+
		(2228.89)		(2371.16)		(9599.02)
R-squared	0.531	0.532	0.517	0.518	0.804	0.804
Observations	36,971	36,971	36,971	36,971	36,639	36,639

Note: Each column is a separate regression. ELL stands for English language learner and FRL stands for eligibility for free or reduced price lunch (i.e., low-income students). Models include covariates that control for differences in local cost including level of urbanicity, geographic cost of wage differentials, and district size. ***indicates statistical significance at the 0.001 level, **indicates statistical significance at the 0.01 level, *indicates statistical significance at the 0.05 level, and + indicates statistical significance at the 0.10 level

among high-poverty schools. Finally, we identify significant variation across states. States that allocate additional funds to special populations through formula funding and those that have larger student weights have more equitable finance systems, but this relationship is not statistically significant and there are several examples of states that do not follow these trends. In other words, changes in state funding formulas will not guarantee more equitable finance systems. We present more detailed information on our findings in the two subsections below.

4.1 Compounded Inequities of High-Poverty High-ELL Districts

Table 3 shows regression coefficients that estimate the relationship between the percent of ELL and FRL students and three different measures of district resources. Measures of district resource levels include state and local funding per student (Model 1 and 2), per-student spending (Models 3 and 4) and average teacher

Table 4 State and local per student funding (adjusted for local differences in cost)

	High-ELL districts	Low-ELL districts	Difference
2007–2008 school year			
All districts	11,200	9843	1357***
	(180.74)	(113.71)	(213.54)
High-poverty districts	10,764	9812	952*
	(268.42)	(301.59)	(403.74)
Low-poverty districts	12,451	10,391	2060***
	(436.56)	(132.63)	(456.26)
Difference	−1687***	−580+	−1108+
	(512.48)	(329.46)	(609.25)
2012–2013 school year			
All districts	10,475	9633	842***
	(149.81)	(76.26)	(168.11)
High-poverty districts	9598	8918	680**
	(135.52)	(165.52)	(213.92)
Low-poverty districts	12,139	10,766	1373**
	(443.00)	(169.70)	(474.39)
Difference	−2541***	−1848***	−693
	(463.26)	(237.05)	(520.39)

Note: This table shows that in 2007–2008, high-ELL districts received $11,200 per students in state and local funding, whereas otherwise similar low-ELL districts received $9843. Thus high-ELL districts received an additional $1357 in funding. However, by 2012–2013, that funding advantage decreased to $842, a 38% reduction. The table also demonstrates that these differences mask variation within high-ELL districts. Among high-ELL districts, those serving high-poverty populations, as measured by the percent of students eligible for free/reduced price lunch (FRL), received, on average, $9598 per student in state and local funding in 2012–2013, compared to $12,139 for lower-poverty districts serving high concentrations of ELL students. Conversely, in 2012–2013, the funding advantage for high-ELL districts in high-poverty settings was $680, compared to $1373 for high-ELL districts in low-poverty settings. High- and low-ELL and FRL districts are defined as those at the 90th percentile within their state. Standard errors are in parentheses. Dollar figures are reported in nominal terms, and overall funding decreased by even more in real terms. ***p &003C; 0.001, **p &003C; 0.01 level, *p &003C; 0.05, and + p &003C; 0.10

salaries (Models 5 and 6). For each outcome, the first model includes the two variables of interest (percent of ELLs and percent of FRL students), as well as the control variables. Next, we add an interaction term that shows how the relationship between resources and the percent of ELLs changes as the percent of FRL students increases.

Model 1 (Column 1) shows results for Research Question 1, which examines how funding for ELLs changed from 2007–2008 to 2012–2013. In the base year (2007–2008), across otherwise similar districts in the same state, a one percentage point increase in the proportion of ELL students is associated with an increase of $38.77 in per-student funding, or about 0.39%. In other words, in 2007–2008, high-ELL districts (those with 35% ELL students, approximately the 95th percentile) received about 14% more state and local funding than otherwise similar low-ELL

Table 5 Differences in state and local funding per student between high-ELL and low-ELL districts, by state for the 25 states with the highest percent of ELL students, 2012–2013

	% ELL	High-ELL	Low-ELL	Difference	% Funding Gap
Regressive/inequitable funding for ELL students (more than 7% funding gap)					
Delaware	6.4%	7896	15,283	−7388	−48.3%
Nevada	15.7%	7466	11,260	−3794+	−33.7%
Arizona	6.2%	5596	7590	−1994**	−26.3%
Arkansas	7.1%	8428	9291	−863*	−9.3%
Idaho	6.1%	12,172	13,183	−1010*	−7.7%
Minnesota	6.4%	11,307	12,190	−883	−7.2%
Flat funding with respect to the percent of ELL students (+/− 7% difference in funding)					
Connecticut	5.8%	17,485	18,092	−607	−3.4%
Massachusetts	7.3%	14,824	15,357	−534	−3.5%
North Carolina	6.6%	7566	7653	−87	−1.1%
California	22.7%	9103	8861	242	2.7%
New Mexico	15.8%	9357	8935	422	4.7%
Texas	15.1%	9443	8941	501*	5.6%
Washington	8.9%	10,776	10,248	528	5.2%
South Carolina	5.8%	11,101	10,566	534	5.1%
Kansas	8.8%	11,165	10,518	647+	6.2%
Progressive/equitable funding for ELL students (at least 7% more funding for high-ELL districts)					
Oklahoma	6.9%	8524	7777	747**	9.6%
Utah	5.7%	8375	7569	806	10.7%
Colorado	12.0%	10,253	8828	1425+	16.1%
Oregon	9.0%	10,465	9011	1454***	16.1%
Florida	9.0%	9626	7642	1983*	26.0%
Illinois	9.4%	8681	6313	2368	37.5%
Alaska	11.3%	19,432	16,183	3250+	20.1%
Rhode Island	5.8%	13,984	11,601	2383	20.5%
Virginia	7.4%	15,406	10,165	5241***	51.6%
Maryland	6.4%	26,307	12,860	13,448***	104.6%

Note: High-ELL and low-ELL are defined as districts at the 5th and 95th percentiles of percent of ELLs. Models include covariates that control for differences in local cost including population density, geographical differences in wage rates, and district size. This table is ordered from least equitable to most equitable state. In previous work (Knight & DeMatthews, 2017), we controlled for district poverty rate over the six-year panel, rather than controlling for district poverty rate individually in each year, as is done in this study. These results therefore differ slightly from those previously reported in related work. ***p &003C; 0.001, **p &003C; 0.01 level, *p &003C; 0.05, and +p &003C; 0.10

districts (those with no ELL students). The second row shows a negative relationship between funding and the percent of low-income students for 2007–2008. Each percentage point increase in the proportion of FRL students is associated with a decrease of $36.58 in state and local funding per student. The bottom panel of Table 3 shows how these relationships changed in 2012–2013, after states cut education funding following the Great Recession. The coefficient for percent of ELL students, −$1471, implies that ELL students were disproportionately impacted by the Great Recession funding cuts. Specifically, relative to funding rates in 2007–2008, each one percentage point increase in the proportion of ELL students across districts in a state is associated with a $14.71 decrease in per-student funding, relative to 2007–2008 levels. The negative coefficient for % FRL (−$1397) implies that high-poverty districts were also disproportionately impacted by recessionary funding cuts by approximately the same degree as high-ELL districts.

The second model of Table 3 captures our results for Research Question 2 of how funding for ELLs varies by poverty rate. This model adds an interaction between percent of ELL students and the percent of FRL students. The coefficient for the percent of ELL students now represents the relationship between funding and the percent of ELL students for districts with zero low-income students. As shown in Table 3, the coefficient for percent of ELL students changes from $3877 to $6281 from Model 1 to Model 2, implying that while the percent of ELLs in a district is positively related to funding, that relationship is stronger among low-poverty districts (those with zero percent FRL students). The interaction term, shown in Row 3, suggests that as the percent of low-income students in a district increases, funding for ELLs decreases. This general trend holds for models 3–6, which show results for spending per student and average teacher salaries. The bottom panel of Table 3 shows that while both high-FRL and high-ELL districts appear to have been disproportionately targeted by Great Recession spending cuts, the negative influence of poverty rate on funding for ELLs did not change significantly (the interaction terms between %ELL and %FRL in the bottom row are not significant for funding and spending rates and marginally significant for average teacher salaries). In summary, both high-poverty and high-ELL districts were disproportionally impacted by recessionary budget cuts. While districts receive greater funding and spend more as the percent of ELL students increases, these resource advantages are strongest among lower-poverty districts. In 2012–2013, average teacher salaries are negatively correlated with the percent of ELL students, and salaries are lowest among higher-poverty high-ELL districts. Resource advantages for ELLs decrease as the percent of low-income students increases. These findings are generally consistent when we consider other types of resources such as average teacher salaries (reported in Table 3) and student-staffing ratios (not shown here).

Table 4 provides predicted values, based on our regression results, which help place our findings in context.[3] The first row demonstrates that in 2007–2008, the difference in funding between high- and low-ELL districts was $1357 (14%), after adjusting for other cost differences. Among high-poverty districts, those at the 95th percentile of % ELL received $10,764, while those with zero ELL students received,

---

[3] The dollar figures presented in Table 4 are considered "predicted values" because they represent the predicted funding rate for districts at the 5th and 95th percentile of percent of ELL students in each state (roughly 0% and 35%), holding other cost-related factors constant. These figures are close approximations to actual funding levels of low- and high-ELL districts, but are adjusted for other differences in the cost of providing education including population density, district size, the percent of students with special needs, and geographic costs of wages.

on average, $9812 per student, a difference of $952 or about 10%. The third row of Table 4 shows that the ELL funding advantage among lower-poverty districts in 2007–2008 was $2060 or about 20%. In other words, although high-ELL districts had a funding advantage prior to the recession, that funding advantage was twice as large among lower-poverty districts on average, within states nationally. The bottom panel of Table 4 shows how these figures changed by 2012–2013, after the Great Recession state budget cuts. The funding advantage for high-ELL districts decreased to $842 per student on average, a 38% decline from the 2007–2008 level of $1357. As before, the funding advantage for ELLs is greater for districts serving lower-poverty student populations. The bottom three rows of Table 4 show that among high-poverty districts, high-ELL districts received only $680 more in per-student funding compared to otherwise similar low-ELL districts (8%), whereas among lower-poverty districts, the funding advantage for high-ELL districts was $1373 (13%).

These figures are plotted in Fig. 1, which shows the relationship between the percent of students classified as ELL in each district and the average funding rates, before and after the recession, for high- and low-poverty districts. As is clear, high-ELL high-poverty school districts are placed a substantial disadvantage through state funding models. Figure 2 shows the same analyses, this time based on average teacher salaries across in districts serving varying levels of ELL students (Fig. 1).

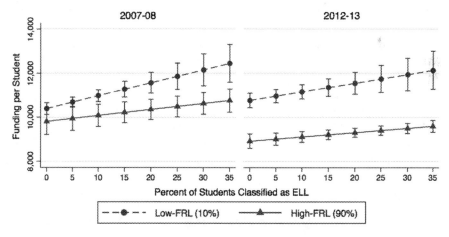

Fig. 1 The relationship between state and local per student funding (adjusted for local differences in cost) and the percent of students classified as ELL, for high- and low-poverty districts
Note: This figure shows that while districts with greater proportions of ELL students receive additional funds on average, there remains a significant gap between high- and low-poverty districts, as measured by the percent of students eligible for free/reduced price lunch (FRL). As a result, high-ELL districts serving high-poverty student populations receive significantly less funding than high-ELL districts serving lower-poverty student populations. Funding for high-ELL high-FRL districts decreased from 2007–2008 both in absolute terms and relative to other districts in the same state. Dollar figures are reported in nominal terms, and overall funding decreased by even more in real terms (after adjusting for inflation)

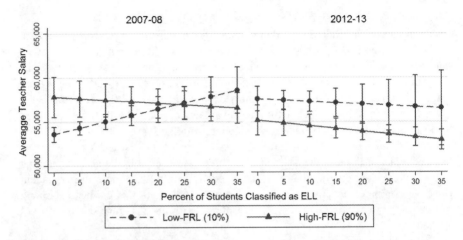

Fig. 2 The relationship between average teacher salaries (adjusted for local differences in cost) and the percent of students classified as ELL, for high and low-poverty districts
Note: This figure shows the relationship between average teacher salaries across districts and the percent of students classified as ELL in the district. Dollar figures are reported in nominal terms, and overall funding decreased by even more in real terms

Figure 2 tells a similar story for average teacher salaries across districts. The panel on the left shows that in 2007–2008 among lower-poverty districts, average teacher salaries across districts were positively correlated with the proportion of students classified as ELLs, whereas among higher-poverty districts, average teacher salaries were negatively correlated with the proportion of students classified as ELLs. The right panel of Fig. 2 shows that five years after the start of the Great Recession, in 2012-13, average teacher salaries had decreased overall (in nominal and real terms) and both high and low-poverty districts had lower average teacher salaries as the percent of ELL students increased. In 2012–2013, high-poverty high-ELL districts offered the lowest teacher salaries among the four groups considered (high-poverty high-ELL, high-poverty low-ELL, low-poverty high-ELL, and low-poverty low ELL).

4.2 Differences in Funding Inequities Across States

Next, we replicate the analyses described above on a state-by-state basis. Results are shown in Table 5, which ranks states according to the funding gap for emergent bilingual students. The first column shows the percent of students in each state classified as ELL students. The next two columns show predicted values of state and local funding per student, by state, for high- and low-ELL districts, holding constant student poverty level and other local cost factors. These results are based on Model 1, where the relationship between funding and % ELL does not vary by poverty level. As expected based on the results for all states nationally, many states provide at least some additional funding for ELL students on average. Maryland, Virginia and Alaska have the most equitable funding systems with respect to emergent bilinguals, while Delaware, Nevada, and Arizona have the least equitable funding systems. The school finance system in Minnesota, which is generally assessed as an equitable system for low-income students, has less equitable funding for ELLs, whereas the finance system in Illinois, which most studies identify as inequitable, is more equitable based on funding for ELL students. Many other states, such as North Carolina, California, New Mexico, and Texas, provide roughly the same level of funding for high- and low-ELL districts. For example, Texas allocates $9443 state and local funding per student to high-ELL districts and $8941 to otherwise similar districts with low concentrations of ELL students, a difference of 5.6%.

What is driving differences across states in school finance equity? We compared the funding mechanisms for ELLs and FRL students across the 25 states shown in Table 2 to the average funding gaps shown in Table 5. We also considered other state-level characteristics including the size of ELL student weights, total overall K-12 spending, the extent to which ELLs are segregated across districts, and the statewide correlation between percent ELL and percent FRL (i.e., the extent to which emergent bilinguals are economically disadvantaged in each state). We found no significant relationship between state funding gaps and the use of either categorical funding or formula funding, although the bivariate correlation between ELL student weights and the funding gap (for the 13 states that use ELL student weights) is −0.77, implying that, not surprisingly, larger student weights are associated with more equitable state funding. The three states that use either reimbursement or have no specific mechanism for funding ELL students tend to have larger funding gaps, other state characteristics held constant. States in which ELL populations are more economically disadvantaged and states that spend less on education have larger funding gaps. The state proportion of students classified as ELL, the degree to which ELLs are segregation, and the relative strength of teachers' unions (based on rankings provided in Winkler, Scull, & Zeehandelaar, 2012) are not associated with funding gaps. In short, states that have some mechanism for funding ELL students other than cost reimbursement, states with larger ELL student weights, states that spend more on K-12 education overall, and states that have less economically disadvantaged ELL populations, on average, provide more equitable financial support for high-ELL districts.

5 Conclusions and Policy Recommendations

Our findings suggest both high-ELL and high-poverty districts were disproportionately impacted by the Great Recession budget cuts. For districts serving high concentrations of emergent bilingual students, the additional resources they received prior to the Recession were significantly reduced during the recessionary budget cuts. In particular, the 12% funding advantage declined to 8% by 2012–2013, after adjusting for local cost factors. Moreover, funding advantages for high-ELL districts are more heavily weighted towards districts serving students from wealthier family backgrounds. Meanwhile, states differ dramatically in the extent to which higher-need districts are under-resourced. These results are consistent for similar analyses of total spending and staffing levels. We provide three policy recommendations for state legislatures, state educational agencies, and the Education Department that we believe would help alleviate the compounded inequities that low-income emergent bilinguals experience.

5.1 Include or Increase Adjustments for ELL and Low-Income Students

Our analysis showed that states that include adjustments for ELL and low-income students, and those with larger funding weights, generally have more progressive funding systems, compared to other states. Although there are exceptions to this rule, the general trend suggests that state legislatures could reduce inequities by introducing or increasing funding weights for special student populations. Several states such as Arizona, Idaho, and Nevada, either provide funding for unduplicated students who identify in any one of a number of different categories including low-income and emergent bilingual, or they simply do not have funding mechanism for certain groups. In other words, districts receive additional funds for each ELL student, but districts do not receive any additional funding if that student is also classified as low-income. Other states such as Maryland, Virginia, and Oregon have designed funding weights that apply doubly for students who are both low-income and classified as ELL. These funding formula decisions recognize the additional resource needs of ELLs, low-income students, and students who fall in both categories.

5.2 Reduce Student Segregation Across School Districts

Disparities in funding across school districts requires some degree of student segregation. A central argument for desegregation is that more integrated school districts necessarily results in more equitably allocated resources. However, studies show that schools are more segregated today than two decades ago, in part because of the ending of court-ordered desegregation mandates (Gándara & Orfield, 2012). Several recent efforts are aimed at re-integrating school districts. For example, in 13 metropolitan areas, inter-district school integration policies aim to reduce inequalities across districts by allowing students to transfer between districts in the same metropolitan area (Finnigan & Holme, 2015; Finnigan et al., 2015). The National Coalition on School Diversity recommends that state education agencies include progress toward racial and socioeconomic integration as a factor in statewide accountability systems. The group also recommends that state education agencies allocate a portion of Title I funding toward programs that foster racial and socioeconomic integration (National Coalition on School Diversity, 2016). State education agencies would need to re-envision the definition of evidence-based Title I interventions (educational programs supported through federal Title I funding) to include strategies for reducing segregation.

5.3 Track Subgroups of Students Classified as ELL in Federal Datasets

The National Center for Education Statistics (NCES) in the Department of Education does not currently collect data on subgroups of students classified as ELL. For example, researchers can measure the percent of students in each district who are classified as ELL and the percent of students in each district in various other classifications (e.g., race/ethnicity, special education enrollment, or free/reduced price lunch), but not students who are ELL and Hispanic or low-income. Current data collection procedures do not allow researchers or policymakers to determine what percent of ELL students in a given district qualify for FRL, or identify in various racial/ethnic groups. In this study, we examined districts with high concentrations of both FRL and ELL students, but we were unable to determine the specific number of students who fall into both categories. More broadly, collecting these data would allow for more fine-grained analyses of how students are distributed across districts, potential disadvantages that emergent bilinguals may face, resources allocated to particular subgroups of ELLs, and the degree of student segregation among ELLs who are also low-income or of color. This level of data would also allow for additional research on the extent to which ELLs are identified as needing special education, perhaps highlighting issues of over- or under-representation. Finally, NCES might consider requiring states to report students' reclassification status as is done in several states. For example, Texas tracks students who were reclassified as non-ELL within the prior 2 years. These data would allow for comparisons across districts in the rate at which schools are reclassifying ELLs as fluent in English.

This chapter focuses on funding for bilingual education and other instructional programs for emergent bilinguals. We measured fiscal support for emerging bilinguals by comparing the revenues, spending, average salaries, and staffing levels in high-ELL districts to that of otherwise similar low-ELL districts. These analyses demonstrate compounded inequities, wherein high-poverty ELLs are not provided with the level of resources that would provide equal educational opportunity. Policy reform that increases funding for high-poverty high-ELL districts would help educators working in these school environments draw on the many assets emergent bilinguals bring to the classroom and may provide for these students with better educational opportunities.

References

Adamson, F., & Darling-Hammond, L. (2012) Funding disparities and the inequitable distribution of teachers: Evaluating sources and solutions. *Education Policy Analysis Archives, 20*(37). Retrieved from http://epaa.asu.edu/ojs/article/view/1053

Arroyo, C. (2008). *The funding gap*. Washington, D.C.: The Education Trust.

Baker, B. D. (2012). *Revisiting the age-old question: Does money matter in education?* Washington, DC: The Albert Shankar Institute.

Baker, B. D. (2014). Evaluating the recession's impact on state school finance systems. *Education Policy Analysis Archives, 22*(91). Retrieved from https://doi.org/10.14507/epaa.v22n91.2014

Baker, B. D., Farrie, D., Johnson, M., Luhm, T., & Sciarra, D. G. (2017). *Is school funding fair? A national report card* (6th ed.). Newark, NJ: Education Law Center.

Candelaria, C. A., & Shores, K. A. (2017). Court-ordered finance reforms in the adequacy era: Heterogeneous causal effects and sensitivity. *Education Finance and Policy*. Advance Online Copy.

Chakrabarti, R., & Setren, E. (2011). *The impact of the Great Recession on school district finances: Evidence from New York*. New York, NY: Federal Reserve Bank of New York.

Chingos, M. M., & Blagg, K. (2017). *Do poor kids get their fair share of school funding?* Washington, DC: Urban Institute.

Coleman, J. S., Campbell, E. Q., Hobson, C. J., McPartland, J., Mood, A. M., Weinfeld, F. D., & York, R. L. (1966). *Equality of educational opportunity* (Report OE-38001). Washington, DC: National Center for Educational Statistics.

Duncombe, W., & Yinger, J. (2008). Measurement of cost differentials. In H. F. Ladd & E. Fiske (Eds.), *Handbook of research in education finance and policy* (pp. 203–221). New York, NY: Routledge.

EdBuild. (2019). *FundEd: Student poverty funding, policies in each state*. Washington, D.C: Author. Retrieved from http://funded.edbuild.org/reports/issue/student-poverty

Finnigan, K. S., Holme, J. J., Orfield, M., Luce, T., Diem, S., Mattheis, A., & Hylton, N. D. (2015). Regional educational policy analysis: Rochester, Omaha, and Minneapolis' inter-district arrangements. *Educational Policy, 29*(5), 780–814.

Finnigan, K. S., & Holme, J. J. (2015). *Regional educational equity policies: Learning from inter-district integration programs. Research Brief No. 9*. Washington, D.C.: National Coalition on School Diversity.

Gándara, P., & Orfield, G. (2012). Segregating Arizona's English learners: A return to the "Mexican Room"? *Teachers College Record, 114*(9), 1–27.

Gándara, P., & Rumberger, R. (2007). *Resource needs for California English learners. Getting down to facts project summary*. Stanford, CA: Institute for Research on Education Policy & Practice, Stanford University.

Gándara, P., & Rumberger, R. (2008). Defining an adequate education for English learners. *Education Finance and Policy, 3*, 130–148.

Gándara, P., & Rumberger, R. (2009). Immigration, language, and education: How does language policy structure opportunity. *Teachers College Record, 111*(3), 750–782.

Gándara P., Rumberger R. W., Maxwell-Jolly J., & Callahan R. M. (2003). English learners in California schools: Unequal resources, unequal outcomes. *Education Policy Analysis Archives*, 11. Retrieved June 13, 2015 from http://epaa.asu.edu/ojs/article/view/264/390

Goldhaber, D., & Callahan, K. (2001). Impact of the Basic Education Program on educational spending and equity in Tennessee. *Journal of Education Finance, 26*(4), 415–435.

Greenwald, R., Hedges, L., & Laine, R. (1996). The effect of school resources on student achievement. *Review of Educational Research, 66*(3), 361–396.

Hanushek, E. A. (1986). Economics of schooling: Production and efficiency in public schools. *Journal of Economic Literature, 24*(3), 1141–1177.

Hanushek, E. A. (1989). The impact of differential expenditures on school performance. *Educational Researcher, 18*(4), 45–62.

Hanushek, E. A. (1997). Assessing the effects of school resources on student performance: An update. *Educational Evaluation and Policy Analysis, 19*(2), 141–164.

Jackson, K. C., Johnson, R. C., & Persico, C. (2015). The effects of school spending on educational and economic outcomes: Evidence from school finance reforms. *Quarterly Journal of Economics, 131*(1), 157–218.

Jimenez-Castellanos, O., & Topper, A. M. (2012). The cost of providing an adequate education to English language learners: A review of the literature. *Review of Educational Research, 82*(2), 179–232.

Knight, D. S., & Strunk, K. O. (2016). Who bears the cost of district funding cuts? Reducing inequality in the distribution of teacher layoffs. *Educational Researcher, 45*(7), 395–406.

Knight, D. S. (2017). Are high-poverty school districts disproportionately impacted by state funding cuts? School finance equity following the Great Recession. *Journal of Education Finance, 43*(2), 169–194.

Knight, D. S. & DeMatthews, D. (2017). *Assessing the educational opportunity of emergent bilingual students: Why are some state school finance systems more equitable than others?* CERPS Working Paper No. 2017-1. El Paso, TX: Center for Education Research and Policy Studies.

Lafortune, J., Rothstein, J., & Schazenbach, D. W. (2016). *School finance reform and the distribution of student achievement* (Working Paper). Berkeley, CA: University of California.

Millard, M. (2015). *State funding mechanisms for English language learners*. Denver, CO: Education Commission of the States.

National Coalition on School Diversity. (2016). *NCSD comments on implementing programs under Title I of the Every Student Succeeds Act*. Retrieved from https://school-diversity.org/pdf/NCSD_Comments_for_ESSA_Title_I_implementation_1-21-16.pdf

Odden, A. R., & Picus, L. O. (2014). *School finance: A policy perspective* (5th ed.). New York, NY: McGraw-Hill.

Organisation for Economic Cooperation and Development. (2016). *Education at a Glance 2016: OECD indicators*. Paris, France: OECD Publishing. Retrieved from https://doi.org/10.1787/eag-2016-en

Parrish, T. B. (1994). A cost analysis of alternative instructional models for limited English proficient students in California. *Journal of Educational Finance, 19*(3), 256–278.

Porter, E. (2013, November). In public education, edge still goes to rich. New York, NY: *New York Times*. Retrieved from: http://www.nytimes.com/2013/11/06/business/a-rich-childs-edge-in-public-education.html

Reardon, S. F., Kalogrides, D., Ho, A., Shear, B., Shores, K., & Fahle, E. (2016). *Stanford Education Data Archive*. http://purl.stanford.edu/db586ns4974

Rolle, A., & Liu, K. (2007). An empirical analysis of horizontal and vertical equity in the public schools of Tennessee, 1994–2003. *Journal of Education Finance, 32*(3), 328–351.

Rolle, A., Torres, M., & Eason, N. (2012). Los elefantes rosas en las cúpulas en la Legislatura: An empirical analysis of the Texas education finance mechanism with special emphasis on bilingual education. *Association of Mexican American Educators Journal, 4*(1), 29–38.

Rolle, R. A., & Jimenez-Castellanos, O. (2014). An efficacy analysis of the Texas school funding formula with particular attention to English language learners. *Journal of Education Finance, 39*(3), 203–221.

Taylor, L. L., & Fowler, W. J., Jr. (2006). *A comparable wage approach to geographic cost adjustment. Research and Development Report. NCES-2006- 321*. Washington, D.C.: National Center for Education Statistics.

Ushomirsky, N., & Williams, D. (2015). *Too many states still spend less on educating students who need the most*. Washington, D.C.: The Education Trust.

Winkler, A. M., Scull, J., & Zeehandelaar, D. (2012). *How strong are U.S. teacher unions? A state-by-state comparison*. Washington, DC: Thomas B. Fordham Institute.

Assessment and English Language Learners in Special Education

Edgar M. Torres Ovando, Danika L. S. Maddocks, and Angela Valenzuela

Abstract Since the implementation of the No Child Left Behind Act in 2001, statewide accountability measures have drastically changed the way schools address achievement gaps among various student populations. One of the negative consequences of this legislation includes the overreliance on standardized assessment programs across all states. However, one of the populations most impacted are students who are classified as English learners and receive special education services. The following chapter highlights some of the issues English learners in special education programs have faced in Texas. This chapter also makes recommendations for appropriately assessing this student population to truly measure their academic achievement.

Keywords English language learners · High-stakes accountability · Special education · Sandardized testing · Education policy · Academic achievement

Since the implementation of the No Child Left Behind Act (NCLB), high-stakes standardized assessments have been used as a primary tool to hold schools accountable for student achievement. In Texas, as well as throughout the United States, students, parents, teachers, administrators, and community members have expressed growing dissatisfaction with the limitations of standardized testing (Hagopian, 2014). Thus, Texas legislators have made strong efforts to revamp the accountability system to employ more holistic assessment systems. Research indicates that alternate assessments systems, including authentic and portfolio-based, provide better measures of student achievement than standardized assessments alone because they are holistic and require students to think critically, use creativity, and apply

E. M. Torres Ovando (✉) · A. Valenzuela
Education Leadership and Policy, University of Texas at Austin, Austin, TX, USA
e-mail: valenz@austin.utexas.edu

D. L. S. Maddocks
Educational Psychology, University of Texas at Austin, Austin, TX, USA

knowledge in multiple ways that reflect understanding (Darling-Hammond, Ancess, & Falk, 1995; Shepard, 2000).

As policymakers work to design and implement new assessment-related policies, it is crucial to first explore the potential impact of these changes on English language learners (ELLs) and students with disabilities (SWD). First, fairness in testing is one of the professional standards for educational assessment and requires that testing practices be appropriate for all test takers in the intended population, including students with disabilities (*Standards for Educational and Psychological Testing*, 2014). Second, specific attention to students with disabilities is essential to uphold the intent of federal legislation which was designed to increase schools' accountability for the academic achievement of traditionally underserved groups of students, including students with disabilities and ELLs. The key mechanism to track such accountability is schools' mandated reporting of school-level standardized assessment outcomes for these subgroups of students. Therefore, it is important to consider whether proposed changes to large-scale, standardized assessments will impact schools' ability to accurately report on the academic progress of specific student subgroups. Third, it is critical to examine the outcomes of special education students separately from those of general education students because students with disabilities may show different responses to reform (Cook, Gerber, & Semmel, 1997). If educational reform movements are to be equitable, reformers must consider the impact that the proposed changes may have on historically underserved groups and subgroups of students and not just focus on the expected benefits for the majority.

To address these concerns, this chapter will discuss key issues in the assessment of English language learners with disabilities and considerations for fair assessment. First, we describe the special education population in the nation and Texas in terms of key issues in the field, including prevalence rates, educational placement, participation in assessment, and educational outcomes. We then provide a historical overview of high-stakes standardized assessments in Texas and describe the participation and performance of students with disabilities on these assessments over time. We critique the current high-stakes assessment system and review research-based suggestions to improve the assessment of students with disabilities within the current framework. Finally, we evaluate the proposal to adopt an authentic, performance-based assessment system for Texas in terms of the potential benefits and challenges for assessing and serving students with disabilities.

1 The Special Education Population in Texas

This section provides an overview of the special education population in Texas and compares it to national trends. Texas served 463,185 students ages 3–21 under IDEA in 2016 (Texas Education Agency, 2016a). Among students in Texas identified with a disability, the most common disabilities were specific learning disability (34.4%), speech impairment (19.8%), other health impairment (13.5%), autism

(11.7%), intellectual disability (10%), and emotional disturbance (5.8%) (Texas Education Agency, 2016a). These proportions are similar to those of the nation as a whole, but the special education population in Texas differs from the national population in several important ways.

Disability prevalence rates in Texas differ from the national averages and suggest both under- and over-identification, depending on the disability type and students' racial and ethnic backgrounds. In the most recent report from the National Center for Educational Statistics (covering 2013–2014), Texas's special education population represented only 8.6% of the state's total public school population—the lowest percentage of any state—suggesting that on the whole Texas under-identifies students with disabilities. This low rate is not an anomaly; Texas has consistently identified and served relatively fewer special education students than most or all other states in the country, and Texas's identification rate has fallen consistently since 2000–2001 (Scull & Winkler, 2011).

One of the factors for underrepresentation of special education students in Texas is attributed to multiple aspects of the state's special education policies and practices. For example, Texas is the only state that does not use the "developmental delay" category, even though it is one of the most common disabilities nationally, representing over 6% of the country's special education students. Similarly, although the federal definition of a specific learning disability includes reading dyslexia, Texas allows schools to serve students with dyslexia under Section 504[1] instead of IDEA. Possibly as a result of this policy, an independent review of Houston ISD special education services found that students with dyslexia often did not receive the educational support services they needed (Hehir and Associates, n.d.).

More recently, the Texas Education Agency (TEA) was under investigation by the U.S. Department of Education as a result of an investigation conducted by the *Houston Chronicle*, which revealed that the agency placed an arbitrary limit on the percentage of students eligible for special education services. This limit required that schools and school districts identify no more than 8.5% of their students as students with disabilities. Under the Performance-Based Monitoring Analysis System (PBMAS), school districts that provide special education services to more than 8.5% of their overall student population are penalized and must take corrective action to decrease that percentage. On October 3, 2016, the agency's Commissioner, Mike Morath, received a letter from the United States Department of Education's Acting Assistant Secretary of Special Education outlining that the agency must demonstrate that this cap has not denied referrals or evaluations to students suspected of having disabilities (Swaby, 2016). Subsequently, the TEA agreed to suspend its 8.5% cap on students receiving special education services.

While misrepresentation of SWD is an area that scholars should continue to examine, the underrepresentation of English language learners (ELLs) is an area of

---

[1] Although not a specific focus herein, it is important to mention that Texas utilizes Section 504 for categories of disability that would otherwise fall under IDEA. For more information, see Blazer (1999) and Madaus and Shaw (2008).

concern for many experts. Latinx[2] students in Texas are underrepresented in various special education programs. For example, Ovando, Combs, and Collier (2006) note that a frequent source of confusion among school personnel occurs when ELLs are placed in language acquisition programs because they believe their academic struggles are language-related when in fact, their deficits should be addressed in special education programs designed for ELLs. This underrepresentation or misrepresentation of ELLs in special education programs is unsettling because linguistically diverse students requiring special education services are not receiving the specialized services they require. For example, a review of Houston ISD services discovered that elementary-age Latinx students were underrepresented in special education in elementary school, with an odds ratio of 0.6 for identification, and were less likely to be identified in schools serving high percentages of Latinx students (Hehir and Associates, n.d.). When children from linguistically diverse backgrounds are misidentified by the school system or it fails to identify them as SWD, the school system is denying a FAPE, as required by federal law. Thus, students' academic development and performance are compromised.

Additionally, Texas has also been criticized for various forms of racial and ethnic disproportionality in identification of students needing special education. For example, during the 2003–2004 school year, African American students made up 14.2% of the overall Texas student population, yet this population also made up 17.7 of the overall population receiving special education services (TEA, 2005). Five years later, this disproportionality increased. During the 2008–2009 school year, 14.1% of all Texas students were African American, yet 18.1% of all students receiving special education services were of the same racial background (TEA, 2009). Furthermore, during the 2013–2014 school year, 12.7% of Texas students were African American, yet the percentage of this population receiving special education services was 16.2% (TEA, 2014b).

During the same academic year, 2,668,315 (51.8%) of all Texas students were Latinx. However, 219,373 Latinxs were identified as SWD, totaling 49.4% of total SWD population. Data also indicate that during this year, schools across the State of Texas identified 62,979 Latinx ELLs as SWD. This indicates that of the overall student population receiving special education services (443,834), 14% were Latinx ELLs. This also indicates that of the overall percentage of ELLs receiving special education services, 93.1% were Latinx (TEA, 2014a, 2014b). During the 2015–2016 school year, data indicates that of the overall student population in the State of Texas, 12.6% were African American, yet 15.7% received special education services. Additionally, 18.5% of Texas students were considered ELLs but only 16.5% were identified as students with disabilities (TEA, 2016a).

Participation rates and student performance have changed over time as the assessment system has changed, so we will discuss assessment participation and performance for Texan SWD in the section below, which also provides a review of the different high-stakes testing programs used in Texas over time.

---

[2] We use the term, *Latinx* rather than Latino or Latina to provide a gender-neutral perspective.

2   Texas High-Stakes Testing for Special Populations

Texas first introduced educational assessments in 1979, when the 66th Texas Legislature enacted a law that required students in grades 3, 5, and 9 to demonstrate basic skill proficiencies in mathematics, reading, and writing (TEA & Pearson, 2012–2013). Since that year, the assessment system as a whole experienced several changes that addressed various legislative requirements. Under the Texas Assessment of Academic Skills (TAAS) assessment program—established in 1990 and ending in 2002—SWD in Texas were exempt from assessment participation and generally did not participate, so little if anything was known about these students' progress on a large-scale basis. In time, assessment options, participation rates, and student performance for SWD shifted such that by 2001, Texas administered its first assessment specifically designed for eligible students in special education in grades 3–8, namely, the State-Developed Alternative Assessment (SDAA). In the year before the implementation of the SDAA, only 46.7% of Texas's students with disabilities participated in assessments for English language arts and mathematics; 50.5% of Texan SWD were considered "ARD [Admission, Review, Dismissal] Exempt," meaning they were exempt from participating in large-scale assessments based on a review of their IEP and academic abilities. In 2001–2002, the first year the SDAA was used, participation of SWD jumped to 89.4%, a 43% increase in participation that could almost entirely be attributed to the SDAA, which was the only test taken by 45.3% of students with disabilities. In the case of the SDAA, the development of an assessment specifically for SWD dramatically increased these students' participation and thus representation in the state's high-stakes assessment.

Between 2005 and 2008, the state developed several other versions of the Texas Assessment of Knowledge and Skills (TAKS) assessment, which were specifically designed to meet the needs of SWD while maintaining some commitment to the Texas Essential Knowledge and Skills (TEKS) curriculum standards. In 2005, the SDAA was revised to align to the statewide TAKS testing program and the resulting test, the SDAA II, was offered to special education students who received instruction in the general TEKS curriculum but for whom the TAKS test was not an appropriate measure of progress according to the student's IEP (McLaughlin & Thurlow, 2007). The following year, the TAKS-Inclusive (TAKS-I) was offered for the first time. It met IDEA requirements for subjects not assessed with the SDAA II and was offered to students in special education for whom TAKS was not appropriate measure, even with use of allowable accommodations. However, the TAKS-I was quickly replaced by the TAKS (Accommodated), which was based on the same grade-level achievement standards as TAKS and was designed to assess the same skills; the accommodations were intended to remove irrelevant barriers that might keep students with disabilities from successfully demonstrating the extent of their knowledge or skills on the content of interest.

Two other versions of the TAKS assessment were also introduced in 2008. The TAKS-Alternate (TAKS-Alt) was based on alternate achievement standards specifically designed for students with severe cognitive disabilities and for whom the

TEKS standards were deemed inappropriate. The TAKS-Modified (TAKS-M) was administered in grades and subjects with federal accountability requirements and was based on modified academic achievement standards which were less rigorous than the typical TAKS standards and which were designed for students receiving special education who meet participation requirements.

When the State of Texas Assessments of Academic Readiness (STAAR) assessment replaced TAKS, STAAR Modified and STAAR Alternate replaced TAKS-M and TAKS-Alt, respectively. Similar to the standard STAAR assessment, the Modified and Alternate versions tested the same subjects and grades as the TAKS in grades 3–8. In high school, the STAAR Modified and STAAR Alternate each included 9 EOC assessments. However, House Bill 5 impacts the STAAR Alternate assessment system because it states that an assessment instrument, including alternate assessment tasks and materials, used to determine school growth [accountability] may not be teacher developed. To comply with this mandate, the TEA amended its contract with Pearson Education, the company used to develop the STAAR system, to redesign the STAAR Alternate to reflect a more standardized assessment. This assessment was renamed to STAAR Alternate 2.

During 2015, the STAAR Alternate 2 was made available for students who meet four eligibility criteria. First, the student must have a significant cognitive disability that interferes with academic performance and which is identified in their IEP. The student must require intensive, individualized instruction in a variety of instructional settings, including assistance with daily tasks related to mobility, social situations, and/or personal needs. Because federal regulations mandate all students have access to grade-level curriculum, students with severe cognitive abilities typically access this curriculum through prerequisite skills that are linked to the grade-level curriculum; this is required for the use of the STAAR-Alternate. Although NCLB, and currently, the Every Student Succeeds Act (ESSA)—passed by Congress on December 9, 2015 caps the percentage of students taking an alternate assessment to 1%, decisions about which students will take the STAAR Alternate 2 must be made by the individual's ARD/IEP committee.

2.1 History of Assessing English Language Learners in Texas

Over the years, Texas has developed various assessments specifically for students whose native language is not English. In 1996, a Spanish-language version of the TAAS was incorporated into the state assessment program for assessments in grades 3–6. Under the TAKS assessment system, Spanish versions of assessments were made available for students in grades 3–6 but in 2009, the Texas legislature removed the Spanish assessment for grade 6 (TEA & Pearson, 2015). Linguistically Accommodated Testing (LAT) was introduced in 2005 for students who qualified for statewide standardized assessments, including those that qualified for TAKS Accommodated or TAKS Modified—two assessments that were regularly administered to SWD (TEA & Pearson, 2010). ELLs and ELLs with disabilities (EWD) that were considered first-year, Limited English Proficiency[3]-exempted, immigrants were not assessed with the reading portion of the TAKS; their assessment to determine reading proficiency was determined by the reading portion of the Texas English Language Proficiency Assessment System (TELPAS) (TEA & Pearson, 2010).

Prior to the development of the TELPAS, the Reading Proficiency Tests in English (RPTE) was a tool developed in 1999 that was used to determine ELLs and EWDs' reading abilities. However, in 2004, the TEA established the Texas Observation Protocol (TOP), which was used to determine ELLs' language acquisition progress (TEA & Pearson, 2011). The TOP required teachers to holistically rate students in listening, speaking, and writing. The TOP and the RPTE were then combined to create the Texas English Language Assessment System (TELPAS). Under this assessment system, students are rated on the English language proficiency standards (ELPS) through the use of a standardized rubric. A composite rating of beginning, intermediate, advanced, or advanced high is given based on students' performance level indicators in the four assessed areas.

Although Texas has made significant progress in determining students' language proficiency, ELL students with disabilities remain at a disadvantage. For example, during the 2015–2016 school year, the only accommodations SWD were allowed to receive on the reading portion of the TELPAS included individualized structured reminders, amplification devices, projection devices, manipulating test materials, basic transcribing, and large print. Allowable accommodations for SWD that require TEA approval included photocopying of test materials, or extra time (up to a day) (TEA, 2016c). Students with disabilities that require additional accommodations beyond those previously mentioned were not allowed to receive those supports, even if their IEPs called for them. This is due to validity concerns—receiving these supports may invalidate a student's assessment. However, students with disabilities that may prevent them from successfully completing any portion of their TELPAS are allowed be exempted from portions of the assessment beforehand with the approval of the ARD and Language Proficiency Assessment Committees (LPAC).

---

[3] A student of limited English proficiency, otherwise known as LEP, is defined by the Texas Education Code (TEC) Sec. 29.052 as a student whose primary language is other than English and whose English language skills are such that the student has difficulty performing ordinary classwork in English. The state's deficient label of LEP and ELL are used interchangeably by the TEA and educators, however, for the purposes of this chapter, we refer to all English language learners, including those who are not enrolled in bilingual or English as second language programs, as ELLs.

2.2 Performance of EWD on Texas Statewide Assessments Over Time

Despite high rates of participation among students receiving special education and linguistic support, these students nevertheless registered lower academic performance on statewide assessments relative to their non-disabled and non-ELL counterparts at every grade level (see Tables 1 and 2) in 2012 and 2016, with the achievement gap widening at higher grade levels. In high school, 40% or less of Texas' ELLs in special education met the passing standards in either math or reading/language arts in 2012 and 2016 in grades 3, 5, 8, and 9, even though the proficiency rates for the high school population as a whole were relatively low.

Table 1 Language arts/reading performance of EWD and all students on STAAR

Language arts/reading				
Subject	2012% of EWD meeting passing standard	2012% of all students meeting passing standard	2016% of EWD meeting passing standard	2016% of all students meeting passing standard
Grade 3	31	37	30	73
Grade 5	21	38	25	81
Grade 8	17	36	22	87
English I	Reading 6	Reading 22	9	65
	Writing 2	Writing 20		
English II	Reading 6	Reading 16	6	67
	Writing 3	Writing 18		

Notes: From TEA (2016b, 2017a). In 2012, the TEA redesigned the accountability system and shifted from administering the TAKS to the STAAR. As such, no state accountability ratings were assigned to campuses and districts. For AYP purposes, different passing standards than those currently used by the TEA were determined by the TAKS Equivalent Information Bridge Study (n.d.)

Table 2 Mathematics performance of EWD and all students on STAAR

Mathematics				
Subject	2012 EWD meeting passing standard	2012 all students meeting passing standard	2016 EWD meeting passing standard	2016 all students meeting passing standard
Grade 3	29	38	42	75
Grade 5	31	41	42	86
Grade 8	29	39	29	82
Algebra I	35	44	38	78

Source: TEA (2016b, 2017b)

3 A Critique of the Current Assessment System for EWD and SWD

Any attempts to improve the assessment of EWD must consider how to address the shortcomings of current practices. Numerous outcomes of the current assessment system harm students with disabilities and general-education students alike—*all* students' learning suffers as a result of a narrowed curriculum, reduced instructional quality, and the erosion of teachers' autonomy and professionalism (McNeil & Valenzuela, 2001; Valenzuela, 2005). However, the national focus on high-stakes testing has also harmed EWD in specific ways above and beyond those experienced by all students. Below, we review three ways that the current assessment system fails special education students specifically—by decreasing individualization in special education, by using methods of questionable validity, and by excluding EWD from participation.

3.1 Standardization Versus Individualization

From a theoretical standpoint, the standardized nature of large-scale assessments is in direct conflict with the goal and mandate of the special education system, which is to provide individualized educational programs specifically designed for each student's personal strengths and needs (Aron & Loprest, 2012). Individualization is essential for special education because students identified for special education services are remarkably diverse in their strengths, abilities, and needs. It is perhaps quite clear that students with specific learning disabilities vary in terms of their specific skills deficits, the severity of their disability, and their response to early intervention.

Under IDEA, each student in special education is entitled to an IEP that lists personalized educational goals chosen through collaboration among school personnel, the child's family, and the child when appropriate. Although the actual implementation of the IEP process is not always as collaborative as intended and many parents and students report wanting more meaningful participation and input, the individualization of the IEP is still considered an essential aspect of special education planning. In fact, in 2002, a President's Commission on Excellence in Special Education reviewed the special education system and concluded that the system actually needed "a new commitment to individual needs."

Unfortunately, in order to prepare EWD for high-stakes tests, IEP goals are increasingly taken from state curriculum standards. Although this practice may serve to integrate special education students into the general education curriculum, IEP goals of this type do not represent true individualization of an educational plan and many argue that they do not fulfill the intent of IDEA. For some students, such as those with intellectual disability, grade-level curriculum may not be appropriate, since these students by definition learn at a slower rate and are not capable of the same level of academic work as their same-age peers.. Even when school personnel recognize that a student will likely not benefit from exposure to the general curriculum, policies do not always provide adequate options for meeting students' educational needs. For example, the elimination of the STAAR Modified and STAAR Accommodated has led to the elimination of self-contained classes for students with mild cognitive disabilities. Because this group of students must now take the STAAR Online, schools are compelled to place these students in classrooms where they will be exposed to the general curriculum, even when that curriculum is inappropriate for their level of ability. When these issues get coupled with a student's lack of proficiency in English, the student is even more likely to struggle in the academic setting.

Furthermore, large-scale assessments are inherently limited in terms of how much information they can provide about student learning and students' instructional needs, and do not provide the type of information needed for IEP planning. One purpose of the response to intervention process and an IEP is to provide more specific learning targets for students who are struggling and to carefully track students' incremental progress towards those targets to determine whether the provided interventions are successful. However, large-scale test results generally provide only a broad indicator of proficiency and provide little or no information about specific skills students have mastered or still need to learn. Therefore, when individualized learning goals are replaced with curriculum standards or skills that are more test-relevant, educators no longer have a framework within which to monitor more specific aspects of students' academic progress at a level that is meaningful for each individual student.

3.2 Concerns About Validity

Further complications regarding assessment of EWD come to light when the validity of the results of high-stakes assessment are questionable. As such, this section addresses issues of test alignment, construct-irrelevant variance, exclusions (or exemptions) from the testing system, and utility. According to Standards for Educational and Psychological Testing, assessment is not a valid or appropriate measure of student learning if the assessment does not align with curriculum. Therefore, one threat to validity already mentioned is the possibility that EWD may not be exposed to the general curriculum covered by large-scale assessments. For example, some EWD may not have access to the appropriate TEKS if they spend part or all of their day in a resource room or self-contained classroom learning content that is not aligned accordingly. In 2011, 14% of the nation's students with disabilities spent less than 40% of their day in the general education classroom, and 19.8% spent between 40 and 79% of their day in the general education classroom.

Another threat to validity can occur even when the content on a standardized assessment is appropriate for certain EWD and they have had adequate access to the relevant curriculum, if the form of the assessment introduces construct-irrelevant variance. Construct-irrelevant variance is variability in test performance that is not attributable to differences in the construct of interest—that is, the ability or quality that the test is designed to measure. For example, a test of math skills will introduce construct-irrelevant variance for an EWD reading disabilities to the degree that the math problems require strong reading skills in a language the student is still learning, because the student will likely have trouble reading and correctly answering math problems even if they understand the math. Thus, construct irrelevant variance can be conceptualized as a barrier that prohibits some students from having an equal opportunity to demonstrate their understanding or knowledge. Accommodations and modifications can be used to reduce the influence of construct-irrelevant variance on special education students' test scores, but Texas has restrictions on the use of these adaptations.

3.3 Exclusion of Students from Testing

Despite the flaws discussed above, one of the most concerning limitations of the current system is actually the regular and disproportionate exclusion of students with disabilities from full participation in accountability processes. Although the current high-stakes assessment system is of questionable validity and educational benefit, the system is still the primary means of assessing students' educational outcomes and is thus the primary way for students to be "represented" or "counted" in major educational decisions.

A main goal NCLB and current goal of ESSA is to increase schools' accountability for the performance of historically under-performing subgroups, and to realize this goal, students with disabilities must be adequately represented. However, research shows that disaggregated Adequate Yearly Progress (AYP) data—the mechanism for enforcing NCLB—consistently misrepresents the performance of students with disabilities. In general, the high-stakes nature of the testing system incentivizes schools and districts to "lose" special education students from their accountability determinations when school officials fear that these students would have caused the school to miss AYP. In order to address the issue of exclusionary practices from state assessments, ESSA requires that the majority of students enrolled in public schools to participate in the statewide assessment program, including SWD. In fact, ESSA allows Texas schools to administer an alternate assessment—the STAAR Alt 2—to no more than 1% of its population.

Although states are nominally required to report the performance of all historically underrepresented subgroups, under NCLB, subgroups were often excluded from AYP measures if a school was not categorized as a Title I campus or if the subgroup's population falls below the state's "minimum *n*," or the minimum population size required for inclusion in AYP calculations. The use of a minimum reporting group size is necessary under the Family Educational Rights and Privacy Act to ensure that student assessment data remains private when small subgroup sizes at a particular school could lead to identification of student data.

The minimum group size also had the advantage of focusing accountability efforts on schools where large groups of students are struggling to perform proficiently. However, states are allowed to set their own "minimum *n*" and thus vary greatly in their reporting rules, with some states reporting data on fewer than 20% of their students with disabilities (Harr-Robins et al., 2012). A frequent criticism is that schools may even assign students a special education status as a way to relieve them from having to take standardized tests and thusly remove them from accountability determinations (Viadero, 2004).

As reviewed earlier, the exclusion of EWD and SWD from Texas accountability measures has varied over time as a result of shifts in state policies. In the first 5 years after the implementation of the high-stakes TAAS assessment, special education enrollment in Texas nearly doubled, with higher increases for African-American and Latinx students (Viadero, 2004). When Texas changed the reporting rules to include students with disabilities in accountability determinations, the special education population stopped growing.

More recently, Texas excluded over half its special education students and almost one-fifth of its English Language Learners from the National Assessment of Academic Progress (NAEP), which produces "The Nation's Report Card". Texas's decision to exclude higher-than-average rates of SWD and EWDs means that the NAEP results do not provide information about whether these groups of students are making adequate progress in the state of Texas on how they fare relative to the non-SWD or non-EWD counterparts. The regular exclusion of students with disabilities from large-scale assessments is a social justice issue because schools are not held accountable for the performance of these students, despite legislation that is specifically justified on this basis.

To wit, most data about students in special education come from administrative processes (Aron & Loprest, 2012) and are not well suited for thorough, critical, or informative analyses of student performance or need. Although states are required to report the number of students in each disability category, and are nominally required to report on the high-stakes assessment performance of these students, in practice there is very little useful data about students served under IDEA at either the state or the federal level (Aron & Loprest, 2012).

For example, little is known about the students' disability characteristics, since states are not required to support severity levels and are only required to report students' primary disability category, despite the fact that comorbidity—the co-occurrence of two or more disabilities within an individual—is fairly common and students may qualify for and receive services related to more than one disability. As a result of all the problems reviewed above, even when students do participate in large-scale assessments, educators rarely receive information that is useful for determining whether the educational program is meeting students' needs or facilitating student progress.

4 Improving the Assessment of Students with Disabilities

Many of the flaws of the current system are in direct contrast to the standards of practice delineated in the *Standards for Educational and Psychological Testing*, a publication of the American Educational Research Association, the American Psychological Association, and the National Council on Measurement in Education (2014). Specifically, Standard 3.0 reads, "All steps in the testing process, including test design, validation, development, administration, and scoring procedures, should be designed in such a manner as to minimize construct-irrelevant variance and to promote valid score interpretations for the intended uses for all examinees in the intended population." Several sections of Standard 3.0 are particularly relevant to the assessment of EWD: Standard 3.9 states that test developers and users must create and provide accommodations to remove construct-irrelevant barriers; Standard 3.10 states that test developers and users must provide standardized procedures for accommodations and monitor their use; and Standard 3.19 states, "In settings where the same authority is responsible for both provision of curriculum and high-stakes decisions based on testing of examinees' curriculum mastery, examinees should not suffer permanent negative consequences if evidence indicates that they have not had the opportunity to learn the test content." Although the Standards acknowledge that these principles of fairness are difficult to accomplish, the pursuit of fairness is essential. Below, we review more specific recommendations for increasing fairness in the assessment of students with disabilities.

4.1 Standardize Disability-Specific Processes

First, assessment practices used for students with disabilities should be as standardized as possible. Schools, districts, and/or states should have formal procedures for granting test accommodations (*Standards for Educational and Psychological Testing*, 2014) and decisions should be made by qualified personnel and based on the individual student's needs. Students who are granted accommodations should receive the accommodations consistently during instruction, as well as during assessment. In the past, Texas decided on a student's accommodations at the student's ARD meeting. The ARD or IEP meeting may be the ideal time to decide accommodation provision because the meeting is a time for determining or refining the student's educational plan, and any accommodations should be an integral part of the plan. School psychologists or special education teachers could be considered "qualified personnel" for this decision if they are knowledgeable about the individual needs of the student as well as best practices for accommodation use. There should also be guidelines that standardize the provision of accommodations during actual test administration. Although schools and districts regularly train and monitor teachers to administer standardized tests, there is less evidence that school personnel know how to provide accommodations in a standardized manner. Therefore, the use of accommodations, modifications, and alternate assessments will likely require extra training and supervision to ensure standardized procedures.

4.2 Increase Inclusion in Assessments and Reporting

Another recommendation to improve the current system is to increase inclusion of students with disabilities in large-scale assessments. Although ESSA requires that all students, including those classified as EWD or SWD, must be assessed on statewide accountability assessments, exclusionary practices exist when selecting students for other large-scale assessments like the NAEP. This should not be taken to mean that we support high-stakes testing, but rather that as long as these testing regimes remain in place, neither schools nor districts should be given the option of "gaming the system" to maintain or improve their accountability ratings. A more perfect world for students, schools, and districts would eliminate high-stakes consequences from the tests and primarily use them for informational purposes.

Second, states can re-examine their policies about the impact of accommodation and modification use on students' scores.

- Define accommodation and impact on results
- Define modification and impact on results

In theory, most accommodations do not change the nature of the underlying construct of interest, and therefore schools could consider scores a fairly valid representation of a student's ability even if an accommodation was used. If schools instituted formal and documented methods for assigning accommodations, as recommended above, this would increase the likelihood that the performance of students with accommodations could be meaningfully and reliably aggregated and compared with the performance of students who do not use accommodations.

Schools could also aggregate the scores of students using modifications, and consider these outcomes separately in an informational manner. Although modifications do make a small change to the construct of interest, tests results using modified procedures are still believed to provide some useful information about student performance. Again, if schools used formalized procedures for granting modifications, they could put more trust into the relevance of modified test score performance and would have the information necessary to interpret the scores. Many advocates for special education students believe that some measurement of student performance—even using modified procedures when necessary—is preferable to no measurement of student performance.

Schools could also report data on students who cannot participate in standardized tests by calculating these students' progress using a more appropriate metric. For example, in South Carolina, students' instructional goals from their IEPs are used to measure student progress; schools are required to report the percentage of students who reach their IEP goals and are thus held accountable for the continued learning of these students even though the students are not cognitively capable of participating in high-stakes tests. Even if a state preferred to use an alternate standardized assessment for students with severe cognitive disabilities, proficiency statistics for this assessment would be meaningful and should be required as part of each school's and district's accountability report. If the state does not believe it is reasonable for their special education students to achieve proficiency on the alternate assessment, then it is not an appropriate assessment and a different form of assessment should be chosen to match the educational goals of that student population.

4.3 Collect Multiple Forms of Data

If these changes were enacted, there would be a marked increase in the quantity and quality of data about the academic achievement of students in special education. Such data are crucial to ensure that students with disabilities benefit from the same quality review procedures as their non-disabled peers. However, in order to improve the special education system, it will be necessary to tie students' outcome data to information about the actual services they receive, as well as the fit between those services and their specific disability (Aron & Loprest, 2012).

To improve the utility of special education assessment data, we also recommend that states collect data on other aspects of special education. For example, states could collect more detailed data about student characteristics, including the severity of the student's diagnosis as well as any comorbid diagnoses. Because student heterogeneity makes it impossible to identify the "best" instructional or assessment practices for students with disabilities as a whole or even specific disability groups as a whole, detailed data on individuals' characteristics is necessary to examine the impact of certain types of practices on more specific strengths, challenges, and needs. It would also be beneficial to have data on specific educational services received and whether teachers use students' recommended accommodations and modifications during instruction, as intended. Furthermore, if detailed data about disability characteristics, instructional practices, and assessment results were combined with demographic data, states will gain new information about racial and ethnic disproportionality in special education, and researchers will be able to conduct systematic analyses into the causes and consequences of disproportionality as well as the effectiveness of attempted solutions. The latter is the type of analysis that until now has been difficult or almost impossible because of missing data (Aron & Loprest, 2012).

If the above suggestions were implemented, the resulting data could contribute to an increasing knowledge base about how different assessment practices relate to students' characteristics and test performance. Such data may even help identify special education programs which do not improve students' test performance and which may need serious change or reform. Despite these possibilities, it is important to note that information from large-scale standardized assessments is inherently limited in the amount of detailed information it can provide about student learning. This limitation may be particularly relevant for students with disabilities who cannot always access the test content as intended, even with the use of careful accommodation and modification. In response to the inherent limitations of large-scale standardized assessments, we will now examine a different approach to assessment that is gaining increasing support in Texas and which may be able to provide more useful and relevant information about the academic performance of students with disabilities as well as students in general education.

5 Principles for a New Era

The data and arguments reviewed above make it clear that NCLB struggled to fulfill its promise of increasing accountability and performance for students with disabilities. In some ways, it is unfortunate that the implementation of IDEA overlapped with general education reforms specifically focused on high-stakes assessment and accountability, because special education advocates were encouraged to fight for equality within the flawed, yet dominant, paradigm of high-stakes standardized assessments. Currently, however, there is increasing dissatisfaction with the high-stakes assessment system, and increasingly angry and urgent cries for reform. As reviewed elsewhere in this special issue, NCLB and its related assessment system was criticized for its erosion of educational quality, irrelevance to students' lives, perpetuation of educational inequalities, undermining of teachers' professionalism, and increases in students' and teachers' stress (Valenzuela, 2005).

The growing dissatisfaction with current assessment systems has led to various proposals for reform and focused reconsideration of assessment values. For example, in 2007, the National Forum on Assessment published a series of principles and indicators for student assessment systems. The National Forum was founded by FairTest and is a coalition of major education and civil rights organizations. Their guidelines are intended to guide ongoing educational reforms in a way that will improve both classroom-based and large-scale assessments, with the ultimate goal of using assessments that are integrated with curriculum and instruction and which support student learning. The Forum acknowledges that the principles are an "ideal," but argues that educational systems must strive to meet these principles if assessments are to provide educational benefits for all students. Readers who wish to read a more detailed overview of the principles or to download the report can do so here: http://www.fairtest.org/principles-and-indicators-student-assessment-syste.

The seven principles are as follows:

1. The primary purpose of assessment is to improve student learning
2. Assessment for other purposes supports student learning
3. Assessment systems are fair to all students
4. Professional collaboration and development support assessment
5. The broad community participates in assessment development
6. Communication about assessment is regular and clear
7. Assessment systems are regularly reviewed and improved

Principle 3 is particularly relevant to students in special education. Several specific stipulations in Principle 3 align with Standard 3.0 from the Standards for Educational and Psychological Testing, which focuses on fairness in testing, as reviewed earlier. For example, Principle 3 calls for instruments, policies, and practices that are unbiased and fair to all students, and states that accommodations should be made to meet the needs of students with disabilities as well as English language learners. Principle 3 also states that assessment practices should allow for multiple methods to assess progress as well as multiple, equivalent ways for students to demonstrate their knowledge and understanding.

Although the shift from NCLB to ESSA has provided some relief from an overreliance on standardized assessments, many states have yet to adopt policies that revamp assessment systems to truly assess student progress and learning. ESSA is unique in the sense that Title I, part B encourages innovative approaches to assessment systems that could be locally developed and used to accountability and reporting purposes.

5.1 Authentic, Performance-Based Assessment Alternatives

With these principles in mind, we turn to a discussion of authentic, performance-based assessment, an assessment framework proposed for use in Texas. As mentioned in the first section of this chapter, it is crucial to consider the impact of reform movements on students with disabilities who may be differentially and negatively impacted by well-meaning educational reforms (Cook et al., 1997). In order for an assessment policy to be equitable and just, it must place value on instructional goals that are meaningful for all students and provide an appropriate way to measure educational success or failure for all students, regardless of their disability status, race, ethnicity, class, or other distinguishing characteristics (standards). Below, we briefly describe authentic, performance-based assessment and then discuss the potential fit between the proposed new assessment framework and the needs of students served by special education.

Authentic, performance-based assessment is based on the principle that both learning and assessment should be rooted in real-life situations and related to meaningful goals (Thurlow, 1994). In a performance assessment, tasks are intended to be authentic, meaning they are valuable in their own right and are rooted in realistic contexts. Students are asked to create products or work out solutions to problems, instead of simply choosing an answer on a multiple-choice test. Some examples of authentic, performance-based assessments are open-ended writing prompts, work portfolios, presentations, or solutions to real-world problems or questions (Thurlow, 1994).

Performance assessments are believed to offer many educational benefits. First, they are expected to encourage teachers to use more authentic, as well as performance-based learning and instructional tasks, just as the spread of high-stakes, multiple-choice tests led teachers to adopt instructional practices that were more restricted and focused on formulaic, memorization-based tasks that mimicked the high-stakes tests.

In contrast, performance-based instruction and assessment demand some degree of flexible problem-solving and thus encourage students to use higher-order thinking skills. In this way, performance-based assessments are learning opportunities in and of themselves, in a way that multiple-choice tests are not. Proponents of performance assessments also argue that students find authentic and performance-based tasks more motivating. Because of their open-ended format, performance tasks are believed to encourage creativity because they allow students to individualize their approach. In sum, performance-based assessments have the potential to improve instruction, student learning, student motivation, and assessment relevance.

When considering the adoption of performance-based assessments, however, it is critical to consider the potential implications for students with disabilities whose needs are sometimes neglected when evaluating educational policy decisions (Thurlow, 1994). A review of the research suggests that authentic, performance-based assessments have the potential to improve both the assessment and the education of students with disabilities. In terms of assessment, performance-based assessments have the potential to address several of the limitations of the current system, as described above. For example, performance-based assessments are inherently more open-ended than assessments with closed-ended, multiple-choice questions. The open-ended nature of the tasks may offer more opportunities for accommodation and modification, which in turn could increase the participation of students with disabilities in large-scale assessment.

From a theoretical perspective, an emphasis on "authentic" tasks aligns perfectly with special education's emphasis on the development of real-life skills that will improve students' abilities to be autonomous in daily life activities. Similarly, performance-based assessments could be tailored to align with students' individualized educational goals from their IEP, and thusly resolve the current discrepancy between the inherently individualized nature of special education services and the standardized "one-size-fits-all" nature of current assessments.

References

American Educational Research Association, American Psychological Association, National Council on Measurement in Education, & Joint Committee on Standards for Educational and Psychological Testing. (2014). *Standards for educational and psychological testing.* Washington, DC: American Educational Research Association.

Aron, L., & Loprest, P. (2012). Disability and the education system. *The Future of Children, 22*(1), 97–122.

Blazer, B. (1999). Developing 504 classroom accommodation plans: A collaborative, systematic parent-student-teacher approach. *Teaching Exceptional Children, 32*(2), 28–33.

Cook, B., Gerber, M., & Semmel, M. (1997). Are effective schools reforms effective for all students? The implications of joint outcome production for school reform. *Exceptionality, 7*(2), 77–95.

Darling-Hammond, L., Ancess, J., & Falk, B. (1995). *Authentic assessment in action: Studies of schools and students at work.* New York, NY: Teachers College Press.

Hagopian, J. (Ed.). (2014). *More than a score: The new uprising against high-stakes testing*. Chicago, IL: Haymarket Books.

Harr-Robins, J., Song, M., Hurlburt, S., Pruce, C., Danielson, L., Garet, M., & Taylor, J. (2012). *The inclusion of students with disabilities in school accountability systems* (Interim report. NCEE 2012-4056). Washington, DC: National Center for Education Evaluation and Regional Assistance.

Hehir, T., & Associates. (n.d.) *Review of special education in the Houston Independent School District* [DM3].

Madaus, J. W., & Shaw, S. F. (2008). The role of school professionals in implementing Section 504 for students with disabilities. *Educational Policy, 22*(3), 363–378. https://doi.org/10.1177/0895904807307069

McLaughlin, M. J., & Thurlow, M. L. (2007). *Profiles of reform: Four states' journeys to implement standards-based reform with students with disabilities* (pp. 1–49). College Park, MD: Educational Policy Reform Research Institute.

McNeil, L., & Valenzuela, A. (2001). The harmful impact of the TAAS system of testing in Texas: Beneath the accountability rhetoric. In M. Kornhaber & G. Orfield (Eds.), *Raising standards or raising barriers? Inequality and high stakes testing in public education* (pp. 127–150). New York, NY: Century Foundation.

Ovando, C. J., Combs, M. C., & Collier, V. P. (2006). *Bilingual and ESL classrooms: Teaching in multicultural contexts* (4th ed.). Boston, MA: McGraw-Hill.

Scull, J., & Winkler, A. M. (2011). *Shifting trends in special education*. Washington, DC: The Thomas B. Fordham Institute.

Shepard, L. A. (2000). The role of assessment in a learning culture. *Educational Researcher, 29*(7), 4–14.

Swaby, A. (2016, November 2). *TEA denies allegations of cap on special education, Texas Tribune*. Retrieved December 1, 2016, from https://www.texastribune.org/2016/11/02/tea-denies-allegations-cap-special-education/

Texas Education Agency. (2005). *Enrollment in Texas public schools, 2003–04*. Retrieved from http://tea.texas.gov/acctres/Enroll_2003-04.pdf

Texas Education Agency. (2009). *Enrollment in Texas public schools, 2008–09*. Retrieved from http://tea.texas.gov/acctres/Enroll_2008-09.pdf

Texas Education Agency. (2014a). *Enrollment in Texas public schools, 2013–14*. Retrieved from http://tea.texas.gov/acctres/Enroll_2013-14.pdf

Texas Education Agency. (2014b). *Enrollment for special populations classified as LEP by race/ethnicity*. Unpublished raw data.

Texas Education Agency. (2016a). *PBMAS state reports*. Retrieved February 27, 2017, from http://tea.texas.gov/pbm/stateReports.aspx

Texas Education Agency. (2016b). *Texas academic performance report: 2015–16 state performance*. Retrieved June 30, 2017, from https://rptsvr1.tea.texas.gov/perfreport/tapr/2016/state.pdf

Texas Education Agency. (2016c). *Texas English language proficiency assessment system: Reading test administrator manual*. Retrieved from http://tea.texas.gov/WorkArea/linkit.aspx?LinkIdentifier=id&ItemID=25769824783&libID=25769824880

Texas Education Agency. (2017a). *STAAR statewide summary data: Reading and EOC English*. Unpublished raw data.

Texas Education Agency. (2017b). *STAAR statewide summary data: Math and EOC Algebra I*. Unpublished raw data.

Texas Education Agency. (n.d.). *STAAR – TAKS equivalent information (bridge study) Tables 2012*. Retrieved June 30, 2017, from http://tea.texas.gov/Student_Testing_and_Accountability/Testing/State_of_Texas_Assessments_of_Academic_Readiness_(STAAR)/STAAR_-_TAKS_Equivalent_Information_(Bridge_Study)_Tables_2012/

Texas Education Agency & Pearson. (2010). Texas assessment of knowledge and skills (TAKS), TAKS (accommodated), and linguistically accommodated testing (LAT). *Technical digest 2008–2009*. Retrieved from http://tea.texas.gov/student.assessment/techdigest/yr0809/

Texas Education Agency & Pearson. (2011). Historical overview of assessment in Texas. *Technical digest 2010–2011*. Retrieved from http://tea.texas.gov/Student_Testing_and_Accountability/Testing/Student_Assessment_Overview/Technical_Digest_2010-2011/

Texas Education Agency & Pearson. (2015). Historical overview of assessment in Texas. *Technical digest 2013–2014*. Retrieved from http://tea.texas.gov/Student_Testing_and_Accountability/Testing/Student_Assessment_Overview/Technical_Digest_2013-2014/

Thurlow, M. L. (1994). *National and state perspectives on performance assessment and students with disabilities. Performance assessment: CEC mini-library*. Reston, VA: Council for Exceptional Children.

Valenzuela, A. (2005). *Leaving children behind: How "Texas-style" accountability fails Latino youth*. Albany, NY: State University of New York Press.

Viadero, D. (2004). Disparately disabled. *Education Week, 17*(22), 25–26.

To Want the Unwanted: Latinx English Language Learners on the Border

Reynaldo Reyes III

> *Violence is initiated by those who oppress, who exploit, who fail to recognize others as persons.*
> *–Paulo Freire, Pedagogy of the Oppressed*

Abstract Scandals rooted in the pressures of high-stakes schooling have pushed school leaders and districts to a tipping point in the education of the marginalized and vulnerable. This chapter explores how some parts of our education system have evolved into ones in which the dehumanization of vulnerable students, their parents, and their communities has become commonplace. In the pursuit of praxis, this author argues that we must consider actions at the individual and local level to bring about localized, incremental change that can result in larger cumulative movements of counter-narratives and counter-pedagogies in response to this trend of dehumanization in our schooling of ethnic, racial, and linguistic minorities.

Keywords Latino English language learners · High-stakes testing · Scandal · Push-out · Dehumanization · Counter-pedagogies

1 Introduction

The adverse effects of the high-stakes testing policy of *No Child Left Behind* (NCLB) on the education of underprivileged and marginalized youth have been well documented and discussed (Darling-Hammond, 2004; Kohn, 2000; McNeil, 2000; McNeil, Coppola, Radigan & Heilig, 2008; Menken, 2006, 2008, 2010; Nichols & Berliner, 2005, 2007, 2008; Valenzuela, 2005; Wood, 2004). Although NCLB was recently replaced with the *Every Student Succeeds Act* (ESSA) (2015),

---

R. Reyes III (✉)
Department of Teacher Education, The University of Texas at El Paso, El Paso, TX, USA
e-mail: rreyes9@utep.edu

accountability remains a central tenet to the education of students. The principle difference in the implementation of accountability practices under ESSA is that less power of oversight is given to the federal department of education, and more to the states and school districts. Under NCLB, administrators quickly became accustomed to extraordinary pressures to improve student test performance. Such pressures have sometimes resulted in various forms of cheating or manipulations of the system (Amrein-Beardsley, Berliner & Rideau, 2010; Nichols & Berliner, 2007), with administrators and teachers having succumb to "Campbell's Law."

Campbell (2011) warned in his seminal 1976 paper, *Assessing the Impact on Planned Social Change*, that "the more any quantitative social indicator is used for social decision-making, the more subject it will be to corruption pressures and the more apt it will be to distort and corrupt the social processes it is intended to monitor" (p. 34). His theory provides an important lens for the acute argument to the consequences of educational policy that breeds a high-stakes testing culture and accountability system, and the intrinsic desire for teachers and administrators to survive and thrive at whatever cost. Ultimately, according to Campbell's Law, cheating within a system that involves critical changes, choices, or consequences based on a pivotal evaluation is to be expected.

Cheating on high-stakes tests has occurred in various forms in US school districts. One of the most egregious examples occurred between 2006 and 2011 in the Border city of El Paso, Texas. Lorenzo Garcia, the superintendent of the El Paso Independent School District (EPISD) at the time, targeted students designated as not fully proficient in English, or those who had a history of "behavior problems," to be discouraged from going to school on testing days. Students were "encouraged" to drop out, seek out their GED, or be artificially demoted or promoted (Llorca, 2012; Michels, 2012; Torres, 2012). This scandal pushed out students seen as threats to performance on the state tests that measure annual yearly progress (AYP).

The EPISD student push-out scandal is more than just administrators and teachers cheating the accountability system. Their actions reveal another level of manipulation. Like the highly-publicized cheating in the Atlanta and Houston school districts, this scandal demonstrates how current accountability policies carry punitive consequences for teachers and administrators. These scandals bring to question what has become of teachers' and administrators' professional identities given that so many within a school district can engage in egregious behavior toward the children and communities they are trusted to serve. This chapter explores the following question: *Does the El Paso scandal illustrate how policies of accountability create an education system that has evolved into one in which the dehumanization of vulnerable students, their parents, and their communities has become normalized?* Using the lens of dehumanization and the pursuit of praxis, this chapter examines the EPISD cheating scandal and the push-out of Mexican-descent, English language learners (ELLs). Close examination of this scandal is necessary to bring to question how current accountability policies of assessment and learning continue to negatively impact so many Latinx communities.

Praxis means creating a more complete understanding of a problem by questioning it, engaging in dialogue, working to arrive at some sort of action to address the problem, and then questioning the results (Freire, 1970). Because praxis is both dialogical and action-oriented, one aim of this chapter is to incite the pursuit of praxis by examining what the cheating scandal actually means – not just for policy and practice, but for individuals as educators, activists, community leaders, and parents – within the context of the education for marginalized Latina/o student populations. This chapter considers how dehumanizing events in our schooling system have become normalized. Along with evidence from local and national news and investigative reports on this scandal, this chapter uses dehumanization as a framework for examining the significance of this scandal not only as a pivotal event in history within our current education paradigm, but as a shakable moment for us and within us as individuals who all have a stake in the schooling of our children.

2 A Need to Know in the Pursuit of Praxis

In the pursuit of new knowledge and understanding, let us begin with the question: *What happened?* The El Paso scandal received award-winning journalistic coverage by the local newspaper, as well as national exposure. But that is where it ended – as another story of scandal in our education system. However, a business-as-usual approach soon reemerged, with more finger-pointing between EPISD officials and the state Texas Education Agency.

The marginalization and disenfranchisement of Mexican-descent students, many of whom are classified as ELLs, is nothing new. Macedo (2006) places our nation's schools among the most pervasive perpetuators of marginalizing discourses and practices, enacting a colonial model that serves to control teachers and students to perpetuate hegemonic ideologies that have systematically disinherited racialized Americans. African-American and Latinx students have especially been victimized by schooling policies and practices that isolate, marginalize, and exclude (Spring, 2012). The EPISD scandal reveals how current policies on assessment, learning, and accountability continues practices of exclusion by institutionalizing a mechanism that inherently places a numerical, test-based value on individual students within a complex, and often confusing, calculation. Today, each student's worth is assigned before and after tests are given. That is, students who are viewed as more difficult to educate and prepare for this test are stigmatized by teachers and administrators. In the EPISD scandal, administrators modified student transcripts to artificially demote or promote students (Torres, 2012). These students' teachers and administrators perceived their capabilities based on state assessments.

In the EPISD scandal, already-marginalized, Mexican-descent students, many of whom were ELLs, were pushed-out, "reassigned" a grade, and made to disappear. Nationally, little has been done beyond rhetoric, re-naming, or re-shuffling to address the roots of corrupt schooling and the targeting and discarding of academically weak and vulnerable students that are seen as threats to high test scores. With the EPISD scandal, we now know such scandals of "disappearing" students can and do happen in our schools. What now? In the pursuit of praxis, reflection is key. So part of this process requires examination of some history of dehumanizing education.

3 A Dehumanizing Education

The dehumanization of individuals and communities in our schools has many faces. Freire (1970) defines dehumanization as a "distortion of the vocation of becoming more fully human" and reflected in "not only those whose humanity has been stolen, but also (though in a different way) those who have stolen it" (p. 44). Drawing on Freire's scholarship, I argue that in the post-NCLB era, dehumanization will *continue to be the norm* in schools and for the most vulnerable communities viewed as "at-risk." Dehumanization will not only continue as long as high-stakes accountability system are present, but as long as individual educators and administrators fail to reflect on and ethically respond to dehumanizing policy and discourses that infiltrate the perception of students as sub-populations and the resultant pedagogy.

Historically, hegemonic and racist ideologies have long denied many Latinx communities access to even the most immediate needs, from land to food, to language and equal education. Latinx communities have experienced institutionalized racism based on immigration status, language, and citizenship (Valencia, Menchaca & Donato, 2002), which has often led to questioning even the physical presence of Latinx individuals within the US and its schools. The case of the EPISD scandal is indicative of how schools that work with ethnically, racially, linguistically, and socioeconomically diverse communities reflect a "language-as-a-problem" view (Ruíz, 1984) that translates into policy and practice (Wiley & Wright, 2004). This mirrors what Menken (2008) has found in her work; that school administrators often express how they do not want ELLs because they present a liability on tests that are given in English. The questioning and suspicions of simple presence in schools further stigmatizes, marginalizes, and segments Latinx students and ELLs from these communities into a deficit narrative and as embodiments of characteristics of liabilities – language, culture, poverty, and difference – that may or may not have value for those in power who are subject to the gravity of Campbell's Law. When students and characteristics of their identities are seen as commodities that are quantified within a "yes-or-no value" dichotomy toward a point-value system, students are no longer students, they are objects and numbers. Students are victims of "cultural and linguistic eradication" because such characteristics are not needed nor desired in schooling, resulting in their dehumanization (Bartolomé, 1994, p. 176). Dehumanization of such students seems inevitable in a high-stakes culture of education that categorizes losers and winners (schools where learning occurs vs schools where learning does not occur) according to point differentials. The former EPISD superintendent involved in the scandal and other administrators developed policy and practice that removed individual students seen as liabilities.

For Latinx students and ELLs, decades of research has shown how public schools continue to struggle with meeting their various needs, graduate them, and have them college-ready (Gándara & Contreras, 2009; Garcia, 2001; Matute-Bianchi, 1991; Romo & Falbo, 1996; Stanton-Salazar, 2001; Valencia, 2002a, 2002b, 2008; Valencia et al., 2002; Valenzuela, 1999). Mexican American students who are ELLs, many immigrant or migrant, historically have had to endure segregation, inferior schooling facilities, and underfunded schools. This reflected a "socially racialized arrangement of White dominance over Mexican Americans", and to "the escalating *barrioization* of Mexican American communities" and school segregation of their children throughout the Southwest from the 1930s to the 1970s" (Valencia, 2008, pp. 9–10). This barrioization has resulted in lowered expectations, weaker curriculum and materials, and overall poor educational experiences for the majority of Mexican American students. A modern-day barrioization of Mexican American students also occurred in the EPISD scandal, as an associate superintendent ordered that students who transferred from out of the country to EPISD be held for a year in the ninth grade, a clear violation of district policy on admitting new students to the district (Torres, 2012). Such a directive from administration suggests that "being Mexican," or coming from Mexico, was reason enough to retain students in the lowest grade possible in the high school, without regard for a Mexican student's language skills, or educational background. Transferring from Mexico not only relegated such students to a grade that would not be counted in the test calculation, but did not consider what repercussions this would have on the student's learning, their social standing because of age difference, or their progress toward graduation. Is this continued inability to meet the educational needs of Latinx students a result of having dehumanized them to the point of being discardable because they are seen as carrying less value for schools, communities, and society?

4 Some Students Not Wanted

Today, in the name of efficiency and convenience, high-stakes standardization and testing has moved many schools to engage in practices and policies of elimination of weak students. As a result, as Giroux (2012) has argued, our consumer culture and neoliberal educational policies have designated many minority youth as "disposable" (p. 5). Teachers and administrators with such a view have removed, re-designated, or pushed out those students who could potentially dilute quality in the schools. Not only in El Paso, but in districts across the US, academically low-performing students have been "counseled" or pushed out to seek alternative forms of education – to get their GED or leave school altogether (Nichols & Berliner, 2005; Darling-Hammond, 2004; Menken, 2010).

It also has been well-documented that high-stakes testing only exacerbates the push out and dropout crisis, further marginalizing vulnerable youth like ELLs, migrants, immigrants, and those from communities of poverty (McNeil et al., 2008; Menken, 2010; Valenzuela, 2005) while depersonalizing the way children are educated (McNeil, 2000). Garnering its roots in widespread school segregation for Mexican students since the 1920s (Menchaca & Valencia, 1990), the current practices of eliminating students as cognitively, academically, socially, and personally unworthy of taking a test or being in school continues. The cumulative effect of this history has created a discourse and perception of inferiority and deficit of the Mexican American student (Acuña, 1995; Valencia, 2002a, 2002b). These deficit discourses have become rampant and intertwined within schools, which contribute to the diminishing of an identity of empowerment and possibility for students. The results of these discources have been devastating– higher dropout rates, disengaging schooling, and victims of pushout (McNeil, 2000; Menken, 2006, 2008, 2010; Valencia, 2008; Valenzuela, 2005).

Teaching and learning today have radically changed in our public schools since the inception of NCLB. This change has especially altered how ELLs are taught and the lens through which they are viewed (Menken, 2006; Pandya, 2011). When teachers of ELLs realize that they are being measured mostly by one test score, innovation in teaching gets reduced, or ceases altogether (Menken, 2010), and such pedagogy minimizes opportunities for culturally, linguistically, and humanizing pedagogy (Freire, 1970; Fránquiz & Salazar, 2004). Ultimately, this history of racialized, linguistic, and ethnically-driven segregation made Latinx youth appear to be inferior to those who were/are privileged. Marginalized and dehumanized youth are now relegated to work harder for mere recognition of their presence. They are now schooled within a *new* hidden curriculum; a curriculum that only considers those who are seen as cognitively, linguistically, economically, personally, and socially legitimized and valued.

5 Looking at What Have We Become

Because Campbell's Law ultimately is about the myopic and relentless focus on the pursuit of numbers, it is natural for those in power to succumb to dehumanizing forces, which are "not a given destiny but the result of an unjust order that engenders violence in the oppressors, which in turn dehumanizes the oppressed," (Freire, 1970, p. 44). The danger in measuring success by numbers is how this process commodifies students. The EPISD scandal also illustrates how what was once "coded language" (Acuña, 1995) and "symbolic violence" (Bourdieu & Passeron, 1977; Shannon & Escamilla, 1999) has now become overt pedagogical and policy practices. It is a perverse game in which, for example, ELLs as a sub-group have always been considered 'failing' in the progress toward AYP until they are re-designated or mainstreamed out of this subgroup (Menken, 2008). The constant labeling of ELLs as "failures" only contributes further to the discardability and liability characteristics assigned to their identity as student and test-taker. And even teachers who want to reverse hints of dehumanizing pedagogy in their classrooms are confined by high-stakes policy. For example, English as a Second Language (ESL) teachers are marginalized and dehumanized in their desire to teach more effectively and humanely (Harper, de Jong, & Platt, 2008). Salazar (2008) found that "even as teachers strive to create humanizing spaces in their classrooms, they are often pulled to conform to rigid language policies that strip students of their dignity" (p. 353). Teachers have lost the power, and even hope, of being that humanizing teacher that they want to be.

Freire's (1970) philosophy of praxis – dialogue, reflection, and action, with more reflection – suggests that teachers and administrators must come together to openly and critically recognize what they have become, not just in schools, but as a community that is allowing dehumanization to occur in themselves and to others. Perhaps the lack of inaction on so many is an indication of what McNeil (2000) has argued:

> The incremental normalizing of a system, the casual use of its language in conversations about education, can silence critique and can stifle the potential to pose countermodels, to envision alternative possibilities. That is the insidious power of an accountability system, to sound just enough like common-sense language that it is not recognized as a language meant to reinforce unequal power relations. (p. 269)

The consequences of NCLB has resulted in many schools essentially shutting the door on ELLs and other student groups (Menken, 2010). We have become a nation of schools so afraid of low test scores that the democratic notion of an education for all has all but disappeared. Teachers, principals, and parents know that this system could be improved, but they feel helpless to do anything about it because they are trapped in a behemoth bureaucratization that has become normalized (McNeil, 2000). Why? Because we have done it for so long? Because we know no other way to teach, learn, and understand how our children are learning? Our current system of accountability simply refuses to allow asset-based pedagogical practices and assessments to become a broader, foundational, and institutionalized part of everyday schooling. Yet, there are many promising counter-narratives in the form of extraordinary pedagogies that create micro pedagogical spaces (Faltis & Abedi, 2013).

6 Humanizing Solutions to Transform

There *are, have been, and continue to be solutions* to our current problems in educating diverse and academically-struggling student populations. We must simply more effectively systematize the locating, understanding, and application of ideas that work. I say "simply" because I believe that in today's infrastructure of communication and exchange of ideas, there are vast capabilities for finding those ideas and solutions in disseminated research, or even of powerful schools, programs, curricula, and/or individual teachers that have not yet been studied or replicated (e.g. the Teaching Excellence Network, i-SEED, the Urban Teaching Quality Index, Roses in Concrete, Urban Hope Project). And we too often complicate pedagogy when it is unnecessary. Sometimes the most effective and empowering approaches and strategies begin with utilizing what makes students feel human, connected, and valued (Bartolomé, 1994).

Ideas and solutions for a humanizing pedagogy exist, but one of the major obstacles to it is sorting through and translating those solutions to fit the local context for which the solution may be applied. Ramanathan and Morgan (2007) have succinctly argued that we must also remember that practice on a local level derives from and is *policy in practice*. It is not simply replicating it, but revealing the complexities, politics, and tensions inherent in the imposition of the law of ideas of curriculum and pedagogy by an often detached governmental structure in the very human endeavor of teaching and learning. Indeed, in this high-stakes paradigm, educators and administrators enact policy on various levels of micro-interactions.

The EPISD scandal was a *tipping point*. It is a call to consider other ways of how we see, comport, and question ourselves within this current system. Conchas (2001) argued that even though schools are places where social and economic injustices can continue, they can just as readily "circumvent inequality if students and teachers work in consort toward academic success" (p. 502). Current practices to humanize students are already present, even in the most obscure spaces within and outside school walls. The spaces where we find these solutions begin at both internal (within ourselves) and external spaces (as small groups, grassroot efforts, advocacy groups, etc. beyond the classroom where dialogue can occur). These spaces are where the concrete ideas emerge to be seen from behind and within the folds of the everyday pedagogies. Individuals in education must internally examine their role(s) and present consciousness in today's schooling and practices of dehumanization vs. humanization. On an external level, finding schooling practices that encompass humanizing pedagogies is about being vigilant in observation and "reading the world" (Freire & Macedo, 1987) in search for those ideas in possibilities and extraordinary pedagogies. Faltis and Abedi (2013) define such pedagogies as those that:

> encompass larger sociocultural issues, bringing attention to how poverty, race, social class, and language interact with local practices in teaching and learning, and in the everyday lives of families, educators, children, and youth…and they point to practices for future generations of children and youth for whom ordinary teaching and learning practices have neither sufficed nor helped in countering the widespread inequities in schooling. (p. viii)

7 Conclusion: Getting Back Our Humanity in Education

In spite of all the research and reform efforts in education, the quality of education for culturally and linguistically diverse students in the U.S. has remained stagnant with little change in the achievement gap. Cummins (1995) argued that even in micro-level efforts by teachers and students to engage in collaborative and empowering efforts of teaching and learning can be limited. The power structures within schools and society elicit discourses of resistance for effective and positive learning to function and be maintained. He found that most efforts to reform education are merely cosmetic and have had a minimal impact on the achievement levels of diverse student populations, which "leave intact the deep structures that reflect patterns of disempowerment in the wider society" (p. V). What the EPISD scandal illustrates is that there must be a call to teachers and administrators to engage in dialogue to question their power, identity, and consciousness in relation to the students and community she/he serves. As such, even in the most alternative, innovative, and reform-minded of schools and programs, the obsession with high test scores and the constant hand-wringing in working with diverse student groups will always dilute this dialogue and any ensuing action.

Newer reform efforts that tout accountability and high standards have not helped in providing an equitable education for culturally, linguistically, and socioeconomically diverse students. Even worse, from the EPISD scandal, we see how such reform efforts have created an educational infrastructure that promotes dehumanization practices that devalue the mere presence of those students who need the most help (Fránquiz & Salazar, 2004), while agencies that are created to oversee such practices fail to respond and protect vulnerable students (Keel, 2013). Solutions begin with raising consciousness about how we are thinking of such problems. Many of these solutions must be sought in those who were victims, or the communities from where they came. For example, by integrating dual language education in the educational framework and approach to ensuring academic success for their ELLs (DeMatthews, Izquierdo, & Knight, 2017), the EPISD is attempting to reverse this dehumanization trend by strategically implementing programming that recognizes the linguistic and cultural capital of their students. Ultimately, Freire (1970) expressed how "only power that springs from the weakness of the oppressed will be sufficiently strong to free" (p. 44) both oppressor and oppressed. In order to eliminate dehumanization in today's public education system, teachers and administrators must recognize their students' agency and dignity. Hutcheson (1999) argues that we must do more than just love our students, which often gets "confused with notions of loving one's student or building self-esteem or in senses of caring that are mistakenly diluted as soft and mushy goals" (p. 17). Dignity in education is "in the moral domain of relationships" (Hutcheson, 1999, p. 17). The consequence of not teaching our students with dignity in mind is marginalization, because when we recognize those we teach with dignity, we acknowledge the need to act and react to the intersection of their history, current lived situation, and the possibilities for them – right there, where they are physically, humanly present.

References

Acuña, R. (1995). *Anything but Mexican*. London, UK: Verso.
Amrein-Beardsley, A., Berliner, D., & Rideau, S. (2010). Cheating in the first, second, and third degree: Educators' responses to high-stakes testing. *Education Policy Analysis Archives, 18*(14), 1–33.
Bartolomé, L. (1994). Beyond the methods fetish: Toward a humanizing pedagogy. *Harvard Educational Review, 64*(2), 173–195.

Bourdieu, P., & Passeron, J. C. (1977). *Reproduction in education, society and culture.* London, UK: Sage.
Campbell, D. T. (2011). Assessing the impact of planned social change. *Journal of Multidisciplinary Evaluation, 7*(15), 3–43.
Conchas, G. Q. (2001). Structuring failure and success: Understanding the variability in Latino school engagement. *Harvard Educational Review, 71*(3), 475–505.
Cummins, J. (1995). *Power and pedagogy in the education of culturally diverse students: A discussion paper.* Toronto, Canada: Ontario Institute for Studies in Education.
Darling-Hammond, L. (2004). From "separate but equal" to "No Child Left Behind": The collisions of new standards and old inequalities. In D. Meier & G. Wood (Eds.), *Many children left behind: How the No Child Left Behind Act is damaging our children and our schools* (pp. 3–32). Boston, MA: Beacon Press.
DeMatthews, D. E., Izquierdo, E., & Knight, D. (2017). Righting past wrongs: A superintendent's social justice leadership for dual language education along the US-Mexico border. *Education Policy Analysis Archives, 25*(1), 1–28.
Every Student Succeeds Act. (2015). Retrieved July 13, 2016, from http://www.ed.gov/essa?src=rn.
Faltis, C., & Abedi, J. (2013). Extraordinary pedagogies for working within school setting serving nondominant students. *Review of Research in Education, 37*(1), vii–vxi.
Fránquiz, M., & Salazar, M. (2004). The transformative potential of humanizing pedagogy: Addressing the diverse needs of Chicano/Mexicano students. *High School Journal, 87*(4), 36–53.
Freire, P. (1970). *Pedagogy of the oppressed.* New York, NY: Continuum.
Freire, P., & Macedo, D. (1987). *Literacy: Reading the word and the world.* Westport, CT: Bergin & Garvey.
Gándara, P., & Contreras, F. (2009). *The Latino education crisis: The consequences of failed social policies.* Cambridge, MA: Harvard University Press.
Garcia, E. (2001). *Hispanic education in the United States: Raíces y alas.* Boulder, CO: Rowman & Littlefield.
Giroux, H. A. (2012). *Disposable youth: Racialized memories and the culture of cruelty.* New York, NY: Routledge.
Harper, C. A., de Jong, E. J., & Platt, E. J. (2008). Marginalizing English as a second language teacher expertise: The exclusionary consequence of No Child Left Behind. *Language Policy, 7*, 267–284.
Hutcheson, J. N. (1999). *Students on the margins: Education, stories, dignity.* Albany, NY: SUNY Press.
Keel, J. (2013). *An audit report on the Texas Education Agency's investigation of the El Paso Independent School District* (Report Number 13-047). Austin, TX: Texas State Auditor's Office.
Kohn, A. (2000). *The case against standardized testing: Raising the scores, ruining the schools.* Portsmouth, NH: Heinemann.
Llorca, J. C. (2012). El Paso School District Rebuilds After Fraudulent Testing Practices by Administrators. *The Huffington Post.* Retrieved from http://www.huffingtonpost.com/2012/10/02/school-district-rebuilds-_0_n_1933327.html.
Macedo, D. (2006). *Literacies of power: What Americans are not allowed to know* (Expanded ed.). Boulder, CO: Westview.
Matute-Bianchi, M. E. (1991). Situational ethnicity and patterns of school performance among immigrant and nonimmigrant Mexican-descent students. In M. A. Gibson & J. U. Ogbu (Eds.), *Minority status and schooling: A comparative study of immigrant and involuntary minorities* (pp. 205–247). New York, NY: Garland Publishing.
McNeil, L. M. (2000). *Contradictions of school reform: Educational costs of standardized testing.* New York, NY: Routledge.
McNeil, L. M., Coppola, E., Radigan, J., & Heilig, J. V. (2008). Avoidable losses: High-stakes accountability and the dropout crisis. *Education Policy Analysis Archives, 16*(3), 1–48.

Menchaca, M., & Valencia, R. R. (1990). Anglo-Saxon ideologies in the 1920s–1930s: Their impact on the segregation of Mexican students in California. *Anthropology & Education Quarterly, 21*(3), 222–249.

Menken, K. (2006). Teaching to the test: How standardized testing promoted by No Child Left Behind impacts language policy, curriculum, and instruction for English language learners. *Bilingual Research Journal, 30*(2), 521–546.

Menken, K. (2008). *English learners left behind: Standardized testing as language policy.* Clevedon, UK: Multilingual Matters.

Menken, K. (2010). No Child Behind and English language learners: Challenges and consequences. *Theory Into Practice, 49*, 121–128.

Michels, P. (2012). *Faking the grade: The nasty truth behind Lorenzo Garcia's miracle school turnaround in El Paso.* Retrieved November 1, 2013, from http://www.texasobserver.org/faking-the-grade-the-nasty-truth-behind-lorenzo-garcias-miracle-school-turnaround-in-el-paso/.

Nichols, S. L., & Berliner, D. C. (2005, March). *The inevitable corruption of indicators and educators through high-stakes testing.* Tempe, AZ: Arizona State University, Education Policy Studies Laboratory, Educational Policy Research Unit.

Nichols, S. L., & Berliner, D. C. (2007). *Collateral damage: How high-stakes testing corrupts America's schools.* Cambridge, MA: Harvard Education Press.

Nichols, S. L., & Berliner, D. C. (2008, May). Why has high-stakes testing so easily slipped into contemporary American life? *Phi Delta Kappan, 89*(9), 672–676.

Pandya, J. Z. (2011). *Overtested: How high-stakes accountability fails English language learners.* New York, NY: Teachers College Press.

Ramanathan, V., & Morgan, B. (2007). TESOL and policy enactments: Perspectives from practice. *TESOL Quarterly, 41*(3), 447–463.

Romo, H., & Falbo, T. (1996). *Latino high school graduation: Defying the odds.* Austin, TX: University of Texas Press.

Ruíz, R. (1984). Orientations in language planning. *NABE: The Journal for the National Association for Bilingual Education, 8*(2), 15–34.

Salazar, M. (2008). English or nothing: The impact of rigid language policies on the inclusion of humanizing practices in a high school ESL program. *Equity & Excellence in Education, 41*(3), 341–356.

Shannon, S., & Escamilla, K. (1999). Mexican immigrants in the United States: Targets of symbolic violence. *Educational Policy, 13*(3), 347–370.

Spring, J. (2012). *Deculturalization and the struggle for equality: A brief history of the education of dominated cultures in the United States.* Boston, MA: McGraw-Hill.

Stanton-Salazar, R. D. (2001). *Manufacturing hope and despair: The school and kin support networks of U.S.-Mexican youth.* New York, NY: Teachers College Press.

Torres, Z. (2012). *Bowie principal, top EPISD administrator reassigned as district Acknowledges massive failings.* Retrieved July 28, 2015, from http://www.elpasotimes.com/episd/ci_20467994/bowie-principal-top-episd-administrator-reassigned-district-acknowledges?source=pkg.

Valencia, R. R. (2002a). The plight of Chicano students: An overview of schooling conditions and outcomes. In R. R. Valencia (Ed.), *Chicano school failure and success: Past, present and future* (2nd ed., pp. 3–51). New York, NY: Routledge.

Valencia, R. R. (Ed.). (2002b). *Chicano school failure and success: Past, present and future.* New York, NY: Routledge.

Valencia, R. R. (2008). *Chicano students and the courts: The Mexican American legal struggle for educational equality.* New York, NY: New York University Press.

Valencia, R. R., Menchaca, M., & Donato, R. (2002). Segregation, desegregation, and integration of Chicano students: Old and new realities. In R. R. Valencia (Ed.), *Chicano school failure and success: Past, present and future* (pp. 70–113). New York, NY: Routledge.

Valenzuela, A. (1999). *Subtractive schooling: U.S. Mexican youth and the politics of caring.* New York, NY: SUNY Press.

Valenzuela, A. (Ed.). (2005). *Leaving children behind: How Texas-style accountability fails Latino youth*. Albany, NY: SUNY Press.

Wiley, T., & Wright, W. (2004). Against the undertow: Language minority education policy and politics in the age of accountability. *Educational Policy, 18*, 142–168.

Wood, G. (2004). NCLB's effects on classrooms and schools. In D. Meier & G. Wood (Eds.), *Many children left behind: How the No Child Left Behind Act is damaging our children and our schools* (pp. 33–50). Boston, MA: Beacon Press.

Part II
Bilingualism, Biliteracy, and Dual Language Education

Dual Language Education for All

Wayne P. Thomas and Virginia P. Collier

Abstract In this chapter key characteristics and the research foundation of dual language schooling (all models—90:10, 50:50, two-way, and one-way) are summarized and contrasted with features of transitional bilingual education, a short-term form of bilingual schooling, developed to serve only English learners. Dual language education (PK-12) is the mainstream curricular program taught through two languages, an enrichment model of schooling designed for all students, including English learners. We have found in our longitudinal research that dual language schooling fully closes the achievement gap for all student groups across ethnicity, social class, and special needs. In our research findings the most powerful outcomes of dual language classes are higher cognitive development as measured by school tests and higher engagement with learning. Dual language education also can result in powerful changes in school districts through innovative teaching practices and administrative reforms. Dual language schooling is rapidly expanding throughout the U.S., as parents and educators acknowledge the need to prepare our students to live and work more effectively as global citizens of the twenty-first century.

Keywords Dual language education · Serving all students together · Cognitive advantages · Closing the achievement gap · Innovative teaching practices · Administrative reforms · Expansion of dual language programs

A phenomenon is currently happening in the United States that no one could have predicted a couple of decades ago—bilingualism is becoming popular. In the 1980s and 1990s, the English-only movement was actively pursuing the agenda of eliminating bilingual schooling for English learners. In the early 1980s the U.S. government significantly reduced the amount of federal funding being used for training bilingual teachers, multilingual curriculum development, and doctoral studies in bilingual education. During these two decades the U.S. media published many

W. P. Thomas · V. P. Collier (✉)
George Mason University, Fairfax, VA, USA
e-mail: wthomas@gmu.edu; vcollier@gmu.edu

© The Author(s) 2019
D. E. DeMatthews, E. Izquierdo (eds.), *Dual Language Education: Teaching and Leading in Two Languages*, Language Policy 18,
https://doi.org/10.1007/978-3-030-10831-1_6

articles written by authors from the English-only movement, and in the late 1990s three states passed English-only voter initiatives—California, Arizona, and Massachusetts.

California native-English-speaking parents who had enrolled their children in integrated, two-way bilingual schools were quite upset with the passage of Proposition 227 in 1998, since that meant ending their children's bilingual classes. These parents succeeded in establishing a state waiver for two-way bilingual schools, and while the waiver application process was cumbersome, these English-speaking parents were determined to provide bilingual schooling for their children, with the English learners in these schools also benefiting when their parents signed the waiver for their children to attend too.

On top of that development, in the first decade of the 2000s, three states not previously known for having large numbers of English learners—North Carolina, Delaware, and Utah—established statewide initiatives, initially proposed by the governor or state board, to expand dual language education to all school districts, mostly for economic development reasons. These programs for both native English speakers and English learners have grown tremendously in popularity throughout the U.S. as more state governments, urban school districts, and parents have become aware of the benefits for everyone involved. This movement is largely fueled by native-English-speaking parents' demand that public schools provide classes taught through two languages (English plus another language), beginning in preschool or kindergarten and continuing throughout Grades K-12. But as the movement has expanded rapidly throughout all regions of the U.S., this type of schooling—now commonly called "dual language education"—has become a means of appropriately serving culturally and linguistically diverse populations, bringing together students of varied socioeconomic backgrounds, while at the same time satisfying the demands of native-English-speaking families. This chapter examines some of the research foundations and effective practices that lead to well-implemented dual language programs.

Transitional Bilingual Education To understand the essential characteristics of dual language schooling, it helps to briefly review some characteristics of the most common type of bilingual program that existed for English learners before dual language became so popular. Transitional bilingual education was developed in the late 1960s and 1970s to serve English learners' needs. The federal government and 30 states enacted legislation that provided funding for schooling through English learners' home language while they were acquiring English as a second language. These bilingual programs were designed to help students get meaningful access to the curriculum for 2–3 years through their primary language, but these classes isolated students from their native-English-speaking peers and tended to be somewhat remedial in nature. Bilingual teachers provided much needed sociocultural support for their students but there was little monitoring of the proportion of instruction in each language. Also, researchers found many bilingual teachers using translation, code-switching, and repetition of lessons in each language, leading to lost instructional time.

How Long? The biggest problem with transitional bilingual education was discovered when longitudinal studies began to examine the number of years that it takes to reach grade level achievement in second language, an average of 6 years (Collier & Thomas, 2017; Lindholm-Leary, 2001; Thomas & Collier, 1997, 2002, 2012). Policy makers had assumed that 2 or 3 years is a sufficient amount of time for support services for English learners, and students were exited from their transitional bilingual classes within a few years, resulting in half-gap closure or less. Once these students were placed in the English educational mainstream, they were no longer able to close the gap, although they reached higher levels of achievement than their peers who received only ESL support. (See Fig. 1 for an overview of longitudinal research findings from Thomas and Collier on English learners' achievement as measured by norm-referenced tests, depending upon the type of program provided during the elementary school years. A detailed summary of interpretation of this figure is provided in Thomas and Collier (2012, pp. 91–96). A comprehensive syn-

Program 1: Two-way Dual Language Education (DLE), including Content ESL
Program 2: One-way DLE, including ESL taught through academic content
Program 3: Transitional BE, including ESL taught through academic content
Program 4: Transitional BE, including ESL, both taught traditionally
Program 5: ESL taught through academic content using current approaches with no L1 use
Program 6: ESL pullout - taught by pullout from mainstream classroom with no L1 use
Program 7: Proposition 227 in California (successive 2-year quasi-longitudinal cohorts)

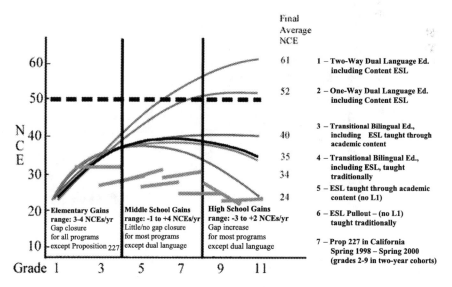

Fig. 1 English learners' long-term K-12 achievement in Normal Curve Equivalents (NCEs) on standardized tests in english reading compared across seven program models (Results aggregated from longitudinal studies of well-implemented, mature programs in five school districts and in California)

thesis of all Thomas and Collier research findings is published in Collier and Thomas (2017).

Current state tests being used for accountability purposes are another way of measuring English learners' progress in English across the school curriculum. In recent years, the Texas Education Agency has collected this information on English learners' performance on the State of Texas Assessments of Academic Readiness (STAAR), along with data on the type of support program in which the students were enrolled. Figures 2, 3, and 4 illustrate the percentage of English learners who reached satisfactory level or above on the Reading, Mathematics, and Writing assessments of the 2015 STAAR. This data shows that two-way and one-way dual language students reach the highest levels of achievement, and students attending either dual language or transitional bilingual classes score significantly higher than their English learner peers who do not receive any support for their native language (those enrolled in ESL, ESL content, and ESL pullout). For example, in Reading the

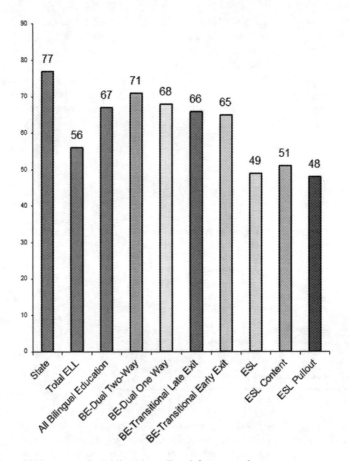

Fig. 2 Texas 2015 staar reading. All grades – % satisfactory or above

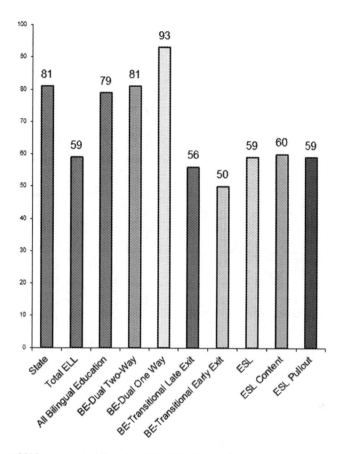

Fig. 3 Texas 2015 staar math. All grades – % satisfactory or above

percentage of "satisfactory and above" performance is in the mid-to-high 60s for bilingual schooling and in the mid-to-high 40s for English-only programs. This is a very large difference in favor of bilingual schooling in general, and for dual language schooling in particular, at 71% passing.

As the research foundation for dual language education has grown, the contrast between characteristics of transitional bilingual programs and dual language schooling that make a big difference in long-term student success are becoming clearer. The combination of native-English-speaking parents' demands and the growing research base are fueling the movement towards dual language education for all students. Let's examine some of the key characteristics of dual language schooling that lead to success for all.

English Learners Benefit First of all, dual language education is the mainstream curricular program, taught through two languages. In the United States, English is required and the other instructional language is the choice of the school and the parent community. The research is clear that English learners benefit enormously from

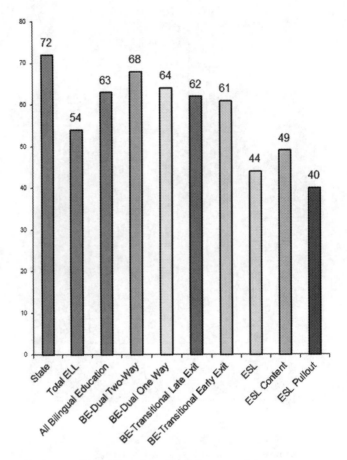

Fig. 4 Texas 2015 staar writing. All grades – % satisfactory or above

this form of bilingual schooling, so most school communities choose the home language of the largest number of English learners, in addition to English. Since Spanish is the primary language of 77% of English learners in the U.S. (*The Condition of Education*, 2017), Spanish-English programs are most commonly chosen. Native-English-speaking parents prefer this language choice, since Spanish is the second largest language of the world after Mandarin Chinese, as defined by number of native speakers (*Ethnologue*, 2017). Also the U.S. is now the second largest Spanish-speaking country in the world, after Mexico (El Instituto Cervantes, 2017).

Parents prefer that their children acquire the new language through interacting with native-Spanish-speaking peers of their children's age. This is the beauty of dual language education—both language groups benefit from the best circumstances for second language acquisition (Krashen, 1981; Wong Fillmore, 1991). These advantages include natural first and second language development, starting at a young age, through interacting with same-age students doing meaningful tasks together across the curriculum (mathematics, science, social studies, language arts, art, music, etc.). Dual language schooling begins in preschool or kindergarten and continues throughout all grades PK-12. Schools usually grow the program one grade at a time.

Dual language Is for All Students The second major characteristic of dual language schooling is that it is for everyone who chooses to enroll. It is not a separate segregated program, designed only for English learners. In fact, English learners do benefit the most dramatically of all participating groups. In our 32 years of longitudinal research analyzing over 7.5 million English learners' records in 36 school districts in 16 U.S. states (Collier & Thomas, 2017; Thomas & Collier, 2012, 2014), we have found that dual language education is the only program that fully closes the achievement gap for all students. English learners have the largest gap to close, starting with zero proficiency in English to reaching grade-level achievement in both first and second languages.

Cognitive Advantages for Proficient Bilinguals In fact, typical English learners attending dual language classes for at least 6 years achieve above-grade-level scores on the state or nationally-normed tests, when tested in both languages. Hundreds of research studies have shown that proficient bilinguals outscore monolinguals on both school and intelligence tests; proficient bilinguals are cognitively advantaged over monolinguals (Baker & Wright, 2017; Collier & Thomas, 2014, 2017). It takes dual language students (of all backgrounds) an average of 6 years to reach grade level in their second language (Collier & Thomas, 2009); whereas English learners in other program types typically do not succeed in reaching grade level achievement in their second language, closing only half or less of the academic achievement gap, and many do not complete high school.

Ethnic Groups' Achievement in Dual Language Programs In the past, Latino students who were tested as "fluent in English" would not have qualified for transitional bilingual education classes. However, when their scores are disaggregated from those of non-Latino native-English speakers they also have an achievement gap to close. When enrolling in dual language classes, Latinos re-connect to their heritage language, become proficient bilinguals, and outscore monolingual English speakers not in dual language. Also, African American students of low-income background in both inner city and agricultural contexts of Texas and North Carolina have dramatically achieved two grades above their peers not in dual language by the middle school years (Thomas & Collier, 2002, 2014).

As can be seen in Figs. 5 and 6, by fifth grade Houston, Texas, public school students attending 90:10 two-way PK-12 dual language programs (green and yellow lines) were significantly above grade level in both Spanish and English on very difficult norm referenced tests (Aprenda and Stanford). These students were mostly of low socioeconomic background (as measured by participation in free and reduced lunch), and three-fourths of the English speakers were of African American

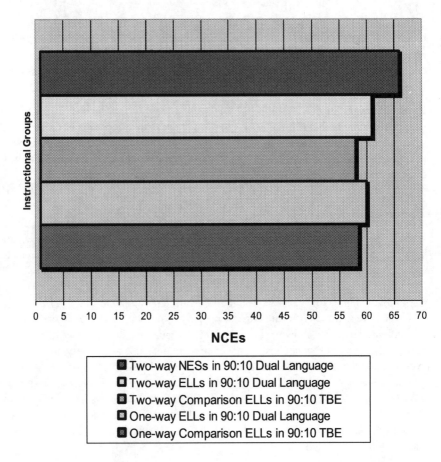

NESs – Native English Speakers
ELLs – English Language Learners
TBE – Transitional Bilingual Education
Comparison – Matched comparison group not in Dual Language

Fig. 5 Houston two-way study 2000. Aprenda total reading at end of grade 5

background (green lines). The African American students even outscored the native Spanish speakers in Spanish!

Other groups that initially test lower than the average, such as students with special needs (such as learning disabilities, speech or health impairment, autism, etc.), also benefit greatly from dual language classes, scoring higher than their peers with similar special needs not in dual language (Thomas & Collier, 2012, 2014). White students and Asian American students also achieve much higher than their peers not in dual language classes (Lindholm-Leary, 2001; Thomas & Collier, 2014).

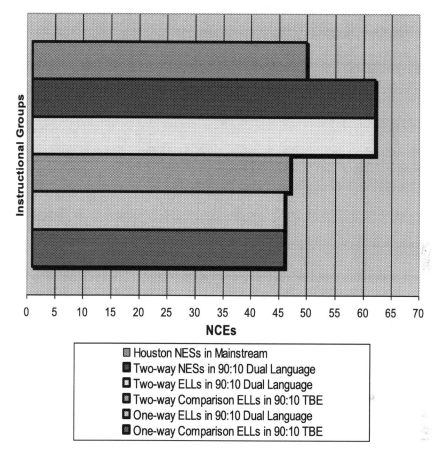

NESs – Native English Speakers
ELLs – English Language Learners
TBE – Transitional Bilingual Education
Comparison – Matched comparison group not in Dual Language

Fig. 6 Houston two-way study 2000. Stanford 9 total reading at end of grade 5

Powerful Outcomes of Dual Language Classes In our research findings, the two most powerful outcomes of dual language programs are higher cognitive development as measured by school tests and higher engagement with learning. Student engagement is visible when we visit dual language classes and watch the students deeply involved with their curricular projects and teaching each other. Also dual language students attend school more consistently, experience fewer behavioral referrals, and develop higher self-esteem, confidence, and motivation, in comparison to students not in dual language classes (Lindholm-Leary, 2001; Lindholm-Leary & Borsato, 2006; Thomas & Collier, 2014). When students graduate from high school, these dual language young adults are receiving scholarships for university study at a high rate and are entering the workforce ready to use their proficient bilingualism. Some have chosen to become bilingual teachers in the school districts from which they graduated (Chapter 7 in Collier & Thomas, 2014).

Additive Bilingualism Also, one of the most powerful outcomes for English learners is that dual language classes solve the problems associated with subtractive bilingualism (Lambert, 1975). Some societies, including many regions of the U.S., have encouraged immigrants and linguistically diverse groups to develop the dominant language by stopping use of their primary language. For example, in the southwest U.S. during the first half of the twentieth century, many Spanish speakers were physically punished for speaking Spanish in school. American Indian children were placed in boarding schools to replace their native language with English. These practices produced what Lambert referred to as subtractive bilingualism, by forcing linguistically diverse groups to lose their heritage language as they acquired the dominant language, English. Lambert also noted that subtractive bilinguals do less well in school. Many studies have examined the relationship between students' first language and cognitive development (Baker & Wright, 2017; Cummins, 1994; Grosjean, 1982). The research shows that additive bilinguals, who acquire their second language while continuing to develop their first language, do exceedingly well in school. When English learners continue to develop cognitively in their first language until at least age 12, they achieve on or above grade level in school. Dual language classes resolve subtractive bilingualism issues—both the native English speakers and English learners become additive bilinguals. Fewer special education referrals are needed and "response to intervention" and other pullout services are no longer required.

Dual Language Non-negotiables There are many "flavors" of dual language education (two-way, one-way, 90:10, 50:50), all of which have the potential to work very well, if the basic non-negotiable components of dual language are followed: (1) at least 50% of the instructional time must be taught in the partner (non-English) language, (2) separation of the two languages for instruction, and (3) PK-12 commitment.

Two-Way "Two-way" and "one-way" are terms used to refer to the demographics of the program. Two-way dual language is the most integrated model, in which two language groups are schooled through their two languages—for example, native English speakers work together with native Spanish speakers. The most important rule for two-way programs is that the two language groups work together at all times—this is the power of this model, because the students teach each other. In particular, if the two language groups are separated to teach reading in the students' native language, this significantly reduces the effectiveness of two-way dual language classes and lowers test scores. When both groups stay together at all times, they teach each other, including serving as peer teachers for developing reading in their L2.

One-Way The demographic situation where only one language group is attending dual language classes is called "one-way." For example, one-way dual language is the common demographic pattern for U.S. school districts close to the border of Mexico, with fewer native English speakers present. The term one-way can also be applied to programs that include only native English speakers, but we are not reviewing those programs in this chapter, since this book focuses on serving linguistically and culturally diverse student populations. One-way dual language programs in the border areas of Texas are flourishing, as students from these programs increasingly do better in school and graduate at significantly higher rates. English-only perspectives still exist in these regions, so it can be difficult to maintain the school leadership needed to sustain dual language classes, but the school districts that have succeeded in long-term dual language schooling are experiencing great success.

90:10 The other "flavors" of dual language—90:10 and 50:50—involve the percentage of time spent in each language in the early grades. The 90:10 model was developed in Canada, for monolingual English speaking students to jump-start their acquisition of French in kindergarten and first grade, by studying 90% in French and 10% in English for the first 2 years of school, followed by gradually increasing English time until the proportion is 50:50 by fourth grade. This model teaches reading in the non-English language first, with formal English reading and writing introduced in second grade. If the classes are two-way, both language groups learn to read in the non-English language first, always working together. This focus on the partner language first is important to provide nonstop cognitive development in L1 for the English learners, which leads to better long-term acquisition of English. The extra partner language at the beginning also helps native English speakers jump-start their L2 acquisition at no cost to L1 development, since they typically have less access to L2 outside of school but plenty of access to English.

50:50 The 50:50 model develops both languages equally each year of school. Because of the tendency for English (the dominant language) to get more emphasis, it is very important to examine all the minutes of a school day, including the specials (art, music, health, physical education, computer lab, etc.), and make sure that half of the total school time is provided in the non-English language. This is the main challenge with the 50:50 model—to provide enough instructional time in the non-English language so that students develop full academic proficiency and maximize cognitive stimulation in that language, because they get less support for it outside of school. While we have found that the 90:10 model is slightly more efficient at getting students to grade level in both languages sooner (Collier & Thomas, 2009), both the 50:50 and 90:10 models are in the long term equally powerful.

Two Teachers Teaming Together Separation of the two languages is another important component of dual language schooling, to be handled with sensitivity to the nuances of this issue. The most practical way to resolve this is by having two teachers team together, sharing two classes, with one teacher teaching in English and the other teaching in the partner language and switching classes as appropriate.

Sharing two classes makes team teaching cost-effective by maintaining the normal student-teacher ratio. In states such as North Carolina where there are fewer bilingual teachers, they have trained the English-medium teachers to use second language (ESL) teaching strategies, while partnering with, for example, a Spanish-medium teacher. (In NC, dual language programs are available in Cherokee, Chinese, French, German, Greek, Japanese, and Spanish.) When the students walk into the other classroom, they know that they must switch to the other instructional language. Team teaching also resolves the issue of the teacher's academic proficiency in the instructional language, by each teacher providing instruction in his/her strongest language.

One Bilingual Teacher In states such as Texas, there are a greater number of proficient bilingual teachers who may teach in a self-contained classroom, serving as the teacher for both languages. One teacher providing instruction through both languages can result in both advantages and disadvantages. It is very important that the teacher maintain the principle of separation of the languages, by time of day or by subject, during the first years of the students' development of their new language. If translation or code-switching is used by the teacher, students come to expect that something they don't understand will be repeated in their primary language, and they lose significant amounts of instructional time because they're not paying attention all the time, leading to less development of the second language. During the first couple of years of the program (Grades K-1), students in a dual language class are allowed to respond in either language (for their comfort zone), but once students have developed enough proficiency in their second language, they should also be able to use the two languages separately. At the same time, as students move along in their development of the two languages, it is important that teachers use bridging between the two languages, to compare and contrast issues in vocabulary and reading and writing, so that students make use of transfer strategies (Beeman & Urow, 2013).

Dual Language Changes Teaching Practices Dual language education is so powerful that it is changing teaching and administrative practices in many school districts (Thomas & Collier, 2017). Teachers in dual language classes must teach very heterogeneous groups of students. Students come from many different socioeconomic backgrounds, and they are culturally and linguistically diverse. Most students in each class have reached varying levels of proficiency in the language of instruction, and immigrant students vary in how much formal schooling they may have received.

To manage these diverse needs, teachers must follow the most up-to-date, innovative, research-based methods of teaching. Cooperative learning is the most important foundation for work in pairs, small groups, and learning centers. As lessons proceed, with the teachers modeling routines and procedures, the teachers must provide lots of clues to meaning through mime, gestures, pictures, word charts, chants, music, movement, graphic organizers, and many more strategies, with peer teaching serving the important role of cognitive development through problem solving and critical thinking across the curriculum. Team teaching also requires coordination and planning, but two heads are better than one for developing innovative teaching strategies and responding to the needs of students.

Dual Language Administrative Reforms As part of program start-up, school leaders must be prepared to provide financial resources for curricular materials in the partner language, a system for finding qualified, certified, academically proficient bilingual teachers, and lots of professional development for teachers to improve their research-supported dual language teaching practices. Central administrators must provide planning and support across feeder schools as the program grows grade by grade, K-12. With this two-way dual language innovation, the directors of world languages and ESOL/bilingual services for English learners must work together and coordinate funding of the program. Since this is a mainstream program, all curricular heads are responsible for understanding the program and sharing resources and joint curricular decisions regarding textbooks in the partner language as well as in English.

Dual Language Expansion As dual language programs expand to all regions of the United States, this type of schooling often starts in one school and then, as other principals see the changes that occur, including test scores improving, they choose to add dual language classes to their schools too. Sometimes the program is implemented district-wide, when the superintendent decides to advocate for dual language classes for all. When this happens, the biggest challenge is finding the qualified bilingual teachers to grow the program grade by grade. A few states have provided some resources and support services at the state level (Delaware, North Carolina and Utah) to encourage the expansion of dual language programs. The Texas state legislature in 2001 endorsed dual language education as a means of graduating more bilingual/biliterate young adults to strengthen the workforce and the state economy.

States Implementing Dual Language Programs; the Biliteracy Seal Dual language programs are spreading in Alaska, California, Colorado, Connecticut, Delaware, the District of Columbia, Florida, Hawaii, Illinois, Louisiana, Massachusetts, Minnesota, New Jersey, New Mexico, New York, Nevada, North Carolina, Oregon, Texas, Utah, Virginia, Washington, and Wisconsin. All of these states have also passed legislation to establish requirements for a Biliteracy Seal to be awarded on a high school diploma, for students who can demonstrate academic proficiency in two languages, and many other states are preparing to join this movement. Representative Roberto Alonzo, who introduced the Texas legislation for the Biliteracy Seal passed in 2014, says "The benefits of having this recognition seal are abundant in this dynamic country of many bilingually populated cities. This Bill truly helps students reach their maximum potential in education."

California was the first state to develop the Biliteracy Seal in 2011, even while the English-only Proposition 227 was still in place. In November, 2016, California voters passed Proposition 58, modifying Proposition 227 by giving schools choice to develop the programs that their communities want, ending the requirement for English-only instruction for English learners. During the two decades of English-only for English learners, two-way dual language schools in California multiplied so that there are now over 400 two-way schools and more being developed with the passage of Proposition 58. In 2017 Massachusetts passed similar legislation, ending the English-only requirements of the voter referendum of 2002 in that state.

Languages of Dual Language Programs in the U.S. We estimate that currently there may be 2500 or more two-way dual language public schools in the U.S. with many more being developed each year. The website "DualLanguageSchools.org" (2019) has registered 1702 dual language schools as of 2019. In many of the states listed, we are aware of twice as many as have registered. The majority of these programs are Spanish-English because Spanish speakers are the largest language group in the U.S. In addition, there are U.S. dual language programs taught in English and Arabic, Armenian, Cantonese, Filipino, French, German, Greek, Haitian Creole, Hebrew, Hmong, Italian, Japanese, Khmer, Korean, Mandarin Chinese, Polish, Portuguese, Russian, Ukranian, Urdu, and Vietnamese, and the list is growing every year. Dual language programs are also provided in the following American Indian languages: Arapahoe, Cherokee, Crow, Diné (Navajo), Hoopa, Inupiaq, Keres, Lakota, Nahuatl, Ojibwe, Passamaquoddy, Shoshoni, Ute, and Yurok (Center for Applied Linguistics, 2019; U.S. Department of Education, 2015).

Dual language education for all students is a reform of U.S. education whose time has come. Through this type of bilingual schooling, we are preparing students to live and work more effectively and "connectedly" as global citizens of the twenty-first century.

References

Baker, C., & Wright, W. E. (2017). *Foundations of bilingual education and bilingualism* (6th ed.). Bristol, UK: Multilingual Matters.

Beeman, K., & Urow, C. (2013). *Teaching for biliteracy: Strengthening bridges between languages*. Philadelphia, PA: Caslon.

Center for Applied Linguistics. (2019). *Two-way immersion directory*. Washington, DC: Center for Applied Linguistics. http://www.cal.org/twi/directory

Collier, V. P., & Thomas, W. P. (2009). *Educating English learners for a transformed world*. Albuquerque, NM: Dual Language Education of New Mexico-Fuente Press. Print, electronic, and Spanish editions. http://www.dlenm.org

Collier, V. P., & Thomas, W. P. (2014). *Creating dual language schools for a transformed world: Administrators speak*. Albuquerque, NM: Dual Language Education of New Mexico-Fuente Press. Print and electronic editions. http://www.dlenm.org

Collier, V. P., & Thomas, W. P. (2017). Validating the power of bilingual schooling: Thirty-two years of large-scale, longitudinal research. In *Annual review of applied linguistics*. Cambridge, UK: Cambridge University Press.

Cummins, J. (1994). Primary language instruction and the education of language minority students. In C. F. Leyba & California State Department of Education (Eds.), *Schooling and *language minority students: A theoretical framework* (2nd ed., pp. 3–46). Los Angeles, CA: California State University, Evaluation, Dissemination, and Assessment Center.

Dual Language Schools. (2019). http://duallanguageschools.org

El Instituto Cervantes. (2017). http://www.cervantes.es.default.htm

Ethnologue: Languages of the world. (2017). http://www.ethnologue.com/statistics/size

Grosjean, F. (1982). *Life with two languages: An introduction to bilingualism.* Cambridge, MA: Harvard University Press.

Krashen, S. D. (1981). *Second language acquisition and second language learning.* Oxford, UK: Pergamon.

Lambert, W. E. (1975). Culture and language as factors in learning and education. In A. Wolfgang (Ed.), *Education of immigrant students.* Toronto, ON: Ontario Institute for Studies in Education.

Lindholm-Leary, K. (2001). *Dual language education.* Bristol, UK: Multilingual Matters.

Lindholm-Leary, K., & Borsato, G. (2006). Academic achievement. In F. Genesee, K. Lindholm-Leary, W. M. Saunders, & D. Christian (Eds.), *Educating English language learners: A synthesis of research evidence* (pp. 176–222). Cambridge, UK: Cambridge University Press.

The Condition of Education. (2017). http://www.rowman.com/ISBN/9781598889567/The-Condition-of-Education-2017

Thomas, W. P., & Collier, V. P. (1997). *School effectiveness for language minority students.* Washington, DC: National Clearinghouse for English Language Acquisition. http://www.thomasandcollier.com

Thomas, W. P., & Collier, V. P. (2002). *A national study of school effectiveness for language minority students' long-term academic achievement.* Santa Cruz, CA: Center for Research on Education, Diversity and Excellence, University of California-Santa Cruz. http://www.thomasandcollier.com

Thomas, W. P., & Collier, V. P. (2012). *Dual language education for a transformed world.* Albuquerque, NM: Dual Language Education of New Mexico-Fuente Press. Print and electronic editions. Spanish edition in press (2017a). http://www.dlenm.org

Thomas, W. P., & Collier, V. P. (2014). *English learners in North Carolina, 2010.* Fairfax, VA: George Mason University. A research report provided to the North Carolina Department of Public Instruction. http://www.thomasandcollier.com

Thomas, W. P., & Collier, V. P. (2017). *Why dual language schooling.* Albuquerque, NM: Dual Language Education of New Mexico-Fuente Press. Print and electronic editions. http://www.dlenm.org

U.S. Department of Education: Office of English Language Acquisition. (2015). *Dual language education programs: Current state policies and practices.* Washington, DC: U.S. Department of Education.

Wong Fillmore, L. (1991). Second language learning in children: A model of language learning in social context. In E. Bialystok (Ed.), *Language processing in bilingual children* (pp. 49–69). Cambridge, UK: Cambridge University Press.

A More Comprehensive Perspective in Understanding the Development and Learning in Dual Language Learners

Eugene E. García

Abstract Millions of children around the globe are acquiring more than one language in their homes and in early care and education (ECE) settings as a consequence of migration and other social/political processes that generate "minority/majority" situations. Growing up within a minority/majority language situation carries a set of particular circumstances that may result in a developmental pathway for these children that differs from that of monolingual children who are part of the majority or dominant language group. A conceptual framework is proposed that provides a more comprehensive understanding of the difficulties that arise from the interaction of presumably universal development and manifestly variable socioculture experiences of these children and students. The conceptual framework proposed in this chapter reflects a concern about the way in which current research, policy and educational practice addresses the development of dual language learners (DLLs) – young children, birth to age five, who are learning a majority language as their second language, while acquiring a minority language as their first language.

Keywords Conceptual framework · Early childhood bilingualism · Dual language · Cognitive development · Asset orientation

1 Introduction

It is common for young children and adolescents around the world to find themselves in circumstances in which they are acquiring more than one language in the home and in early care and formal education settings (Castro, 2014). In the United States, this population of children and students includes both long term native populations as well as recent immigrants to the country (Garcia & Cuellar, 2006) and has

E. E. García (✉)
Arizona State University, Tempe, AZ, USA
e-mail: genegar@asu.edu

received significant research, policy, and practice attention at various levels of schooling (California Department of Education, 2010; U.S. Department of Education, 2008; Garcia, Weise, & Cuellar, 2013) and is of particular interest to the study of the increasing number and diversity of dual language learners[1] in the United States (Takanishi & Le Menestrel, 2017).

Currently, theoretical and research contributions have added to a more complex and layered understanding regarding the development of dual language learners (DLLs) who are developing two languages simultaneously (McCabe et al., 2013; Hammer, Hoff, Uchikoshi, Gallanders, & Castro, 2013). However, findings from critical reviews of the literature recently revealed key limitations in the existing research (García & Náñez, 2011). For instance, this research focused on differences between the DLL and non-DLL populations, but neglected the heterogeneity *within* the DLL population, and, very few studies offered longitudinal evidence related to DLLs' trajectories across various developmental domains (language, cognitive and social-emotional domains) (Castro, 2014). The bulk of this scholarship, not surprisingly, foregrounds attention to linguistic and cognitive factors while other developmental and contextual influences too often tend to be considered only as secondary variables of interest (García & Markos, 2015).

In light of this state of affairs, a more comprehensive perspective that recognizes language development as interdependent and situated within social and cultural practices and specific institutions and contexts is proposed here to better understand DLL development and learning. Moreover, this perspective is cognizant of biological and neurological factors that support language development (Shonkoff & Phillips, 2000). The conceptual perspective recognized the link between language and culture. It recognizes that culture as instantiated in people's everyday practices, views culture as patterned, dynamic, and historically grounded instrumental, and as a product of human history and its evolution (Artiles, 2003). This means culture affords and constrains human behavior, including language even as language is itself a transmitter of culture. DLLs are active participants in the environments influencing their linguistic development and in turn influence that same environment. This is an important departure from many views of child and language development perspectives for this perspective goes beyond the exclusive analytic focus on individual characteristics related only to cognitive and linguistic elements.

The perspective is also mindful of the role of biological and neurological factors linked to perceptual and cognitive development and learning, language development (as recognized by other National Research Council Committees' attention to the complex nature of child development (Allen & Kelly, 2015; Shonkoff & Phillips, 2000)), and elaborations of this linkage of biological, neurological and behavior functions (Goldman & Pellegrino, 2015). The development of the brain from before birth through early adulthood, and the effects and consequences of that develop-

---

[1] When referring to young children aged birth to 8 in their homes, communities, or early care and education programs, this I use the term "dual language learners" or "DLLs." This is consistent with definition adopted by the National Academies of Science, Engineering and Medicine's 2017 report focusing on research practice and policy from birth to grade 12 (Takanishi & Le Menestrel, 2017).

ment, specifically relevant to the experiences of DLLs is an important part of this perspective. Understanding how the brain responds to and processes one, two, or more languages is a large, complex and ongoing field of inquiry.

The ability to learn and understand language relies on distinct neural processing mechanisms that lie in different areas of the brain and develop at different ages. Brain development begins before birth with cell division, followed by cell migration – which is mostly complete by birth. Neurons then grow from axons and dendrites. When the axon of one neuron meets the dendrites of another neuron, a connection between them (or synapses) is made. The formation of synapses is thought to begin around birth. Over time, neurons that do not make connections with other neurons die, a process called synaptic pruning. The formation of synapse (synaptogenesis) together with synaptic pruning leads to the formation of neural networks such as those used to produce and process language. Patterns in the input determine which neurons will fire together and develop into networks; neurons that do not make connections die. ***Thus, infants are not born already "wired for" language***. Instead they are born with the capacity to form the neural networks that connect the pieces of language that they hear with what they see in their environments (and with how those sounds are produced). This "dance" between the brain and the environment leads us to adopt a more dynamic model of development (Conboy & Kuhl, 2011).

In summary, the perspective builds on the significant contributions by the National Research Council regarding issue of development and learning and DLLs (Allen & Kelly, 2015; August & Hakuta, 1997; Bransford, Brown &and Cocking, 1999; Bowerman, Donovan, & Burns, 2000; Shonkoff & Phillips, 2000). The perspective serves as an archetype for guiding a review of the knowledge base and addressing implications for practice, policy and research, believing it is helpful for determining factors that need to be taken into consideration when designing, conducting, and interpreting findings from new studies of the DLL experience as they relate to identifying and implementing educational practices and informed federal, state and local policies. As previously stated, this constellation of elements is known to interact in complex ways, but are listed here in a linear order for ease of exposition.

2 Neural Foundations for Dual Language Learning

Many parts of the brain are involved in language processing in both the left and right hemispheres. They include the frontal lobe in which Broca's area is located (and is also involved in cognitive control), the temporal lobe which contains the auditory cortex and Wernicke's area, the motor cortex, and the parietal and occipital cortices. Experience with language plays a critical role in the development of these networks; both in determining the connections that are created and retained, and in setting and closing the sensitive period windows (e.g., in the auditor cortex) via the neurochemistry of making and keeping connections (Werker & Hensch, 2015). Highly relevant to dual language learners, who may not be exposed to both of their languages from birth, this does not happen in all areas of the brain at the same time. The frontal cortex, for example, is critical for planning the order in which words of a sentence will be spoken, develops last. In the case of DLLs who learn two languages from birth or very early on, the neural mechanisms that underlie language processing overlap considerably with infants and children who only learn one language, or at least they overlap more than in the case where a second language is learned later. When the second language is learned later, it is supported by the later developing neural areas. The brain develops a lot like muscles in the body; the more certain areas are used, the larger, more efficient and stronger those areas become (Swanson, Wolff, Elison et al., in press).

The *neoconstructivist* theoretical approach of cognitive development allows for the framing of the relationship between experiences in language domains and brain development by assuming a dynamic relationship between "nature" and "nurture" (Westerman et al., 2007). This theoretical underpinning has led to direct exploration of bilingual development and speech perception and vocabulary development in DLLs (Conboy & Mills, 2006; Conboy & Kuhl, 2011). What is becoming more evident is that the interaction of the neurological systems and the environment, particularly the formation of the brain architecture during periods of plasticity, is highly relevant to our understanding of the behavioral indicators of development and learning (Allen & Kelly, 2015;). What is also emerging is a better understanding of the specific influence of multilingual environments on the neurological connections for developmental and learning trajectories of DLLs (Takanishi & Le Menestrel, 2017).

3 Socio-Cultural Foundations for Dual Language Learning

3.1 Family Circumstances

For most children, the immediate structures and individuals providing care is the family which serves as the most salient and enduring context in which DLLs learn and develop. Understanding the demographic profile of the family is an important step in understanding what DLL families "look like," but is not sufficient for uncovering the rich processes that both characterize – and distinguish – the contexts of DLL families related to language development. For example, debates over the relationship between language development and the influence of poverty have been highlighted in both the developmental and educational literatures. One popular stance in this debate views the difference in linguistic environments between wealthier families and those who live in poverty as producing a significant language gap (aka, "word gap") that contributes to children's trajectory of educational success or failure. For instance, Hart and Risley (1995) report that by the age of three, children from wealthier households are exposed to approximately 30 million more words than children from families receiving welfare. This is conceptually linked to the low academic achievement of students from economically impoverished backgrounds.

It is important to note that major findings of this study and related "word gap" studies have been critiqued for substantive methodological flaws and their deficit theoretical orientation (Dudley-Marling & Lucas, 2009). In contrast, others suggest and have adopted a language socialization lens for viewing educational disparities across socioeconomic groups (Miller & Sperry, 2012). While this debate is based on attempts to better understand the role that language plays in academic challenges, placing the blame on parents for not providing the appropriate language environments is unfortunately rooted in the same dominant group norms that perpetuate educational inequities (Johnson, 2015). Moreover, considering the disproportionate number of ethnic minorities who are DLLs (especially Latinos, Native Americans and recent immigrants) who live in poverty and have a record of lower academic achievement, it is significant to recognize the significance of exploring how cultural diversity intersects with discussions of poverty, language and education. Expecting parents to change their linguistic profiles and their interactions with their children to support their children's academic progress minimizes the responsibility that schools have accepted to build on their students' home experiences and skills as a way to enhance classroom learning.

Processes related to culture-specific parenting goals, practices, and beliefs and home language and literacy practices related to bilingualism serve as key aspects of the family that are unique to DLLs. While family demographics, such as SES, are often relied on to discuss family level influences on development, reliance on demographic characteristics may be inadequate for describing how family features influence development. For example, DLLs are more likely to live in homes with grandparents, other relatives, or non-relatives, than their monolingual English-speaking peers. While such living environments might be viewed as overcrowded (and a detriment to development), upon further investigation, the more people living in the home provides DLLs with additional learning opportunities for enriched language and other cultural experiences (García & Garcia, 2012). In parent interviews and public hearings reported by Takanishi and Le Menestrel (2017), one recurrent highly emotional theme in those discussions was the fear that the home language of the family would be lost to the children when they participated in formal education delivered only in English, and thus minimizing the critical supportive relations between students and family members who are not fluent in English.

3.2 *Formal Care and Education Circumstances*

A premise of this conceptual perspective is that developmental and learning capacities are the result of the interaction between what children bring into the "educational" situation and what is being offered to them in that setting. Moreover, this perspective acknowledges that formal "schooling" is critical for academic achievement and the general wellbeing of DLLs. However, in formal care and education settings, it is important to understand what is being offered to students in the form of personnel designing and implementing services, assessments, curriculum and instruction, how the learning environment interacts with characteristics of the child (e.g., level of L1 and L2 language abilities, social-emotional strengths, background knowledge, etc.), and how learning opportunities are related to developmental capacities and academic achievement.

Participation in some form of out-of-home early care setting has become the norm for monolingual English-speaking and DLL preschoolers in the United States (Hernandez & Li, 2011; Castro, 2014). For those DLLs participating in early childhood education, that participation has been associated with improved school readiness particularly in the academic areas of language, literacy, and mathematics (Gormley, Gayer, Phillips, & Dawson, 2004; Karoly & Gonzalez, 2011; Takanishi, 2016). The features of successful academic programs serving DLLs from Pre-K to grade 12 highlight the need for well qualified DLL teachers, intensive professional development, support for teachers, adequate teacher-child ratios, as well as instructionally focused features, such as responsive and enriched language interactions, individualized adult-child conversations that promote language and positive relationships, opportunities for children to learn and practice new vocabulary and complex literacy, frequent assessment and parent engagement (Barnett, Yarosz, Thomas, & Blanco, 2006; Genessee, Lindholm-Leary, Sanders, & Christian, 2006).

It is critical to note that the specific needs of students vary as a result of ethnic origin and cultural attributes associated with ethnicity and individual learning capacities. Asian American students, for example, are aided in their academic success in English based on family and community structures that are available to support students—not all "Asians" generate positive academic achievement profiles (Asian American Legal Defense Fund, 2008). And, students of any ethnic group with special needs require special instructional attention, but do not seem to be placed at any risk by exposure to multiple languages and may be instructionally enriched by instruction in multiple languages (Artiles & Klinger, 2006). The DLLs come from a great diversity of social, linguistic and cultural communities, which must be considered in any examination of effectiveness of any instructional programs and practices intended for them.

Addressing the complex educational needs of these children would be difficult for educators, even without the challenges stemming from poverty. Educators require an abundance of professional preparation to work effectively with these children and their families for whom the world of the American schooling may be unfamiliar. In classrooms where students come from many different cultures, teachers should know how to learn about their students' worlds—their origins, their families and communities, how learning is structured in their homes, and the roles parents play in the education of their children. To be able to do so is a matter of professional training; thus, the preparation required for the programs and practices is crucial (García & Markos, 2015).

3.3 Instructional Circumstances

It hardly needs to be said that there is no one best way to educate ELLs/DLLs effectively. DLL students come with a great enthusiasm and capacities to learn but are generallyimmersed in an educational system that is unprepared to act on the enthusiasm and capacities (Takanishi & Le Menestrel, 2017). Educators seem well aware of their obligations to serve the complex needs of these students, which require resources and solutions that are not always readily available (García & Náñez, 2012).

The U.S. National Academies of Sciences, the National Research Council (Takanishi & LeMenstrel) provide a set of constructs that optimize instructional support for DLLs summarized here:

- Learning requires (or is enhanced by) understanding
- Prior knowledge is the basis of new learning
- Identity development and ways of learning have their roots in cultural practices. Learning in one language transfers to second language when the first language or L1 is adequately developed.
- Language learning – whether of a first or subsequent language – takes place in a sociocultural environment and depends on social interaction with speakers of the language, which provides necessary support for learning the language.

DLL s come to new development and learning experiences with the resources of their primary languages: they have an underlying neural architecture for language, with existing connections between various components such as how sounds perceived are related to sounds produced; they have a system of concepts on which the language is built; they know that elements of a language (e.g., words) can be combined to make sentences; they know about the referential functions of language, what people might say in various socio-cultural situations (e.g., greetings, expressions of appreciation, politeness rituals, etc.), and most importantly, an inclination to read or guess at the intentions of others in events and interactions in which they are engaged (Tomasello, 2003).

With regard to specific educational programming, some researchers have found that enrollment in high quality pre-kindergarten programs can boost the English language scores of Hispanic/Latino DLLs (Barnett, Yarosz, Thomas, Jung, & Blanco, 2007; Gormley, 2008; Hammer, Davinson, Lawrence & Miccio, 2009; Winsler, Díaz, Espinosa, & Rodríguez, 1999). These studies have shown that when preschool programs systematically expose DLLs to English within the context of a high-quality program, their English proficiency scores at kindergarten entry improve. Furthermore, there is a convergence of evidence that supporting a student's home language while adding English promotes higher levels of achievement *in English* (Castro, Páez, Dickinson, & Frede, 2011). At best, instruction that systematically includes L1 contributes to growth in both English and home language skills; at worst, there is no difference in English language skills, but an advantage in home language growth (Durán, Roseth, & Hoffman, 2010; García, 2005).

Lastly, the perspective recognizes that strong school-family partnerships have been a hallmark of high-quality early education for decades. The empirical research base for parent education, family visitation, parent conferences, and home-school communication interventions with DLL populations is "minimal, but promising" (Mathematica Policy Research, 2010, p.22). Researchers have found that sending literacy materials home in the family's primary language and sharing with parents strategies for literacy activities can increase the frequency of home literacy activities and promote literacy skill development in DLLs (Zentella, 2005). Reaching out to families and recognizing children are learning important related academic skills outside of school. These are "funds of knowledge" that can be utilized by teachers in school (Gonzalez, Moll, & Amanti, 2005). Establishing partnerships with families implies engaging in a dialogue through which teachers learn about families' childrearing beliefs and practices, as well as their expectations for their children's development and learning (Delgado-Gaitan, 2004).

3.4 Community and Societal Circumstances

In relation to the societal context, features of the community in which DLLs live are particular to DLLs' daily experiences. For example, one community feature of significance is the presence and value of different languages in a community as observed in spaces where the people who live in that community come together and socialize (for example public political events, festivities/celebrations, churches and other spiritual gatherings). It is within these spaces that DLLs and their families have more or fewer opportunities to hear different languages, to interact with speakers of different languages, to observe every day and academic uses of language and literacy, and to value their heritage languages and bilingualism (Valdés, 2005).

The development and learning of language for DLLs must include attention to a variety of social policies those related to the immigration and integration history of DLLs' families. Social policies, such as anti-immigrant policies that may disrupt family unification, can have detrimental effects on DLL development and negatively shaping the way young children form their own psychological and social identities (Bean, Brown, & Bachmeier, 2015). In academic learning settings, evidence related to classroom practices indicates that immigrant and refugee DLL children may have their learning experiences narrowed due to teacher's negative perceptions about their capacities to learn in English—a direct form of discrimination other children do not experience (Migration Policy Institute, 2015).

Also, within the society context, whether the DLL is a child of an immigrant or native-born parent, and the extent to which the DLL's family has integrated into mainstream society are all associated with DLLs' development and learning. While all the parents we interviewed for this report desired that their children learn English so that they could take advantage of opportunities in the United States, they also wanted their children to maintain their heritage language. For Native American children, many of whom are from language groups that are disappearing because few young people are learning and using the Native American languages, the development of the heritage language is key for participation in their own community and in development of their personal and spiritual identity—a critical element considered important by the family-- while English development assists in broader capacities to enhance their academic learning (McCarty, 2014).

4 Conclusion: The Implications of This Perspective

This perspective encompasses the following:

- the development and learning of language is a common and critical element in every child's development, learning and well-being;
- the development and learning of multiple languages in DLLs are critically important in understanding the development, learning and well-being of DLLs;
- DLL experiences influence and are influenced by neurological development and brain architecture;
- the acquisition of two languages in young children has no inherent negative social, linguistic, cognitive or educational consequences and, to the contrary, may generate advantages in a variety of social, linguistic, cognitive and academic domains;
- dual language learning is a socially-embedded process residing within family, community and societal contexts;
- understanding development and learning of DLLs requires understanding the array of activities that are practiced by children in and outside of formal care and in the learning opportunities in families, communities and societies in which they reside;
- ways in which children participate in day-to-day activities should inform the design and implementation of early care and formal learning opportunities/environments, Prek-12;
- educational policies at all levels in the U. S. play a particularly important role in shaping the formal educational experience of DLLs;
- educational and institutional practices play a critical role in the development and learning of DLLs with an emerging consensus that effectiveness and outcomes can be significantly advanced from the present state of academic underachievement.

The conceptual perspective is offered here as a more integrative, comprehensive and a functional approach to positively advancing the developmental and learning circumstances of DLLs in the United States.

References

Allen, L., & Kelly, B. B. (2015). *Professional learning for the early care and education workforce.* Washington, DC: National Research Council.

Artiles, A. J. (2003). Special education's changing identity: Paradoxes and dilemmas in views of culture and space. *Harvard Educational Review, 73,* 164–202.

Artiles, A. J., & Klingner, J. K. (2006). Forging a knowledge base on English language learners with special needs. *Teachers College Record, 108,* 2187–2194.

Asian American Legal Defense Fund. (2008). *Left in the margins: Asian Americans students and the no child left behind act.* New York, NY: Author.

August, D., & Hakuta, K. (1997). *Improving schooling for language-minority children: A research agenda.* Washington, DC: National Research Council, Institute of Medicine, National Academy Press.

Barnett, W. S., Yarosz, D. J., Thomas, J., & Blanco, D. (2006). *Two-way and monolingual English immersion in preschool education: An experimental comparison.* New Brunswick, NJ: National Institute for Early Education Research.

Barnett, W. S., Yarosz, D. J., Thomas, J., & Blanco, D. (2007). *Two-way and monolingual English immersion in preschool education: An experimental comparison.* New Brunswick, NJ: National Institute for Early Education Research.

Bean, F. D., Brown, S. K., & Bachmeier, J. (2015). *Parents without papers: The progress and pitfalls of Mexican American Integration.* New York, NY: Russell Sage Foundation.

Bowerman, B. T., Donovan, S. M., & Burns, M. S. (2000). *Eager to learn: Educating our preschoolers.* National Research Council, Washington, DC.

Bransford, J. D., Brown, A., & Cocking, R. R. (1999). *How people learn.* National Research Council.

California Department of Education. (2010). *Improving education for English learners: Research-based approaches.* Standards, Curriculum Frameworks and Instructional Resources Division.

Castro, D. (2014). The development of early care and education of dual language learners: Examining the state of the knowledge. *Early Childhood Research Quarterly, 29,* 693–698.

Castro, D. C., Páez, M. M., Dickinson, D. K., & Frede, E. (2011). Promoting language and literacy in young dual language learners: Research, practice, and policy. Child Development Perspectives, v5 n1: 15-21

Conboy, B. T., & Kuhl, P. K. (2011). Impact of second language experience in infancy: Brain measures of first and second language speech perception. *Developmental Science, 14,* 242–248.

Conboy, B. T., & Mills, D. L. (2006). Two languages, one developing brain: Effects of vocabulary size on bilingual toddlers' event-related potentials to auditory words. *Developmental Science, 9*(1), F1–F11.

Delgado-Gaitan, C. (2004). *Involving Latino families in schools: Raising student achievement through home-school partnerships.* Thousand Oaks, CA: Corwin.

Dudley-Marling, C., & Lucas, K. (2009). Pathologizing the language and culture of poor children. *Language Arts, 86*(5), 77–92.

Durán, L., Roseth, C., & Hoffman, P. (2010). An experimental study comparing English-only and transitional bilingual education on Spanish-speaking preschoolers' early literacy development. *Early Childhood Research Quarterly, 25*(2), 207–217.

García, E. E. (2005). *Teaching and learning in two languages: Bilingualism and schooling in the United States.* New York, NY: Teachers College Press.

García, E.E., & Cuellar, D. (2006). Who are these linguistically and culturally diverse students? *Teachers College Record, 108*(11), 2220–2246.

García, E., & Markos, A. (2015). Early childhood education and dual language learners. In W. E. Wright, S. Boun, & O. Garcia (Eds.), *The handbook of bilingual and multilingual education.* Malden, MA: Wiley.

García, E., & Náñez, J. (2011). *Bilingualism and cognition: Joining cognitive psychology and education to enhance bilingual research, pedagogy and policy*. Washington, DC: American Psychological Association.

García, E. E., & Náñez, J. (2012). *Bilingualism and cognition: Joining cognitive psychology and education to enhance bilingual research, pedagogy and policy*. Washington, DC: American Psychological Association.

García, E., Wiese, A.-M., & Cuéllar, D. (2013) Language, public policy, and schooling. In R. R. Valencia (Ed.), *Chicano school failure and success: Past, present, and future* (3rd ed., pp. 143–159). New York, NY: Routledge.

García, E. E., & Garcia, E. H. (2012). *Understanding the language development and early education of hispanic children*. New York, NY: Teachers College Press.

Genessee, F., Lindholm-Leary, K., Sanders, B., & Christian, D. (2006). *Educating English language learners: A synthesis of research evidence*. New York, NY: Cambridge University Press.

Goldman, S., & Pellegrino, J. W. (2015). Research on learning and instruction: Implications for curriculum, instruction and assessment. *Behavioral and Brain Sciences, 2*(1), 33–41.

Gonzalez, N., Moll, L., & Amanti, C. (2005). *Funds of knowledge: Theorizing practices in households, communities, and classrooms*. Mahwah, NJ: Taylor & Francis Group.

Gormley, W. (2008). The effects of Oklahoma's pre-K program on hispanic students. *Social Science Quarterly, 89*(4), 916–936.

Gormley, W., Gayer, T., Phillips, D., & Dawson, B. (2004). *The effects of Oklahoma's Universal Pre-K Program on school readiness: An executive summary*. Washington, D.C.: Georgetown University. Center for Research on Children in the U.S. Retrieved from http://www.crocus.georgetown.edu/reports/executive_summary_11_04.pdf

Hammer, C. S., Davison, M. D., Lawrence, F. R., & Miccio, A. W. (2009). The effect of maternal language on bilingual children's vocabulary and emergent literacy development during head start and kindergarten. *Scientific Studies of Reading, 13*(2), 99–121.

Hammer, C. S., Hoff, E., Uchikoshi, Y., Gallanders, C., & Castro, D. (2013). The language and literacy development of dual language learners: A critical review. *Early Childhood Research Quarterly, 29*, 715–733.

Hart, B., & Risley, T. (1995). *Meaningful differences in the everyday experience of young American children*. Baltimore, MD: Paul H. Brookes Publishing.

Hernandez, A. E., & Li, P. (2011). Age of acquisition: Its neural and computational mechanisms. *Psychological Bulletin, 133*(4), 638–650.

Johnson, E. J. (2015). Debunking the "language gap". *Journal for Multicultural Education, 9*(1), 42–50.

Karoly, L. A., & Gonzalez, G. (2011). Early learning environments: Child care and preschool arrangements for children in immigrant families. *Future of Children, 211*, 71–101.

Mathematica Policy Research. (2010). *Identifying enhanced instructional practices that support English language learners: Background literature review*. Washington, DC: Author.

McCabe, A., Tamis-Lemonde, C. S., Bornstein, M. H., Brockmeyer Cates, C., Golinkoff, R., Guerra, A. W., … Song, L. (2013). Multilingual children: Beyond myths and toward best practices. *Social Policy Report, 27*(4), 1–29.

McCarty, T. L. (2014). Reclaiming indigenous languages: A reconsideration of roles and responsibilities of schools. In K. M. Borman, T. G. Wiley, D. R. Garcia, & A. B. Danzig (Eds.), *Review of research in education*. Washington, D. C.: American Educational Research Association.

Migration Policy Institute. (2015). *The impact of discrimination on the early schooling experiences of children of immigrant families*. Washington, DC: Author.

Miller, P. J., & Sperry, D. E. (2012). Deja 'vu: The continuing misrecognition of low –income children's verbal abilities. In S. T. Fiske & H. R. Markus (Eds.), *Facing social class: How social rank influences interaction* (pp. 190–130). New York, NY: Russell Sage.

Shonkoff, J., & Phillips, D. (2000). From neurons to neighborhoods: The science of early childhood development. In *National Research Council*. Washington, DC.

Takanishi, R. (2016). *First thing first: Creating the new American Primary School*. New York, NY: Teachers College Press.

Takanishi, R., & Le Menestrel, S. (2017). *Promoting the educational success of children and youth learning English: Promising futures*. Washington, DC: National Academic Press.

Tomasello, M. (2003). *Constructing a language: A usage-based theory of language acquisition*. Harvard University Press.

United Sates Department of Education. (2008). *Biennial report to congress on the implementation of the title III state formula Grant program*. Washington, DC: Author.

Valdés, G. (2005). Con respeto: Bridging the distances between culturally diverse families and schools—An ethnographic portrait. New York, NY: Teachers College Press.

Werker, J. F., & Hensch, T. K. (2015). Perceptual foundations of bilingual acquisition in infancy. *Annual Review of Psychology, 66*, 173–196.

Westerman, G. D., Mareschal, D., Johnson, M. H., Sirios, S., Spratling, M. W., & Thomas, M. S. C. (2007). Nueroconstructivism. *Developmental Science, 10*(1), 75–83.

Winsler, A., Diaz, R. M., Espinosa, L., & Rodriguez, J. L. (1999). When learning a second language does not mean losing the first: Bilingual language development in low-income, Spanish-speaking children attending bilingual preschool. *Child Development, 70*(2), 349–362.

Zentella, A. C. (2005). *Building on strengths: Language and literacy in Latino families and communities*. New York, NY: Teachers College Press.

Biliteracy and Translanguaging in Dual-Language Bilingual Education

Susana Ibarra Johnson, Ofelia García, and Kate Seltzer

Abstract Using translanguaging as a resource has the potential to transform biliteracy instruction in dual-language bilingual education (DLBE). In a flexible model of biliteracy, the students' full repertoire of resources is used to interact with texts that are written in different named languages as they think discuss, interact with, and produce written texts (García O. Bilingual education in the 21st century: a global perspective. Malden/Oxford, Wiley/Blackwell, 2009). In this article, we provide an example of this flexible model of biliteracy from a case study involving a third-grade dual-language bilingual teacher. The teacher designed a translanguaging space to create more holistic ways of doing biliteracy that allowed students to use their full linguistic repertoire for literacy performances. To do this, the teacher's *stance* about keeping the two languages in her DLBE class separate first had to change. She started consciously integrating what students were learning to do during English literacy and social studies instruction into her Spanish literacy instruction. She then designed a translanguaging instructional and assessment space she called *Los círculos*. In that space bilingual students take what they have learned across other content areas in instructional spaces dedicated to English and Spanish and do biliteracy juntos.

Keywords Biliteracy *juntos* · Translanguaging pedagogy · Dual-language bilingual education · *Corriente* · Emergent bilinguals · Assessment

---

S. I. Johnson (✉)
Department of Language and Cultural Equity, Albuquerque Public Schools, Albuquerque, NM, USA
e-mail: Susana.johnson@aps.edu

O. García
Graduate Center, The City University of New York, New York, NY, USA
e-mail: ogarcia@gc.cuny.edu

K. Seltzer
Department of Language, Literacy and Sociocultural Education, Rowan University, Glassboro, NJ, USA
e-mail: seltzerk@rowan.edu

© The Author(s) 2019
D. E. DeMatthews, E. Izquierdo (eds.), *Dual Language Education: Teaching and Leading in Two Languages*, Language Policy 18,
https://doi.org/10.1007/978-3-030-10831-1_8

1 Introduction

Imagine a river that serves as the fluid border between two riverbanks; on one side is the riverbank of English language life and instruction, on the other side is that of Spanish language life and instruction. The teacher in our case study, Marisol, knew that providing an equitable education to her students needed to involve the two riverbanks. That is precisely why she was happy being a dual language bilingual education teacher. However, the dual language allocation policy followed in her school in New Mexico demanded that English and Spanish be kept completely separate at all times. In fact, Marisol who taught in Spanish was paired with another teacher who taught in English only, Tammy. Little by little, however, Marisol became disillusioned with the strict language allocation policy followed in her school. She wasn't completely satisfied with having students hop from one riverbank to the other without being immersed in the energy of the dynamic bilingual corriente of their own language practices.

During her instruction in Spanish, Marisol often would experience what she called the corriente, the river current produced by students' energy and engagement when their dynamic and fluid bilingualism was allowed to flow. The students' dynamic bilingual practices would dissolve the shape and strict separation of the riverbanks (one language on one side and the other language on the other) and allowed the positive power of students' bilingualism to surge beyond the two riverbanks. On those occasions, Marisol glimpsed the power of the corriente and started thinking that the two riverbanks (the language and literacy practices in English and those in Spanish) were not so separate as her DLBE's language allocation policy indicated. Perhaps, she thought, it would be important to capture the students' energy that flowed through the corriente so that the separate riverbanks would disappear and *bilingual* students' lived realities would be put at the center of instruction. Marisol started learning about translanguaging theory in relationship to bilingualism and decided to design a translanguaging space (Li Wei, 2011) for biliteracy instruction.

This chapter, based on research conducted by Susana Ibarra Johnson (2013), describes how Marisol's stance toward literacy instruction shifted from a language separation model where the Spanish literacy activities always occurred separately from those in English to a literacy juntos model. Reading to learn relies on a juntos model, integrating the students' full language and semiotic resources, that is, all the resources human beings have to make meaning (García, Johnson, & Seltzer, 2017). Marisol eventually developed a *translanguaging stance* towards language practices. This enabled her to adopt a flexible model of biliteracy by designing a translanguaging instructional and assessment space within her DLBE classroom that opened up the potential to make use of all the students' linguistic and meaning-making features. In that space, she leveraged a translanguaging pedagogy that consists of strategies to both support and scaffold instruction when one language is being used, as well as go beyond the named languages of the instructional spaces and transform the hierarchical power relationship in which English and Spanish are held in the United States.

Marisol is a *transladora/translatera,* a teacher able to merge both lados/sides of the riverbanks, of students' lived experiences, so as to create equitable instruction for all. As we will see, Marisol's translanguaging pedagogy for biliteracy instruction leveraged the translanguaging corriente produced by students and transformed their subjectivities. Before we describe Marisol's translanguaging pedagogy for biliteracy in a DLBE program, it is important to consider how this work rests on and extends the theoretical frameworks of many scholars of bilingualism and biliteracy.

2 Biliteracy and Translanguaging: A Juntos Theory

One of the most important goals of all types of developmental bilingual education is to develop biliteracy. Biliteracy, as defined by Hornberger (1989) is "any and all instances in which communication occurs in two or more languages in or around writing" (xii). All communication, oral or otherwise, around a written text, is considered literacy. Literacy is not an autonomous skill, but as Street (1985) has demonstrated, all literacy practices are influenced by social, cultural, political and economic factors. Literacy practices are not only associated with different cultural contexts and social structures, but are also multimodal, that is, meaning is bound up with other visual, audio, and spatial semiotic systems (Kress, 2003; New London Group, 1996). García, Bartlett, and Kleifgen (2007) referred to pluriliteracy practices as moving "away from the dichotomy of the traditional L1/L2 pairing, emphasizing instead that language and literacy practices are interrelated and flexible, positing that all literacy practices have equal value, and acknowledging the agency involved in communicating around writing" (García, 2009, pp. 339–40; italics in original).

This pluriliteracy approach is not new. Gutiérrez and her colleagues (Gutiérrez, Baquedano-López, & Alvarez, 2001) and Reyes (1992, 2001) have demonstrated the diversity of, and interplay between, linguistic codes and literacy practices in multilingual classrooms. And yet, most dual language bilingual education programs adopt the concept of biliteracy as that of functional literacy in two separate named languages, that is, as an autonomous skill of reading and writing in two languages that can be measured by standardized forms of assessment. The model of biliteracy espoused by most DLBE programs is what García (2009) calls the *separation biliterate model,* ignoring the potential of a pluriliteracy approach. In a separation biliterate model, children and teachers match the language in which they are communicating around writing to the language of the written text.

This model of separation biliteracy corresponds in most DLBE programs with a sequential perspective on biliteracy, that is, the view that literacy in an additional language should not be introduced until a child has competence in speaking, reading, and writing in what is considered a first language (Wong-Fillmore & Valadez, 1986). The idea, following Jim Cummins (1979) is that what is learned in one language can then be transferred to the other because of a common underlying proficiency.

Recently, some scholars have argued that biliteracy does not need to be developed sequentially, and that paired literacy instruction works (Escamilla et al., 2014). Beeman and Urow (2013) have proposed the concept of the Bridge, or "the instructional moment when teachers purposefully bring the two languages together, guiding students to transfer the academic context they have learned in one language to the other language, engage in contrastive analysis of the two languages, and strengthen their knowledge of both languages" (p. v).

These perspectives on biliteracy provide ways of bringing the two named languages closer together, English and Spanish. However, the flexible model of biliteracy that Marisol enacts in this case study goes beyond providing a bridge between the two riverbanks of the language of power and prestige (English) and the language of Latinx homes and communities (Spanish). The flexible model of biliteracy is based on translanguaging theory, and thus does not start with the named languages of societies, but with the actual language repertoire and practices of bilingual speakers.

Translanguaging theory differentiates between named languages—English, Spanish, Chinese and others—as an important *social* construction that has had many real material effects, and the *internal* language of human beings (Otheguy, García, & Reid, 2015) with its potential to make meaning, to imagine, to construct, to liberate and generate ideas. This language of human beings is usually constrained by the notion that there are two riverbanks. But underneath the surface, where the human potential of the corriente lies, true language flows in torrents that disturb the riverbanks, that shape them differently, that show their true interrelationship as one territory. Herein lies the power of translanguaging, not constrained by social definitions of what is English and what is Spanish, but more flexible ways of doing language. It magnifies people's ability to make meaning, to use their full linguistic repertoire, to imagine, to be creative and critical (García & Li Wei, 2014).

Anyone who has ever read a good book knows that all aspects of our meaning-making repertoire come to our assistance as we imagine colors, smells, and situations, as we visualize characters and events, and as we make our own meaning based on the verbal hints that authors give us in written texts. Oral dialogue around written text is always generative because it reveals the power of readers over authors, authors who can only give readers and listeners clues for constructing messages. And those messages that we derive from texts are always dependent on our individual background knowledge, our context, our situation, and our cultural and linguistic practices.

A translanguaging space in which a flexible model of biliteracy is enacted liberates readers, writers and speakers from the constraints imposed by the standardized named languages of nation-states and their schools. Even when we define the language of a written or oral text as being English or being Spanish, we know that it contains within it many voices, the heteroglossia that Bakhtin (1981) taught us to recognize in texts so long ago. Here is where translanguaging dwells, in the understanding that for biliteracy to develop we must let go of our conception of autonomous named languages that mean denotatively, and instead recognize that languages are made up of features, linguistic and otherwise, that the speaker or writer selects as best they can to communicate a message to the reader (Otheguy et al., 2015). But in the *selection* of some linguistic features by the writer (and the inhibition of others that may not be socially acceptable for the particular situation), and also in the ways in which the features are interpreted by the reader, there are differences, openings and interstices through which different meanings are made. Translanguaging works then within these interstices, as teachers and bilingual students construct meanings with their own resources of texts that are said to be in one or another language or even both.

Dual language bilingual education classrooms should potentialize the meaning-making performances of bilingual students, allowing them maximum freedom in *selecting* features from their unitary repertoire, in being *agentive* learners, speakers, readers, writers, scholars. Instead, many DLBE classrooms, following strict language allocation policies, do not allow students this freedom to imagine, to construct meaning, because they are seen as incapable of making meaning of all their features in interrelationship. True, bilingual students must be given practice selecting certain features and not others in specific situations, and an instructional space in one named language or another is important to make this possible. But alongside these instructional spaces in different named languages, translanguaging spaces where students are given agency over the selection of the linguistic features with which they want to construct messages is a most important learning endeavor for bilingual students.

Only when bilingual teachers become aware of the meaning-making potential of translanguaging, beyond it being simply a scaffold, can a flexible model of biliteracy become possible within a DLBE classroom. The case study that we introduce next shows how Marisol, the teacher, changed her *stance* towards translanguaging while working within a dual language framework of language separation. She was able to *design* a translanguaging space that she called Los Círculos, and also was liberated to *shift* her language use to tend to individual students who needed support at times. Together, the translanguaging stance, design and shifts make up the three strands of translanguaging pedagogy as defined by García, Johnson, and Seltzer (2017).

3 The Case Study

Data for this case study were drawn from a qualitative case study of a third grade DLBE teacher conducted by Susana Ibarra Johnson (2013). The study took place during a 5-month period of participant observation.

Marisol, a Latina teacher, grew up speaking Spanish, having been born in Barranquilla, Colombia. She first learned English in a dual language bilingual secondary school in Colombia where language separation was strictly implemented. She began her teaching career 17 years ago in Colombia as an English as a second language teacher for adults. In the United States, Marisol became the Spanish language arts teacher in a middle school dual language bilingual program. We meet her at Vista del Sol Elementary School, where she has been teaching for 7 years as a third-grade dual-language bilingual teacher, responsible for instruction in Spanish.

Vista del Sol Elementary School is located in an older section of a large urban city in New Mexico. The students and their families are from the neighborhood and the majority have resided in this community for many years. The school is inspired by the work of a native New Mexican who was often referred to as *La doctora* (the professor). A long-time pioneer in bilingual education, *La doctora* believed strongly in the "importance of bilingual education and that children should learn both Spanish and English so that their culture, history, traditions and most importantly, the Spanish language would be preserved" (Program Brochure, 2010). *La doctora's* legacy in bilingual/multicultural education continues in this school. The majority of the students in the school are Spanish-speaking Latinx, about half of whom are designated as "English learners."

In the 1990s, many immigrants arrived from Mexico. In order to meet the linguistic and cultural needs brought about by the shift in demographics, the school established a 50/50 Spanish/English dual-language bilingual education strand kindergarten through fifth grade. In the third grade, two teachers distribute the content areas (language arts, social studies, science, and mathematics) by language and teach for an entire theme or unit in that selected language and content area. Marisol is team-teaching with Tammy. Marisol teaches language arts and science instruction in Spanish, whereas Tammy teaches social studies and mathematics instruction in English year around. This case study is about Marisol; however, in this work we also include Tammy since one of the examples we draw from includes Tammy's instruction which prompted Marisol's concerns of her students learning. Thus, Tammy will be mentioned in several sections given that she team-taught with Marisol and needed to be included in this work to fully explain how both classrooms were connected and changed even though they taught within a DLBE language separation model.

Marisol's third grade classroom is full of print in Spanish. For example, the school schedule and homework assignments for the week appears on a whiteboard, as does "Lo que vamos aprender..." (What we will learn...). There are shelves with leveled books and chapter books in Spanish used for literature circles that were done twice a week. Marisol has a rug at the center of the classroom. This space allows the students to sit next to their peers and listen to a book being read aloud by the teacher or discuss el dicho del día (the saying of the day), which is one of the students' favorite activities. In Marisol's classroom, there is a poster depicting a Columbian scene with flowers and mountains in the background. Marisol often speaks to the students about her own dual language schooling experience, and following the bilingual approach she learned in Colombia, she has always insisted that her students use only Spanish during her Spanish instructional period.

Marisol and Tammy often plan lessons together, developing theme studies that connect concepts and ideas across content areas, but never across the languages in which they teach during their instructional time. Occasionally, Marisol and Tammy combine the two classes of about 36 students and teach them together, but always in either English or Spanish. It was during one of these joint classroom lessons, a lesson about historical figures from the Civil War and the Civil Rights Movement, that

Marisol had her "aha moment" about the inadequacy of the strict language separation. The next section describes why and how the walls between languages came tumbling down, as Marisol and her students used the corriente to surge forward.

4 The "Aha Moment": Developing a Translanguaging Stance

It was during instruction led by Tammy in English that Marisol was first explicitly confronted with her "aha moment." Tammy had been trained in the Guided Language Acquisition Design (GLAD) model that consisted of many differentiated strategies to integrate instruction in English and grade-level content. Project GLAD is a K-12 instructional model consisting of 35 strategies (Bretchel, 2005). Tammy was introducing a unit about the history of race relations in the United States and important historical figures. She used a Project GLAD comparative input chart activity that depicted President Abraham Lincoln and Dr. Martin Luther King Jr.

Tammy began by introducing key concepts or vocabulary about the Civil War and Civil Rights Movement (i.e.: presidency, American Civil War, access, North, South, campaign, battlefield, slavery, Civil Rights Movement, integration, nonviolence, boycott, and preacher). Tammy placed pictures of Abraham Lincoln and Martin Luther King Jr. on a timeline located in the front of the classroom and explained the similarities of these two historical figures. She emphasized that both Lincoln and King had fought for the rights of African Americans in the U.S. and sought to unite the nation. As students shared what they knew about the two figures, Tammy continued adding information to the comparative input chart. She then asked students to talk to an elbow partner in English about two new ideas or vocabulary words that they learned about Abraham Lincoln or Dr. Martin Luther King Jr.

As she observed, Marisol became concerned. Although some students were participating, especially her emergent bilingual students were silent. She had seen these students be vivacious and smart during her Spanish language instruction. She wondered whether they were making sense of what was going on. She then heard a student say, *"¿No estoy seguro de lo que tengo que hacer?* (I am not sure what to do?) At this point, Marisol decided to pull out a small group of five students who had remained silent and disengaged. When she asked them yes or no questions like: "Was Abraham Lincoln our 16th president?" the students were able to answer correctly. But when she asked opinion questions like: "Why do you think Lincoln and Martin Luther King were important historical figures?" the students were unable to say much more than: "He was a good person" or "He was for black people."

Marisol was alarmed. She understood that although the strict content and language separation was a good division of labor for the two teachers, it was not working for all students. She read, thought and discussed with other teachers the potential of translanguaging. She argued with some teachers in the school who did not think that introducing a translanguaging space was a good idea, for they were convinced that to develop Spanish literacy, the Spanish language had to be protected. But Marisol wanted to protect her students, not simply the Spanish language of which she had been given charge. Marisol wanted to make sure that her students were learning at all times, whether they were immersed in the English language space or the Spanish language space. Furthermore, she wanted to recognize and leverage their own bilingual practices that made up who they were and to develop a bilingual subjectivity that was firm and strong.

She started realizing that teaching bilingually in Colombia was not the same as teaching bilingually in the United States. Unlike in Colombia, these U.S. Latinx students were minoritized, rendered voiceless and powerless, forced to live a bilingual life in a society that was determined to construct them as illegal, poor, and criminal. By observing her students intently, Marisol developed a committed translanguaging stance, a view of the students as whole, a view of the students' linguistic repertoire as unitary. She determined that her responsibility would have to be to help students select the appropriate linguistic features for the task at hand, and leverage their full linguistic repertoire to make meaning at all times, and not simply keep the two languages apart.

When Marisol questioned Tammy about her ability to assess their students' progress, Tammy confessed that she really couldn't do so in English only. When students seemed not to understand a reading, Tammy shared that she didn't know whether students did not understand the English language itself, or they didn't understand how to make meaning from written texts. She also admitted that she had no idea whether students who performed poorly in writing had ideas they wanted to share in writing, since they couldn't express them in Spanish. As she and Marisol talked, Tammy was also developing a translanguaging stance, understanding that she was instructing and assessing these bilingual students monolingually, acknowledging only part their linguistic and semiotic repertoire. Tammy realized that she rarely made use of other students' bilingual capacities, or of those of her fellow teachers, or of technology and electronic translation. Tammy came to see that more was needed.

In talking with Tammy, Marisol came to see that she controlled the Spanish language intently, only allowing multimodal or English texts, when scaffolds were necessary. Now she wanted to understand how she would be able to "re-see" this translanguaging corriente as one that could flow unbridled across the surface of the classroom, rather than covertly beneath it. The teachers' stances regarding the potential of leveraging the translanguaging corriente in teaching had been transformed. But now it was necessary to design instruction and assessment in ways that made sense for a dual language bilingual program.

5 Biliteracy and a Translanguaging Juntos Design

Marisol and Tammy decided they were going to integrate the English and Spanish language instruction river banks because they needed to focus on their bilingual and biliteracy development juntos, not separately. They started slowly, with Marisol leading the instruction. Together they developed Los círculos, a biliteracy juntos activity adapted from Literature Circles (Daniels, 2002). They selected bilingual, English and Spanish texts related to historical figures to make connections between what was learned during the students' English social studies work and their biliteracy work.

Marisol shared that doing biliteracy juntos supports the stance that "*la voz del estudiante es necesario siempre.*" (the students' voice is always necessary) During this biliteracy translanguaging space Marisol's design was based on how these bilingual students were experiencing their lives, not as speakers of English and speakers of Spanish, but as bilingual Americans, with pride and recognition of their bilingual subjectivities. The students' language performances fell at multiple points along the bilingual continua, with all being emergent bilinguals of one type or another, that is, for some students some features said to be English had to be developed for some tasks, for other students it was features said to be Spanish.

The first thing that the translanguaging design allowed was the ability of the teachers to document and assess seriously what it was that students knew content-wise and language-wise, in what García, Sánchez and Solorza (2018), call the *translanguaging documentation space*. The books that Marisol and Tammy gathered for Los círculos consisted of texts in English only, Spanish only, those that had bilingual translations in the same text, and those that used translanguaging at times, but no translations. Marisol led the instruction in Los círculos.

Los círculos book baskets the teachers set up provided an opportunity for students to select a text that met their literacy interests and that responded to the way that they wanted language to be represented in the text. This gave Marisol a better idea of the students' preferences, as well as reading abilities. Conferencing with students about their individual reading often consisted of questions such as:

- Why did you select this particular book?
- ¿Qué te gusta o no de este libro? [What do you like or not from this book?]
- Which parts did you enjoy, y ¿cuáles no disfrutaste? ¿Por qué? and Why?
- Tell me what is happening in this picture in English. Ahora dímelo en español [Now tell me in Spanish].

By asking some questions in English, some in Spanish, some in both, and allowing students to select whichever features of their repertoire (either those said to be from English or those said to be from Spanish) in most instances, but not in all (as in the last question), Marisol was able to assess the content knowledge and linguistic knowledge that the student had about the topic.

Once Marisol had a better assessment of the students' understandings and ability to use language to make meaning, she proceeded with the translanguaging design of

Los Círculos. In these small groups, the students first read for 20 min with a partner. Half the students read the book *Pink and Say* by Patricia Polacco (1994) in English, whereas the other half read the Spanish version, *Pink y Say*. The story, about Say, a white soldier injured during the American Civil War saved by Pink, a former slave, was linked to their study of racism and slavery in the social studies lesson conducted in English by Tammy. Marisol carefully selected the student pairs, as well as the language in which students read, ensuring that a strong reader in that particular language was paired off with a reader who needed more support. The pair of students read in one language, stopped often to ask each other questions, and discussed the book with a torrent of language and ideas.

The whole class then came together to discuss the book with Marisol. Rather than direct students to answer questions in the language that they have just read or in one language only, Marisol made *translanguaging shifts*, appropriate moment-by-moment decisions that deepened the conversation. For example, student said: "*Mejor parte es Pink le dijo a Say que lo toque porque el tocó a Abraham Lincoln,*" to which Marisol replied, ¿Por qué? Marisol continued her discussion about Pink saving Say after getting wounded from battle and then abandoning his unit. Pink and his family took Say in and nursed him back to health. Another student soon says: "*A mí me gustó esta historia porque Pink rescató a Say y le ayudó bastante.*" (I like this part because Pink saved Say and helped him alot) To which Marisol adds: "*¿Piensas que Say hubiera hecho lo mismo para Pink? Es decir, rescatarlo y ayudarle siendo que él era un esclavo.*" (Do you think Say would have done the same for Pink?) The student who had the first reaction then says: "*No creo porque es por eso que tenían The Civil War unos querían esclavos, the south, y otros no, the north. Y donde Pink estaba en Georgia no podían ayudarles a los esclavos.*" (I don't think so because this is why we have The Civil War some want slaves, the south, and others do not, the north) Marisol doesn't provide the students now with the lexical ítems for Civil War, south, north. What is important is to deepen the conversation about slavery and to get others involved in the conversation. "Why?" Marisol asks, "what did you learn in social studies que pueden compartir conmigo ahora." The effect is immediate. Many students' trip over each others' words to participate. One says: "*Say no podía rescatar a Pink porque tenía miedo que lo arrestaran por ayudar a un esclavo.*" (Say could not save Pink because he would be afraid to get caught helping a slave.) Yet another one says: "*Say lo hubiera ayudado porque él peleaba por for the North.*" (Say would help him out since he was fighting for the North.) After which Marisol asks: "*Y ¿por qué, durante la Guerra Civil, Say peleaba por el norte y no el sur?*" (Why during The Civil War, did Say fight for the north and not the south.) Marisol has become aware that the students need the lexical item norte y sur, but she doesn't interrupt them. She merely introduces the lexical items in her own discourse. In this way, the students are adding new lexical features to their repertoire, while nor marking them as "we speak Spanish here, not English." At the same time language is used to learn, to make sense, to infer, to deepen connections, rather than simply adding structures.

Using the flexible biliteracy approach of *Los círculos* students found *sus voces* to make sense, to make connections, and to make inferences of the text in their own words, thus improving their reading comprehension. These students were able to discuss their understandings about slavery and the division between North and the South during the Civil War, on a deeper level than when Tammy insisted English only.

In the flexible model of biliteracy, students are engaged in using all their language resources to read texts in different languages, think, discuss, interact with, and produce written texts. If students are to have deeper levels of comprehension while they read or discuss a text, teachers must ask reflective questions in *both* languages that prompt students to interact with the text. To facilitate this, Marisol developed a Círculos Wheel, as appears in Fig. 1. Marisol changed the prompt questions throughout the year to keep the activity interesting and to generate a rich dialogue. She provided the questions in Spanish and English in order for students to use as a prompt as they got started in their discussions. Sometimes a student would begin with a question in Spanish other times in English. Marisol often provided texts in both languages and students selected the text they wanted to read and discuss in during Los círculos activity.

Los Círculos opened up a space for deeper levels of comprehension which resulted in students leveraging their translanguaging to make meaning of the texts.

Because Marisol and Tammy were now aware that the school and the home/community needed to be included in their instruction they drew from their student's funds of knowledge (Moll, Amanti, Neff, & Gonzalez, 1992) and planned assignments that involved community and family participants. For example, Marisol and Tammy asked their students to interview people at home or in the community about

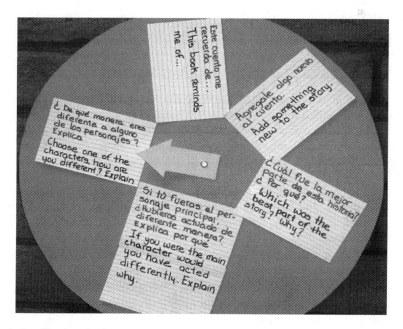

Fig. 1 Los Círculos wheel

what they knew about racism, civil rights, and historical figures that fought for liberation and civil rights. They explicitly told them that they could interview whomever in English, Spanish or both. Students came back with stories that went beyond Abraham Lincoln and Martin Luther King Jr. Civil rights activists César Chavez and Dolores Huerta received much mention, but also Benito Juárez, Miguel Hidalgo and Emiliano Zapata. Beyond Mexican historical figures, the family narratives also included mention of those considered the liberators of Latin America from Spain, Simón Bolivar and José de San Martín, and also included was José Martí and Che Guevara. Not only did individual students learn from each other but the teachers themselves extended their understandings of Latin American and Latinx histories. Little by little the borders not only between languages and subject matter content, but also home and school, past and present, Latin America and the United States began to crumble. Students began to see their language practices as important and useful, regardless of where those language performances fell along the bilingual continuum.

6 Conclusion: Merging Borders to Take Up Students' Translanguaging Corriente

Marisol shifted towards a more flexible model of biliteracy during her Spanish literacy instruction because she came to realize after observing Tammy's lesson about historical figures from the Civil War and the Civil Rights Movement the inadequacy of the strict language separation. Her "aha moment" was that students needed to use their entire linguistic repertoire to make meaning of texts. By creating Los Círculos, a unit organized around biliteracy juntos activities, she drew from her student's bilingualism and understandings as they connected what they learned about historical figures in social studies in English to the bilingual texts presented to them during Spanish literacy, as well as to their families and communities. The separate riverbanks dissolved as the students' translanguaging capacity flooded the translanguaging space. Marisol was a transladora, a linguistic and worlds merger, able to understand the students' experiences holistically and drawing on them juntos.

Planning and enacting a flexible model of biliteracy is necessary if bilingual educators are to sustain the rich ways that bilingual students do literacy. Taking up a flexible model of biliteracy has the potential to connect with bilingual students' translanguaging and transcend the borders that keep them hopping from one riverbank to the other without rest. It allows teachers to document their linguistic performances holistically, and to assess fairly.

Marisol and Tammy developed a translanguaging stance that led them to design a translanguaging space design for instruction and assessment. In particular, Marisol was a transladora who was able to understand the difference between the *social* importance of named languages, English and/or Spanish, and the *internal* language capacity of human beings. As such, Marisol and Tammy maintained the separate instructional spaces for English and Spanish, but opened up the translanguaging space of Los Círculos that enabled the two riverbanks to come together, integrating bilingual students' language practices in ways that gave rise to their thinking, imagination, creativity, and criticality without the social constraint of doing so only with certain language features. Just as making space for English and space for Spanish is important in a dual language bilingual education programs, making space for *translanguaging* is equally important. This space is not simply to scaffold instruction, but to transform the hierarchical positions of the social power of the named languages. The edges of riverbanks are softened as linguistic features are recognized for their potential to make meaning, rather than simply whether they fit the appropriate conventions demanded at certain times.

In the United States, strict models of dual language bilingual education substituted the developmental maintenance bilingual education programs supported by minoritized communities in the civil rights era. And although the strict language separation supported by DLBE programs might work for language majorities students for whom Spanish is just a commodity, it simply is inappropriate for language minoritized students, unless translanguaging spaces are designed. Though bilingual teachers have always been certain that for bilingual students to learn they must draw from their funds of knowledge (Moll et al., 1992), they have too often fallen prey to these strict language separations and conventional understandings of language and bilingualism that exist precisely to keep the power in the hands of the powerful majority.

This article shows how a dual language bilingual teacher and her teaching partner became aware of the potential of translanguaging and designed a flexible biliteracy space where students' translanguaging was leveraged. In that space, students learned to select the features of their linguistic repertoires in ways that put them in control of language use and learning, rather than following language allocation policies that will always leave out their bilingual capacities and exclude their ways of languaging and knowing.

References

Bakhtin, M. (1981). *Dialogic imagination: Four essays*. Austin, TX: University of Texas Press.
Beeman, K., & Urrow, C. (2013). *Teaching for biliteracy: Strengthening bridges between languages*. Philadelphia, PA: Caslon Publishing.
Bretchel, M. (2005). *Bringing it all together: An integrated whole language approach for the multilingual classroom*. Carlsbad, CA: Dominie Press.
Cummins, J. (1979). Lingistic interdependence and the educational development of bilingual children. *Review of Educational Research, 49*, 222–251.
Daniels, H. (2002). *Literature circles: Voice and choice in book clubs and reading groups*. Markham, ON: Pembroke Publishers.
Escamilla, K., Hopewell, S., Butvilofsky, S., Sparrow, W., Soltero-González, L., Ruiz-Figueroa, O., & Escamilla, M. (2014). *Biliteracy from the Start. Literacy squared in action*. Philadelphia, PA: Caslon.

García, O. (2009). *Bilingual education in the 21st century: A global perspective.* Malden, MA/Oxford, UK: Wiley/Blackwell.

García, O., Bartlett, L., & Kleifgen, J. (2007). From biliteracy to pluriliteracies. In P. Auer & L. Wei (Eds.), *Handbook of applied linguistics, Vol. 5: Multilingualism* (pp. 207–228). Berlin, Germany: Mouton de Gruyter.

García, G., Johnson, S. I., & Seltzer, K. (2017). *The Translanguaging classroom: Leveraging student bilingualism for learning.* Philadelphia, PA: Caslon.

García, O., & Li, W. (2014). *Translanguaging: Language, bilingualism and education.* London, UK: Palgrave Macmillan.

García, O., Sánchez, M. & Solorza, C. (2018). Reframing language allocation policy in dual language bilingual education.

Gutiérrez, K., Baquedano-López, P., & Alvarez, H. H. (2001). Literacy as hybridity: Moving beyond bilingualism in urban classrooms. In M. Reyes & J. J. Halcón (Eds.), *The best for our children: Critical perspectives on literacy for Latino students* (pp. 122–141). New York, NY: Teachers College Press.

Hornberger, N. (1989). Continua of biliteracy. *Review of Educational Research, 59,* 271–296.

Johnson, S. I. (2013). *Dual language teachers changing views of Spanish literacy teaching and learning as influenced by critical dialogue.* Unpublished doctoral dissertation. University of New Mexico.

Kress, G. (2003). *Literacy in the new media age.* London, UK/New York, NY: Routledge.

Moll, L. C., Amanti, C., Neff, D., & Gonzalez, N. (1992). Funds of knowledge for teaching: Using a qualitative approach to connect homes and classrooms. *Theory Into Practice, 31*(2), 132–141.

New London Group. (1996). A pedagogy of multiliteracies: Designing social futures. *Harvard Educational Review, 66*(1), 60–92.

Otheguy, R., García, O., & Reid, W. (2015). Clarifying translanguaging and deconstructing named languages: A perspective from linguistics. *Applied Linguistics Review, 6*(3), 281–307.

Program Brochure. (2010). Albuquerque Public Schools Publications.

Reyes, M. (1992). Challenging venerable assumptions: Literacy instruction for linguistically different students. *Harvard Educational Review, 62,* 427–446.

Reyes, M., & Halcón, J. (Eds.). (2001). *The best for our children: Critical perspectives on literacy for Latino students.* New York, NY: Teachers College Press.

Street, B. (1985). *Literacy in theory and practice.* Cambridge, UK: Cambridge University Press.

Wei, L. (2011). Moment analysis and translanguaging space: Discursive construction of identities by multilingual Chinese youth in Britain. *Journal of Pragmatics, 43,* 1222–1235.

Wong-Fillmore, L., & Valadez, C. (1986). Teaching bilingual learners. In M. C. Wittrock (Ed.), *Handbook of research on teaching* (pp. 648–685). New York, NY: Macmillan.

Literature References

Polacco, P. (1994). *Pink and say.* New York: Philomel.

Preparing Leaders for Latina/o Academic and Language Success: Frameworks, Perspectives and Strategies

Juan Manuel Niño and Enrique Alemán Jr.

Abstract Despite the increased enrollment of students of color in Texas schools, many school leaders still need to become more knowledgeable and pedagogically prepared to better serve the needs of diverse students. This chapter highlights how current school practices are not sufficiently responsive to the cultural and linguistic assets of students from diverse backgrounds. In this chapter, the authors offer practical strategies and frameworks to facilitate a change process in schools and communities. By drawing on these strategies and frameworks, school leaders can engage in a grassroots approach to create more socially just schools and educational experiences for students of color.

Keywords Latinos in education · Equity leadership · Community engagement · Cultural assets · Social justice leadership preparation · Culturally responsive leadership

1 Introduction

Public school enrollment in the U.S. consists increasingly of students of color, and students with varying linguistic backgrounds. In Texas schools, in every major urban center and across each region, Latina/o students are no longer a "minority" (Murdock, Cline, Zey, Jeanty, & Perez, 2014). Higher education institutions and school districts of all sizes are being challenged to implement academic programming that produces success with and for this type of diversity (López & Moreno, 2014). The decisions made by educational leaders and practices utilized by educators have direct impact on these communities, and what they ultimately implement will have long-term impact on the future of the state. We contend that educators and school leaders must do a better job at addressing their deficiencies in leadership

---

J. M. Niño (✉) · E. Alemán Jr.
Department of Educational Leadership & Policy Studies, University of Texas at San Antonio, San Antonio, TX, USA
e-mail: Juan.nino@utsa.edu; Enrique.aleman@utsa.edu

© The Author(s) 2019
D. E. DeMatthews, E. Izquierdo (eds.), *Dual Language Education: Teaching and Leading in Two Languages*, Language Policy 18,
https://doi.org/10.1007/978-3-030-10831-1_9

practice especially concerning cultural and linguistic responsiveness. Many educators and leaders are not well equipped to serve Latina/o students or to engage Latina/o parents and families. Policymakers and educational leaders need to know that the fastest growing and youngest student group is Latina/o, and that this sustained growth will persist over the next several decades (Murdock et al., 2014). Capable and culturally competent educators and administrative personnel must be prepared in response to these demographic changes (Valenzuela, 2016). Despite the irrefutable fact that Texas schools are among the most diverse and that students bring multilingual abilities, educational polices fail to address pervasive segregation (Orfield, Kucsera, & Siegel-Hawley, 2012), funding continues to be distributed in unequal and inequitable ways (Alemán, 2007; Maxcy, Rorrer, & Alemán, 2009), and academic standards are enforced as doctrines without much considersation of students' cultural and linguistic assets (Valenzuela, 2004). In this chapter we argue that school leaders need to face these challenges head on, recognize the inherent complexities of engaging in such efforts, and embrace the cultural assets of their communities – including the racial and linguistic diversity – if they are to create spaces for all children to succeed. We outline practices and strategic activities that center Latina/o student experiences, engage communities by providing a model of inclusion for emergent bilingual students, and call on educational policymakers to utilize their role and institutional power to enhance awareness of cultural diversity in schools, rather than to enact deficit-oriented practices and policies that have resulted in unequal educational opportunities for the majority of Texas students.

2 The Browning of U.S. and Texas Schools

Public schools are typically among the first institutions to experience shifts in demographics, and remain among the most vital organizations in providing access to upward social mobility for young people and their families. According to the National Center for Education Statistics (NCES), from 1990 to 2010, the number of Latina/o students rose from 5.1 million to 12.1 million, an increase of 11% of the student population. The trend is not subsiding as the Latina/o population is projected to double from 53.3 million in 2012 to 128.8 million in 2060, resulting in one in three U.S. residents identifying as Latina/o compared to the current one in six (U.S. Census Bureau, 2012). Considering these demographic shifts, the U.S. population growth from 2000 to 2010 accounted for a 43% rise within the Latina/o population. This accounts for an increase of 15.2 million individuals. Most of this growth in the United States occurred in the South (57%) and in the Midwest (49%). The five so-called majority-minority states or territories in 2011 were Hawaii 77.1%, the District of Columbia 64.7%, California 60.3%, New Mexico 59.8% and Texas 55.2% (U.S. Census Bureau, 2012). However, California, Texas, and Florida reported having over half of the Latina/o residents.

Furthermore, the change in school population is not only seen in the Latina/o population. According to NCES, student enrollment of White and Black students has been decreasing in U.S. public schools. Between 2001 and 2011, the enrollment of White students decreased by 8% and Black students decreased by 1% (NCES, 2014). During the same time period, the Latina/o student population increased by 7%, while the Asian student population increased by 1% (NCES, 2014). With these population shifts in mind, it is now necessary to critically consider how educators are prepared to welcome and properly serve the new student population. Educating the diverse student population is still a very White educator profession, where 82% of teachers were White and 80% of principals were White during 2010–2011 academic year (U.S. Department of Education, 2014). Therefore, as the population continues to shift across the country, educators must consider how their racial identities reflect their students. Moreover, educator and leader preparation pipelines need to change to embrace the diversification of schools across the nation.

In Texas, the demographic shifts have been more pronounced. According to the Texas Education Agency (TEA), Latina/o students accounted for the largest percentage of total enrollment (51.8%) in 2013–14, followed by White (29.5%), African American (12.7%), Asian (3.7%), and multiracial (1.9%) students. Furthermore, across racial/ethnic groups in 2013–14, the percentages of individual group enrollment by students identified as economically disadvantaged were larger for Latina/o (77.7%) and Black (73.1%) students than for multiracial (43.9%), Asian (30.4%), and White (28.3%) students. Higher Latina/o enrollment was also evident in instructional programs for special populations. For example, Latina/o enrollment for English Language Learner enrollment was at 90.6%; 98.4% for migrant education; 62.7% for Title I; and 49.4% for special education. However, in the same year, 3.3% of Black and 2.8% of Latina/o students dropped out of high school, in comparison to 1.1% of Whites, 0.8% of Asians, and 2.2% of Pacific Islanders. A closer look at drop out rates reveals how schools are failing Latina/x students. In Texas, Latina/o student dropout rates in ESL were 4.1%. For students identified as "migrant" or receiving special education their drop out rates were 3.9% and 3.2% respectively, much higher than the state average of 2.2% (Texas Education Agency, 2014).

Due to higher enrollment of Latina/o students in schools, educational policymakers and leaders need to examine data trends to determine where schools can better assist students to successfully navigate the public school experience and provide support to achieve academic success. It is important for schools and school leaders to become understanding of the programmatic needs of the diverse student population they serve to ensure students have the proper instructional support to successfully navigate the educational process. This new perspective calls for educators to be more culturally aware of the new Texas demographics so that schools can recognize and celebrate the differences of students, families, and staff.

3 From Deculturalizing Spaces to Asset-Based Schools

The shifting nature of public school enrollment requires a renewed focus on leadership development and a re-tooling of leadership and educator practice. When put into proper context, the histories of public education, migration, and racial diversity adds additional significance to the preparation of school leaders. As many scholars have documented, public schools have historically disadvantaged and discriminated against students of color (Anderson, 2007), and against Latina/os in particular (Acuña, 1988; Donato, 1997; San Miguel & Valencia, 1998). Egregiously, Native American students experienced boarding schools after being forcefully removed from their families and communities (Lomawaima, 1999). Japanese American students were held captive and marked as foreign threats in internment camps across the West and Southwest after the attack on Pearl Harbor (Takaki, 2000). And the long history of Black segregation and violence, from slavery to Reconstruction to Jim Crow, is well documented (Anderson, 2007; Carmichael & Hamilton, 1967). The historical remnants of these periods of U.S. racial injustice are institutionalized and thriving today (Bonilla-Silva, 2003; Gillborn, 2009; Love, 2004; Tatum, 1992; Teranishi, Behringer, Grey, & Parker, 2009).

For Latina/o students, schools have also been sites of disadvantage and deculturalization. Defined by Spring (2016) as the conscious attempt to replace one culture and language with another that is considered to be "superior" (p. 1), scholars (DePouw, 2012; Lomawaima, 1999) have demonstrated that the framing of any language other than English as an indicator of academic inferiority has been one form of deculturalization. Tracking students and categorizing them as academically deficient, has further disadvantaged students who attend school with a home or primary language of Spanish. Valencia (2008), in his book on litigation pursued by Mexican American educators, activists and parents, dedicates a whole chapter to the numerous court cases specifically about language, bilingual education policy, and the treatment of Latina/ox students. Unfortunately, many of the same deficit notions and practices – especially around language and bilingualism – continue to persist across K-12 institutions (García & Guerra, 2004).

With her conceptualization of community cultural wealth, Yosso (2005) lays out forms of capital that many communities of color posses but that do not always get "counted" or acknowledged as assets. Social, familial, resistant, navigational and linguistic forms of capital enable students and families with little or no material wealth to not only survive but to also thrive in conditions that most would consider unbearable. Linguistic capital, in particular, is relevant to communities where most students and family members might not necessarily speak English or have strong command of it, but who nonetheless possess the ability to communicate in Spanish. Many children, who because they may act as translators or brokers for their parent, thus possess linguistic and navigational capital because they are able to communicate on behalf of their family member and learn from an early age in life how to navigate complex governmental agencies or institutional policies. Despite having these forms of capital, many mainstream or traditional notions of "wealth" or "capital" might not view the community cultural wealth of these children or families. Similar to the way that Valencia and Black note in their work, educators might "blame the victim" for their academic failure, rather than note the tremendous assets that Latina/o families possess, or fail to acknowledge the "funds of knowledge" that are passed onto their children.

4 Preparing Teacher-Leaders and School Leaders for Social Justice

Teacher preparation has traditionally been focused on pedagogical skills and content training. Lenski, Crumpler, Stallworth, and Crawford (2005) found that teachers complete their preparation programs and perpetuate one of three common practices in the classroom:

> [a] curriculum centered on the dominant culture, which ignores bias and fails to address inequity, a curriculum that pretends that differences do not exist, thereby denying the experiences of many children in the classroom, a curriculum that treats multicultural as tourism, in which superficial aspect of the culture (holidays/food, etc.) are introduced. (p. 50)

As such, educators continue to reflect the practices and ideologies that were passed to them in their preparation programs and often do not embrace the differences that students come with as forms of assets. Delpit (2006) maintained that teacher preparation "usually focuses on research that links failure and social economic status, failure and cultural differences, and failure and single-parent households" (p. 34). Therefore, teacher preparation needs to address the tendency educators have of blaming students with differences, particularly, immigrants, for failure in public schools because they are the innocent/victims (Valencia, 1997). Similarly, language diversity and home languages other than English have historically been deemed as markers of inferiority (Spring, 2016). Educators must shift the thinking and practice of education for students, particularly students who speak another language other than English. What is missing in the training of teacher programs is the development of educators as cultural responsive educators, who learn and lead for social justice. Using various pedagogical practices, educators can become more familiar with the various needs of the changing demographics. These approaches can facilitate a process to assist educators view themselves as leaders able to create equitable opportunity for all students.

4.1 Innovative Educator Preparation in Texas

Over the years, many scholars have focused on developing awareness about the oppressive systems found in schools and communities (Bordas, 2012; Freire, 1993; Ladson-Billings, 2009; Marshall & Oliva, 2010; Murakami-Ramalho, Garza, & Merchant, 2009; Theoharis, 2009; Valenzuela, 1999). Such scholars highlight the need to be more socially just in school systems if educators are committed to increase academic performance for all students. Valenzuela (1999) found that teachers who embraced an authentic care towards Latina/o students have a much better opportunity of engaging students in schools. Nieto (2007) worked with teachers who embodied particular behaviors characteristic of what she conceptualized as teacher leadership. According to Nieto, teacher leaders are those who practice believing in, and advocating for, public education, challenging conventional wisdom, improvise to meet students' diverse needs, model social justice, and use power inside and outside the classroom.

In order to move the work from the conventional practices of teacher leaders as department heads or master teachers, teacher leadership development needs to be embedded in professional environments. A single training will not facilitate the development of vital teacher leadership traits. While there are no particular skillsets required for teacher leaders, Nieto suggests that educators can foster certain conditions to enact teacher leadership. Within the scope of their practice, Nieto asserts certain concepts must be present to enact teacher leadership. Respect and support from administration and colleagues, the time and resources to practice leadership and the opportunity to work collaboratively with colleagues are hallmarks of this practice. Teachers need to embrace a mentoring mindset where the mentor/mentee relationship is reciprocal. A reciprocal mentor/mentee relationship is critical when attempting to develop teacher leadership. This reciprocal approach allows teachers to collaborate and share experiences, ways of knowing, and knowledge relevant to supporting the needs of marginalized students. The relationship fostered between teachers is one of respect and care. These powerful relationships are then institutionalized within schools and passed through other interactions with other colleagues, administrators, students, and families.

Teachers who embody leadership traits understand the authentic role of educating a child holistically. Teacher leaders do not neglect the multidimensional needs of students. Given the demographic shifts across the nation, a teacher leader's knowledge and practice on how to address the culture, language, abilities and lived experiences of students is critical. This approach invites teachers to reject deficit notions of students with diverse backgrounds. The development of teacher leaders challenges the hegemonic practices that helps some students while neglecting to properly serve culturally and linguistically diverse students. Nieto (2007) argued that the practice of teacher leadership can provide a teacher who is interested in becoming a social change agent the opportunity to become a "moral compass for the nation" (p. 307).

4.2 *Educators as Teacher Leaders*

Teachers as leaders is not a novel concept. While their roles and responsibilities vary, what is the heart of their work is the desire to help students and colleagues succeed. Context is crucial for the work of teacher leaders. With the demographic shift our nation and schools are undergoing, it is important for teacher leaders to get to know the communities and schools they serve. With this approach, teacher leaders can advance a social justice perspective to support and advocate for culturally and linguistically diverse students. Furthermore, while not every practitioner may have gone through a teacher education program that focused on equity and social justice, teachers still have potential to be powerful agents of change.

Fitzgerald and Gunter (2008) contend that educators are in a position to use their agency as a catalyst for activism. "Teachers are in control of their work with an agenda to not only work for children in their immediate care but also having a wider social justice imperative" (p. 336). Unfortunately, many of these teachers who advance this form of work may be viewed as uncompliant and radicals. As such, minimal research exists on the work these types of teacher leaders are doing as many times teacher leaders are conditioned to embrace traditional managerial tasks. According to Yendol-Silva, Gimbert, and Nolan (2000), missing from the literature are the voices of educators who have enacted the third wave of teacher leadership. The first wave of teacher leadership consisted of those teachers who fulfilled formal management roles such as department head and team leader. As the teaching profession evolved so did the responsibilities. In the second wave of teacher leadership, such practice was characterized by teachers who provided pedagogical expertise as specialists out of the classroom. Many public schools have adopted this model as instructional specialists, instructional coaches or master teachers. However, these types of leadership practices are still centered on pedagogical and content knowledge and not focused on the multidimensional needs of students. As such, the third way of teacher leadership, as suggested by Yendol-Silva, Gimbert, and Nolan is characterized by teachers who lead from within the classroom and "navigate the structures of the school, nurture relationships, encourage professional growth, help others with change, and challenge the status quo by raising children's voices" (p. 12). These educators embrace the teaching aspect of the profession while simultaneously advancing the social and emotional needs of the students they serve. This form of teacher leadership is focused on adopting the tenets of social justice leadership from the classroom. Teachers with the adequate support and creative space can engage in multidimensional experiences that can help them lead and teach in an equitable manner.

4.3 Preparing Culturally Responsive School Leaders

In preparing to teach and lead for a more culturally and linguistically diverse Texas, educational leaders must be culturally aware of and competent to lead in schools with students of color. Educators, as instructional leaders, need to be familiar with cultural relevant pedagogies to ensure equitable learning opportunities for all. According to Ladson-Billings (1995a), educational leaders must consider the academic success that all students need to experience. Ladson-Billings (1995b) also highlights that, "Despite the current social inequities and hostile classroom environments, students must develop their academic skills….[as well as] literacy, numeracy, technological, social, and political skills….to be active participants in democracy" (p. 160). To do so, she argues that schools must develop and maintain student's cultural competence, which can partly be achieved by utilizing a student's culture as a vehicle for learning. Finally, Ladson-Billings argues that schools should help students develop a critical consciousness to challenge the status quo and critique social norms, values, and morals.

One approach educators can model in schools to better serve culturally and linguistically diverse students is to create inclusive instructional classrooms. Using this model, students are afforded with additional instructional assistance which results in higher participation in class. Also, the learning experiences a student brings from his/her cultural background needs to be reflected in curriculum and classroom activities. This adds value to the student's new content knowledge and bridges connections from her or his prior knowledge. As a principal, one must ensure this form of environment allows students to become engaged in their learning.

5 Strategies for Engaging Schools in the Success of Latina/o Students and Families

5.1 Equity Audits

Equity audits can help familiarize educators with their school and community and help them identify challenges and inequities that exist within the school (Skrla, McKenzie, & Scheurich, 2009). Equity audits provide the guidance and structure for educators to collect and critically analyze data on school profiles. Areas in which educators collect and analyze data include the following: General and Social Class Data; Status of Labeling at the School, General Achievement Data; Race and Ethnicity Data; English Language Learners (ELL) and Bilingual Education Data; (Dis)ability Data; and Sexual Orientation and Gender Identity (LGBT support and alliances).

Specifically, the equity audit experience calls for educators to collect qualitative and quantitative data. The quantitative data is collected from state and district reports, surveys and other quantifiable information schools collect throughout the school year. For the qualitative data, educators are encouraged to interview fellow teachers, counselors and administrators to elicit information beyond the traditional information schools generate. In this exercise, educators analyze the data from their campus to generate common themes about their instructional programs, teacher quality, and programmatic practices. In sum, this collection of information creates a more transparent report of how and where school resources are prioritized. Furthermore, educators are encouraged to collaborate with others in the campus to make this a more organic learning opportunity for all educational professionals in the school. Additionally, educators can then identify at least two leadership recommendations they would make based on their findings that could improve campus equity and/or student achievement.

For servicing bilingual students, Frattura and Capper (2007) suggest for all teachers to become bilingual certified, since knowledge of language acquisition and pedagogical techniques associated with bilingual education can benefit all students. They also suggest for all faculty and staff to learn a second language in order to experience the first-hand challenges, frustrations, and nuances of learning a second language. It also opens up learning about literacy that will benefit all students. In sum, conducting an equity audit will not only provide basic information about the students' needs, but more importantly, give educators the knowledge needed to value the knowledge capital students come to school with and be able to share cultural wealth with the community. It may also inspire teachers to expand their professional capacities to better serve their students.

5.2 Leaders for Community Engagement

Schools are essential institutions within communities. As educational institutions, one of their goals is to prepare individuals that will be able to contribute to the growth and progress of the social groups they belong. However, this is not a one-way endeavor. In fact, the development of meaningful relationships between a school and its community will impact positively the two entities, and thus the wellness of all members. In order to establish a foundation for such connections, it is imperative for schools to be proactive and to go out of their comfort zone. Teachers and school staff are to experience the community and its assets in a way that opens their minds to learning. Interacting with community members in daily life situations provides significant insights to teachers because they are no longer outsiders of the community, but rather they become insiders (Pollock, 2008). According to Sullivan (2001), a community has both an historical record and current resources that can enhance teaching and learning. Teachers can learn from collective memories and people's ways of living and can incorporate that cultural richness into their classroom instruction.

In addition to the equity audit, educators are also encouraged to engage in a more collaborative approach to building ties between the school and community. As such, a community scan provides an opportunity for educators to extend the learning beyond the walls of the schools and into the neighborhoods. In this experience, educators are encouraged to solicit information from families, students, business members, and community stakeholders. For example, brief surveys can be conducted with students and parents to gauge the sentiment of the community and to better understand what community members feel is either lacking or working in the district as well as the community. Additionally, soliciting this information from parents and students reminds them of their vital role in the educational process. Businesses are key stakeholders who are essential in the development of instructional programs and partnerships. As educators, inviting them to contribute to the growth and improvement of schools helps generate investments.

Traditionally, schools are active in conducting neighborhood walks at the beginning of the school year to introduce themselves to the community. However, this singular attempt to create community with the neighborhood has little impact to sustain a promising partnership between schools and the neighborhood. What is needed is a more organic and grassroots approach where educators visit with community members throughout the school year. This ongoing effort entices families, business and community stakeholders as active participants in the schooling process. Having periodic meetings with the stakeholders is another attempt to increase family engagement with the school. Such meetings can highlight concerns with the students' attendance, social emotional issues, negative environmental factors, and poverty issues. Due to this approach, educators can be made aware of the resources the community offers.

Furthermore, educators can organize a community walk in the neighborhood of the school. This is a great opportunity for the teachers, staff and administration to know more about the culture, language, abilities and diverse knowledge available to the school from the community. This discovery process can then be used to engage a reciprocal relationship between the school and community. When educators understand the histories of the diverse populations they serve in schools, they are able to recognize community strategies that are used to cope with everyday challenges (Rodriguez & Fabionar, 2010). In order for a school to thrive they must reach out into their community.

5.3 Reflective Practitioner Practices

Lastly, a teacher leader must be willing to engage in critical reflection. This reflection provides an opportunity for an educator to look at their role in practice. How do teachers practice a balance of promoting change, conservation, coalition, and confrontation for students of diverse backgrounds? This mindset of reflection allows teacher leaders to negotiate the tension between curriculum standards and their agency as critical educators. Teacher leaders who are reflective can integrate their knowledge, the knowledge of their communities, and their own critical observations of self to modify their practices and curriculum to be more culturally responsive to their students. Through critical reflection teacher leaders also find their authentic purpose for teaching.

Journaling provides another opportunity for educators to reflect about their experiences and express their thoughts in a written format. In the journaling experience, educators are able to share how certain practices, behaviors and attitudes influence their pedagogy. During their reflective experience, educators are able to intimately challenge themselves. In the journal, educators are encouraged to share concerns, fears, celebrations, comments from readings, reactions to readings, and anything they feel compelled to share. The reflective journal is a simple process with the purpose of helping educators be reflexive about their practice.

5.4 Principals as Agents of Support

Researchers suggest the principal's position is critical for increasing levels of student performance, especially for culturally and linguistically diverse students (Lyons & Algozzine, 2006). Glover-Blackwell, Kwoh, and Pastor (2010) contend that, "minority concerns are no longer strictly minority concerns" (p. 35). Therefore, school leaders must create a practice to gain a deeper understanding of inequalities that impact the lives of students of color and invest in their economic and social growth. This can be a challenge for principals given the demands of high-stakes accountability and resources challenges described in other chapters. However, if principals are working collaboratively with teacher leaders and communities, they will be able to better understand their school-community resources and use them in ways that support equitable and inclusive schools and classrooms.

Given the historical trends of Latina/o students, it is of urgency that school leadership development, training and preparation address how school leaders can foster a culture of academic success given the current and future population projections of Latinos. Scholars, such as Ylimaki, Brunderman, Bennett, and Dugan (2014), for example continue to find the need to prepare principals to lead in culturally diverse schools. In order to facilitate the development of this type of school leader, principal preparation programs have seen the need to integrate issues of diversity into coursework by proposing a variety of models and approaches to developing social justice leaders (Cambron-McCabe, 2010; McKenzie et al., 2008). This important practice must be adopted by leadership preparation programs that address issues of equity, justice and academic advancement.

6 Conclusion

The story of the United States and Texas is not complete without the contributions of immigrants from all over the world. Yet, current political and economic conditions have created a backlash against immigration, particularly immigration from Central and Latin America. As communities in Texas continue to become more diverse, preparation programs must be responsive to better prepare educators to serve Texas public school students. Given the historical context, it is imperative that educator preparation programs provide pre-service teachers and leaders with the tools to advocate for students who identify as immigrants and non-native English speakers so that all students are given an equal opportunity. Moreover, to prepare pre-service educators during their preparation programs with the mindsets and skills necessary to take action and to advocate for immigrant students, some university professors have created opportunities and strategies for students to engage the community and schools during their university experience.

While most leadership preparation programs are focused on narrowly adhering to state certification standards, the Urban School Leaders Collaborative offers a model for developing leaders for social justice (Merchant & Garza, 2015). This program is unique in its pedagogical approach for leadership development. The pedagogy is centered on developing all educators as leaders for a more equitable learning environment. Adopting this leadership development program, aspiring school leaders participate in leadership exercises to develop a mindset of equitable practices. In this space, aspiring school leaders are able to see the strengths of students from diverse backgrounds. They are able to recognize a student's lived experience as part of the student's knowledge base and incorporate that knowledge in how they teach. School leaders and teachers must refuse to think of students as passive learners waiting for intellectual deposits from the omniscient teacher. Educator programs can begin the change we need in schools by challenging and resisting cultural and linguistic hegemony in their classrooms.

References

Acuña, R. (1988). *Occupied America: A history of Chicanos* (3rd ed.). New York, NY: Harper Collins.
Alemán, E., Jr. (2007). Situating Texas school finance policy in a CRT framework: How "substantially equal" yields racial inequity. *Educational Administration Quarterly, 43*(5), 525–558.
Anderson, J. D. (2007). Race-conscious educational policies versus a "color-blind constitution": A historical perspective. *Educational Researcher, 36*(5), 249–257.
Bonilla-Silva, E. (2003). *Racism without racists: Color-blind racism and the persistence of racial inequality in the United States*. Oxford, UK: Rowman & Littlefield Publishers.
Bordas, J. (2012). *Salsa, soul, and spirit: Leadership for the multicultural age* (2nd ed., pp. 46–56). San Francisco, CA: Berrett-Koehler Publishers.
Cambron-McCabe, N. (2010). Preparation and development of school leaders: Implications for social justice policies. In C. Marshall & M. Oliva (Eds.), *Leadership for social justice: Making revolutions in education* (2nd ed., pp. 110–129). New York, NY: Pearson.
Carmichael, S., & Hamilton, C. V. (1967). *Black power: The politics of liberation in America*. New York, NY: Vintage Books.
Delpit, L. (2006). *Other people's children: Cultural conflict in the classroom*. New York, NY: The New Press.
DePouw, C. (2012). When culture implies deficit: Placing race at the center of Hmong American education. *Race Ethnicity and Education, 15*(2), 223–239.
Donato, R. (1997). *The other struggle for equal schools: Mexican Americans during the civil rights era*. Albany, NY: SUNY Press.
Fitzgerald, T., & Gunter, H. M. (2008). Contesting the orthodoxy of teacher leadership. *International Journal of Leadership in Education, 11*(4), 331–340.
Frattura, E. M., & Capper, C. A. (2007). *Leading for social justice: Transforming schools for all learners*. Thousand Oaks, CA: Corwin Press.
Freire, P. (1993). *Pedagogy of the oppressed* (30th Anniversary edn). New York, NY: Continuum.
García, S., & Guerra, P. (2004). Deconstructing deficit thinking: Working with educators to create more equitable learning environments. *Education and Urban Society, 36*(2), 150–168.
Gillborn, D. (2009). Education policy as an act of white supremacy: Whiteness, critical race theory, and education reform. In E. Taylor, D. Gillborn, & G. Ladson-Billings (Eds.), *Foundations of critical race theory in education* (pp. 51–72). New York, NY: Routledge.
Glover-Blackwell, A., Kwoh, S., & Pastor, M. (2010). *Uncommon common ground: Race and America's future*. New York, NY: W.W. Norton.
Ladson-Billings, G. (1995a). Toward a theory of culturally relevant pedagogy. *American Educational Research Journal, 32*(3), 465–491.
Ladson-Billings, G. (1995b). But that's just good teaching! The case for culturally relevant pedagogy. *Theory Into Practice, 34*(3), 159–165.
Ladson-Billings, G. (2009). *The dreamkeepers: Successful teachers of African American children*. San Francisco, CA: Jossey-Bass.

Lenski, S. D., Cumpler, T. P., Stallworth, C., & Crawford, K. M. (2005). Beyond awareness: Preparing culturally responsive preservice teachers. *Teacher Education Quarterly, 32*(2), 85–100.

Lomawaima, K. T. (1999). The unnatural history of American Indian education. In K. G. Swisher & J. W. Tippeconnic (Eds.), *Next steps: Research and practice to advance Indian education* (pp. 1–32). Charleston, WV: Clearinghouse on Rural Education and Small Schools.

López, P. D., & Moreno, C. (2014). *A Latina/o K-12 and Higher Education Policy Agenda in Texas*. Retrieved from Senate Hispanic Caucus, Mexican American Legislative Caucus and Latina/o Education Task Force

Love, B. J. (2004). *Brown* plus 50 counter-storytelling: A critical race theory analysis of the "majoritarian achievement gap" story. *Equity & Excellence in Education, 37*, 227–246.

Lyons, J. E., & Algozzine, B. (2006). Perceptions of the impact of accountability on the role of principals. *Education Policy Analysis Archives, 14*(16), 1–19.

Marshall, C., & Oliva, M. (2010). *Leadership for social justice: Making revolutions in education*. Boston, MA: Allyn & Bacon.

Maxcy, B. D., Rorrer, A. K., & Alemán, E. (2009). Texas. In B. C. Fusarelli & B. S. Cooper (Eds.), *The rising state: How state power is transforming our nation's schools* (pp. 89–132). Albany, NY: SUNY Press.

McKenzie, K. B., Christman, D., Hernandez, F., Fierro, E., Capper, C., Dantley, M., … Scheurich, J. J. (2008). From the field: A proposal for educating leaders for social justice. *Educational Administration Quarterly, 44*.

Merchant, B., & Garza, E., Jr. (2015). The urban school leaders collaborative: Twelve years of promoting leadership for social justice. *Journal of Research on Leadership Education, 10*(1), 39–62.

Murakami-Ramalho, E., Garza, E., & Merchant, B. (2009). Lessons from country borders: Preparing leaders for social justice and diversity through a district and university partnership. *Journal of School-University Partnerships, 3*(2), 80–97.

Murdock, S. H., Cline, M. E., Zey, M., Jeanty, P. W., & Perez, D. (2014). *Changing Texas: Implications of addresing or ignoring the Texas challenge*. College Station, TX: Texas A&M University Press.

National Center for Education Statistics. (2014). *The condition of education*. Retrieved from http://nces.ed.gov/pubs2014/2014083.pdf

Nieto, S. (2007). Latinos and the elusive quest for equal education. In J. Flores & R. Rosaldo (Eds.), *Latino studies companion* (pp. 217–228). Oxford, UK: Blackwell Publishers.

O'Sullivan, M. (2001). *Community awareness and community mapping*.

Orfield, G., Kucsera, J., & Siegel-Hawley, G. (2012). E pluribus… separation: Deepening double segregation for more students. Retrieved from.

Pollock, M. (Ed.). (2008). *Everyday antiracism: Getting real about race in school*. New York, NY: The New Press.

Rodriguez, G. M., & Fabionar, J. O. (2010). The impact of poverty on students and schools: Exploring the social justice leadership implications. In C. Marshall & M. Oliva (Eds.), *Leadership for social justice: Making revolution in education* (pp. 55–73). Boston, MA: Allyn & Bacon.

San Miguel, G., & Valencia, R. R. (1998). From the treaty of Guadalupe Hidalgo to *Hopwood*: The educational plight and struggle of Mexican Americans in the Southwest. *Harvard Educational Review, 68*(3), 353–412.

Skrla, L., McKenzie, K. B., & Scheurich, J. J. (2009). *Using equity audits to create equitable and excellent schools*. Thousand Oaks, CA: Corwin Press.

Spring, J. (2016). *Deculturalilzation and the struggle for equality: A brief history of the education of dominated cultures in the United States* (8th ed.). New York, NY: Routledge.

Takaki, R. (2000). *Iron cages: Race and culture in 19th century America* (Revised edition ed.). New York, NY: Oxford University Press.

Tatum, B. D. (1992). Talking about race, learning about racism: The application of racial identity development theory in the classroom. *Harvard Educational Review, 62*(1), 1–24.

Teranishi, R. T., Behringer, L. B., Grey, E. A., & Parker, T. L. (2009). Critical race theory and research on Asian Americans and Pacific Islanders in higher education. *New Directions for Institutional Research, Summer*(142), 57–68.

Texas Education Agency. (2014). *Student Enrollment Report, 2013–2014*. Retrieved from https://rptsvr1.tea.texas.gov/cgi/sas/broker

Theoharis, G. (2009). *The school leaders our children deserve: Seven keys to equity, social justice and school reform*. New York, NY: Teachers College Press.

U.S Census Bureau. (2012). *U.S. Census Bureau projections show a slower growing, older, more diverse nation a half century from now*. Retrieved from http://www.census.gov/newsroom/releases/archives/population/cb12-243.html

U.S. Department of Education. (2014). *Law and guidance: Elementary and secondary education*. Retrieved from http://www2.ed.gov/policy/elsec/guid/esea-flexibility/index.html

Valencia, R. (1997). *The evolution of deficit thinking: Educational thought and practice*. Bristol, PA: The Falmer Press.

Valencia, R. R. (2008). *Chicano students and the courts: The Mexican American legal struggle for educational equity*. New York, NY: New York University Press.

Valenzuela, A. (1999). *Subtractive schooling: U.S.-Mexican youth and the politics of caring*. Albany, NY: State University of New York Press.

Valenzuela, A. (Ed.). (2004). *Leaving children behind: How Texas-style accountability fails Latino youth*. Albany, NY: State University of New York Press.

Valenzuela, A. (Ed.). (2016). *Growing critically conscious teachers: A social justice curriculum for educators of Latino/a youth*. New York, NY: Teachers College Press.

Yendol-Silva, D., Gimbert, B., & Nolan, J. (2000). Sliding the doors: Locking and unlocking possibilities for teacher leadership. *Teachers College Record, 102*(4), 779–804.

Ylimaki, R. M., Brunderman, L., Bennett, J. V., & Dugan, T. (2014). Developing Arizona turnaround leaders to build high-capacity schools in the midst of accountability pressures and changing demographics. *Leadership and Policy in Schools, 13*(1), 28–60.

Yosso, T. J. (2005). Whose culture has capital? A critical race theory discussion of community cultural wealth. *Race Ethnicity and Education, 8*(1), 69–91.

Part III
Leading the Way to Dual Language Education

Dual Language for All: Central Office Leadership in the El Paso Independent School District

Elena Izquierdo, David E. DeMatthews, David S. Knight, and James Coviello

Abstract Despite intentions to promote academic achievement among Latinx student populations, many districts continue to provide exclusionary and subtractive educational programs. Dual language education has been put forth by many researchers, social justice advocates, and practitioners as an approach to transforming schools through its emphasis on valuing linguistic diversity, inclusivity, and rigorous and culturally sustaining curriculum. Drawing upon theories of social justice leadership, we explore how one superintendent in the El Paso Independent School District (EPISD) in Texas engaged in leadership to address injustices against Mexican and Mexican American emergent bilinguals through the implementation of district-wide dual language education. This study highlights the important role of the superintendent in supporting dual language education, identifies specific actions and values pertinent to social justice leadership at the district level, and distinguishes some of the ways personal values, context, and continual learning can positively influence leadership.

This article has been adapted with permission from DeMatthews, D. E., Izquierdo, E., & Knight, D. (2017). Righting past wrongs: A superintendent's social justice leadership for dual language education along the US-Mexico border. *Education Policy Analysis Archives*, 25(1), 1–28.

E. Izquierdo (✉)
Department of Teacher Education, University of Texas at El Paso, El Paso, TX, USA
e-mail: ielena@utep.edu

D. E. DeMatthews
Department of Educational Leadership and Policy, University of Texas at Austin, Austin, TX, USA
e-mail: ddematthews@austin.utexas.edu

D. S. Knight
University of Washington, Seattle, WA, USA
e-mail: dsknight84@gmail.com

J. Coviello
Department of Educational Leadership, Saint Joseph's University, Philadelphia, PA, USA
e-mail: James.Coviello@sju.edu

© The Author(s) 2019
D. E. DeMatthews, E. Izquierdo (eds.), *Dual Language Education: Teaching and Leading in Two Languages*, Language Policy 18,
https://doi.org/10.1007/978-3-030-10831-1_10

Keywords Social justice leadership · Superintendents · Dual language · English Language Learners (ELL) · Emergent bilinguals · District leadership · District improvement · Latinx

1 Introduction

Dual language education has been put forth by many researchers, community activists, and practitioners as an approach to transforming schools through its emphasis on valuing linguistic diversity, inclusivity, and rigorous and culturally sustaining curriculum (Collier & Thomas, 2004; Lindholm-Leary & Block, 2010). Without consideration of dual language research, many districts continue to maintain the status quo, fail to value family language as an asset or right, and leave Latinx students vulnerable to academic failure in subtractive and substandard programs (Menken & Kleyn, 2010; Valenzuela, 2010; Wiley & Wright, 2004). It should come as no surprise, therefore, that emergent bilinguals, the overwhelming majority of whom are Latinx, are rarely proficient in reading (4%) or mathematics (6%) by eighth grade and are not graduating at the same rate as those students who are English proficient (NCES, 2015).

Research on second language learning has documented that English proficiency is not quickly obtained by one hard-working teacher or a result of 1 or 2 years of targeted instructional support (Hakuta, Butler, & Witt, 2000). Instead, schools cultivate academic English proficiency over a four to seven-year period (Cummins, 1981). Supporting Latinx emergent bilinguals requires that teachers and principals have access to extensive professional development and ongoing coaching that can perhaps only come through a long-term district-wide improvement process (Cheung & Slavin, 2012; Elfers & Stritikus, 2014). Given their positional authority to make such investments at the district level, the role of superintendents is therefore critical. At the same time, superintendents' power is shaped by social, political, and economic forces stemming from financial concerns, influential constituent groups, state and federal policies, and local power dynamics.

Drawing upon theories of social justice leadership (Anderson, 2009; DeMatthews, 2016, 2018; Ryan, 2016; Theoharis, 2007), this chapter explores how one superintendent in the El Paso Independent School District (EPISD) in Texas engaged in leadership to address injustices against Mexican and Mexican American emergent bilinguals through the implementation of district-wide dual language education (DeMatthews, Izquierdo, & Knight, 2017). Three central research questions guided this study: (a) What was the role of the superintendent in supporting dual language; (b) What specific actions and orientations were necessary to bring about dual language; and (c) What beliefs and understandings did the superintendent draw from to inform his action? EPISD provided a strategic site for this study because a new superintendent and school board instituted a district-wide dual language model soon after a large-scale cheating scandal that "disappeared" hundreds of Mexican and Mexican American students through improper promotion, demotion, and forced dropout/pushout. This scandal is the primary reason for the study being undisguised, as multiple national and regional media outlets reported this story (Anderson, 2016; Kreighbaum, 2013; Weaver & Tidwell, 2013).

What follows is a brief overview of literature focused on the miseducation of Latinx emergent bilinguals and the justification of dual language as a social justice-oriented approach to schooling. Next, a theoretical framework focused on social justice leadership from the position of the superintendent is presented. Following this is a section describing the methods used to conduct this study. Findings are presented beginning with a brief overview of the EPISD cheating scandal followed by major themes that emerged through the analysis of data. Finally, the chapter concludes with a discussion of the superintendent's role in creating dual language education as well as implications for future research and practice.

2 Emergent Bilinguals and Dual Language Education

Latinx emergent bilinguals have long been marginalized, but the current testing and accountability context makes these students more vulnerable. Educators are under increased pressure and are more likely to view Latinx students as liabilities on state-mandated assessments (Menken, 2010; Reyes, 2016; Valenzuela, 2010; Wiley & Wright, 2004). Framing Latinx students as liabilities also creates a perception that students need to be separated, immersed in English, and subjected to a narrow curriculum rather than building on their cultural and linguistic assets. Emergent bilinguals who learn English while further developing their first language to a high cognitive level are likely to outperform other similar students in English-only programs and also narrow achievement gaps with their English-speaking peers (Genesee, Lindholm-Leary, Saunders, & Christian, 2006).

Closing academic gaps are important, but not sufficient. Student achievement is inextricably linked to a well-rounded and socially-just education that respects and builds upon the cultural resources that are present in Latinx families and communities (Good, Masewicz, & Vogel, 2010; Huerta, 2011). Dual language education is centered upon this notion due to its academic rigor, related social and cultural outcomes – such as healthy multi-generational cultural and linguistic communities – and the presentation of a counter-narrative to dominant racial ideologies that disregard Latinx culture (Fránquiz, Salazar, & DeNicolo, 2011; Wiemelt & Welton, 2015). Dual language education also requires collaborative, flexible professional development for educators and parents; welcomes and connects different communities; maintains high expectations for students; and develops curricula that are developmentally appropriate and attentive to context and culture (García, 2005; McLaughlin, 2013; Schachter & Gass, 2013). The academic and cultural imperatives of dual language education make it a social justice-oriented approach to addressing the educational and cultural injustices currently facing Latinx emergent bilinguals.

3 Theoretical Framework

Three theoretical concepts are useful in thinking about how superintendents engage in social justice leadership. All educational leaders pursuing a social justice agenda need to have situational awareness, an understanding of advocacy, and a refined ability to enact a leadership praxis that is dialogical and critical (DeMatthews & Izquierdo, 2018). Before exploring these concepts, we briefly discuss how social justice leadership has been conceptualized and linked to the role of the superintendent.

3.1 Positioning Superintendents as Social Justice Leaders

Few studies have investigated how superintendents support equity-oriented reforms or the development of dual language education. However, the superintendent's relevance to such reforms is apparent given their unique structural position. The superintendent's "pivotal organizational perch has direct and proximate access to board members, building principals, and community residents, as well as direct and proximate influence on vision inception, resource distribution, and operational procedures" (Bird, Dunaway, Hancock, & Wang, 2013, p. 77). The superintendent can support the structures, resource allocations, and long-term commitments necessary for dual language education or other equity-oriented reforms, especially if she is aware of the broad range of educational injustices present within schools/communities and critically reflective of her practice (Beard, 2012). A superintendent, as with any educational leader acting to advance a social justice agenda, can help to change organizational and cultural values, structures, and practices that marginalize students.

3.2 Components of Superintendent Social Justice Leadership

Situational Awareness Superintendents confront powerful constituent groups, including business leaders, school boards, politicians, and other organizations with diverse sets of interests. Waters, Marzano, and McNulty (2003) defined situational awareness for educational leaders as the extent to which one is "aware of the details and undercurrents in the running of the school and uses this information to address current and potential problems" (p. 12). Leadership at the district level necessitates a deep understanding of power and influence and how it relates to the marginalization of communities and student groups since equity-oriented reform is typically political and complicated. Similar to principals and the micro-politics of schools (Blasé & Anderson, 1995; Iannaccone, 1991; Malen, 1994; Mawhinney, 1999), superintendents need to be aware of and engaged in ongoing political interactions.

This inquisitive awareness provides an opportunity to gain more profound insights into inequities and how different stakeholders conceive notions of the public good and the purposes of education.

Advocacy The context of district leadership necessitates a form of advocacy leadership that is critical, problem-posing, and process- and problem-solving oriented. For Anderson and Cohen (2015), advocacy is part of a broad strategy to build a new alliance of educators, students, parents, and communities who can "advocate for diverse, equitable and culturally responsive schools" (p. 17). For DeMatthews (2018), advocacy is about being visible, strategic, growing networks, and positioning organizations to advance social justice agendas. Additionally, a district leader might strategically "frame" issues in ways that propel communities and districts to act on their behalf or can legitimate an equity-oriented reform. Benford and Snow (2000), describe "framing" as a tool of organizers and social movements, which refers to "action-oriented sets of beliefs and meaning that inspire and legitimate the activities and campaigns of a social movement organization" (Benford & Snow, 2000, p. 614). This kind of action allows leaders to talk about their struggle in ways that unite a variety of stakeholders.

Praxis The merging of situational awareness and advocacy contributes to a superintendent praxis for social justice. Numerous definitions of praxis emerge across education and educational leadership literature (Dantley & Tillman, 2010; Furman, 2012). Freire (2007) uses the term "conscientização" as "learning to perceive social, political, and economic contradictions, and to take action against the oppressive elements of reality" (p. 35). In this chapter, we define praxis as an iterative and ongoing process where individual and/or community/organizational-based learning instigates action and subsequent reflection. Praxis leads to further knowledge with a more extensive purpose of bringing about equitable changes in a complex and changing world. Superintendents leading for social justice engage in praxis through traditional superintendent practices aligned with social justice principles and their situational awareness and ongoing advocacy.

4 Methodology

This qualitative case study examined the leadership of the EPISD superintendent in supporting dual language education, his specific actions and orientations, and his beliefs and understandings that informed his leadership. Data came from observations of school board meetings, task force meetings, and district professional development sessions and interviews with the superintendent, deputy superintendent, and other key stakeholders. Following each observation, the researchers reviewed observation notes, linked any collected documents to the notes, and created a file for the observation. Additional interviews were conducted with central office administrators, task force members, principals, teachers, and parents to triangulate interview responses from the superintendent and deputy superintendent. Although the case reports the actual names of the district, superintendent, and deputy superintendent, we used pseudonyms for all other participants and schools described.

After the initial report was completed with pseudonyms and shared with the district, the superintendent and deputy superintendent believed the study should include the identification of the school district, which would then indirectly identify themselves given their high-level positions. Together with EPISD, we recognized the uniqueness of this case: a large urban district along the U.S.-Mexico border that had previously been involved in a large-scale cheating scandal that would go on to implement dual language for all emergent bilinguals. Although findings may seem provocative to a reader outside of the region, our findings broadly represent what has been openly discussed in national and local media, city council and school board meetings, and other public forums. Moreover, EPISD was interested in having other districts learn from their successes, mistakes, and ongoing challenges. The district made no attempts to change the findings or conclusions. This chapter presents findings, analysis, and conclusions of the authors.

We coded data using NVivo 10 software in multiple phases. First, we read all field notes, documents, and transcripts several times and recorded data by type, source, and began with an initial coding phase that involved low-inference codes derived from our theoretical framework. Then, we inductively coded data related to social justice leadership in the following areas: advocacy, vision, challenging the status quo, leadership orientation and beliefs, politics/power/influence, and social/personal interactions. We also maintained prolonged engagement at the research site over the course of the study that allowed us to build trust with the superintendent, deputy superintendent, and other participants (Miles & Huberman, 1994).

5 Findings

We present findings across five sections related to the context of EPISD and the role of Superintendent Cabrera's leadership. First, we describe the district context and culture before Superintendent Cabrera's arrival. Second, we highlight Cabrera's initial perspectives and steps to move dual language from a boutique program to a district-wide reform. Third, we examine the institutional and organizational challenges of dual language. Fourth, we detail Cabrera's role as an advocate at the school, community, and state level to show how a well-organized movement solved seemingly impossible problems. Finally, we conclude with the specific district practices that contributed to teacher/principal capacity building.

5.1 Setting the Stage: Injustice, Disappearances, and Dual for Some

EPISD is a large urban school district located in Texas along the U.S.-Mexico border and serves some of the poorest zip codes in the nation. The district enrolls more than 60,000 students – approximately 80% of students are Hispanic, 12% White, 70% economically disadvantaged, and 25% emergent bilinguals. District demographics mask stratification, as some schools have emergent bilingual populations over 70% while others serve very low percentages of Hispanic students and economically disadvantaged families.

A cheating scandal associated with the former superintendent as well as numerous district administrators and principals inappropriately kept low-performing students out of tested grade levels by improperly promoting or holding back students, preventing students from enrollment, or forcing students to drop out (Weaver & Tidwell, 2013). The local media, a state senator, and other community stakeholders implored the U.S. Department of Education and the Texas Education Agency (TEA) to investigate the district. Eventually, an independent audit found that numerous district administrators encouraged cheating or looked the other way. The report noted that EPISD was involved in "an extensive scheme that deprived students of an education by denying them access to school, manipulating their official records and providing scam credit-recovery methods disguised as legitimate education" (Weaver & Tidwell, 2013, p. 1).

Meanwhile, in a more affluent part of the city, nine elementary schools, one high school, and one middle school independently developed dual language models starting in the late 1990s. Reveles ES, one of the city's most reputable elementary schools, had received national attention for its excellence in dual language education and eventually partnered with a middle school and high school to continue the program for their students. These schools primarily served students from higher socio-economic backgrounds with more engaged parents interested in dual language as an additive program for their native English-speaking children. For the rest of EPISD, early exit bilingual education was the policy norm.

At the beginning of school year 2013–2014, Juan Cabrera, an attorney and businessman, was appointed superintendent. His appointment came with criticism as he lacked school leadership experience and was considered by some to be an outsider. Despite the fact that he was a Texas-born Mexican-American and grew up in a Spanish-speaking household, Cabrera's selection represented the power of conservative Texas politics. In December 2013, the district's Board of Managers commissioned a community task force on dual language with three goals: (a) to identify and describe successful dual language models with associated costs; (b) to propose a timeline for district-wide implementation; and (c) to recommend a plan for parental and community support. In February, the group recommended the district implement dual language district-wide from grades Pre-K through 12. These events created a sense of immediacy within the central office and produced numerous challenges to be addressed within schools, the central office, and at the state level.

5.2 Initial Perspectives and Framing a Crisis

The emergence of dual language was initially driven by high-SES families. Cabrera and others used grassroots momentum to frame dual language as a needed response to the EPISD cheating scandal. Cabrera framed this injustice as a necessity for systemic and ideological change. He drew personal connections to dual language, stating: "I grew up as an English language learner. I know what it's like trying to learn English and what those experiences are like." Cabrera began by recruiting a deputy superintendent with the experience and passion for dual language district-wide. Deputy Superintendent (DS) Ivonne Durant is a veteran principal and chief academic officer who implemented dual language as a principal and district administrator. She is a Mexican-American woman born in Mexico and a native Spanish speaker. Like Superintendent Cabrera, she was dismayed by the actions of the previous administration and returned to the region to support the implementation of dual language.

5.3 Institutional Challenges

Superintendent Cabrera demonstrated a situational awareness of the challenges associated with implementing dual language across the district, which included teacher certification challenges and competing interests within the district bureaucracy. Both challenges had the potential to impact the district's climate and stop the implementation of dual language at a district level.

District Bureaucracy and Culture In the initial stages of planning for dual language, EPISD recognized an organizational obstacle: the general education curriculum and bilingual education maintained separate offices. Cabrera believed this was problematic because it provided a structural separation in "thought, resources, and objectives." Cabrera added, "For an organization to be effective, its priorities should be aligned." He also recognized the negative cultural impact of the cheating scandal on principals and teachers as well as the ongoing effects of an active federal investigation. Some stakeholders talked about a culture of "complacency and a CYA ['Cover Your Ass'] mentality." Cabrera recognized these difficulties and empowered DS Durant to create a more cohesive central office "where general education and dual language are at the table together... and that the people we hire in the district and as principals and assistant principals are supportive and knowledgeable of dual language." Cabrera's recognition of both the culture and structure of the central office led to a shift in hiring policies and created a more inclusive bureaucracy that did not view the needs of emergent bilinguals as separate from the general education curriculum.

State Compliance Issues Cabrera learned of a state policy requiring English-only teachers in dual language programs to be certified in bilingual education even if they taught only the English component. Even more problematic was the high proportion of teachers with bilingual certifications teaching in English-only classrooms. TEA, therefore, had doubts about granting certification waivers since, on paper, the district had a significant number of bilingual certified teachers – but they would necessarily have to be reassigned. Cabrera recognized the power dynamics that would make dual language untenable if the district was forced to move teachers to different schools, grades, and teaching areas. He decided to challenge the policy through formal channels and recruited principals, a state senator, a U.S. Congressman, the city's mayor, and others to strategize on how to address the certification problems. Cabrera and other EPISD leaders and educators visited the state capitol, testified in legislative sessions, met with representatives, and helped to have the policy changed, thereby allowing EPISD to keep their current teachers.

5.4 Rebuilding Trust and Moral Standing

Cabrera recognized EPISD's reputation was injured. One former task force member and EPISD parent said: "It's horrible what they did and it really set back the district. There's no trust, plus, the harm they did to so many kids. You can't just repair that damage overnight." According to Cabrera, the situation dictated a need for the district to listen to parent concerns and use those concerns to drive reform. He explicitly said "I must be an advocate for our ELL's. They must be our priority now." As Cabrera engaged with the school board, community members, principals, and teachers, he continually retold how emergent bilinguals were historically marginalized and must be offered a more ideal future. Cabrera and DS Durant framed injustices as a cause for action, an opportunity for change, and a sense of purpose connected to their own stories of isolation and embarrassment during their own public schooling.

Cabrera advocated to empower parents to engage in district-level shared governance while also acting strategically in elevating powerful voices to promote equity. He reflected, "It [dual language] was really a grassroots community effort. I think that there were a number of parents who started dual language in the nine schools and their primary concern was getting more middle schools." These parents were mostly from high socio-economic status (SES) communities. Cabrera's situational awareness helped him recognize how these influential parents' power could be used to advocate for dual language for all emergent bilinguals in the district and combat potential resistance to needed changes.

Despite ongoing attempts, parent, teacher, and principal interviews revealed that trust had not been fully restored. Observations revealed most stakeholders agreed with dual language at a general level but were less optimistic about implementation. Many principals reported that their schools were unprepared to roll out dual language and worried about test scores in the short term. One principal asked, "Do they really want us to do this well? If so, wouldn't we have more training and more time?" Many teachers felt unprepared as well. Conversely, few parents were against dual language for emergent bilinguals or as an option for native English-speaking students. Cabrera listened and publicly acknowledged these challenges were real, but argued that change should happen despite potential dips in test scores or self-doubts over preparedness. Privately, he admitted that it was essential to ensure dual language was implemented and solidified given the potential for shifting beliefs with new school boards and Texas state policies.

5.5 Managing Frustration and Building Capacity

EPISD had a short time window between the task force recommendation and the next school year when dual language implementation in pre-k and kindergarten would begin district-wide. Recognizing the need, and given the complexity and the ideological shift required, Cabrera and DS Durant initiated professional development for principals, teachers, and parents the day after approval. Cabrera recognized the symbolism of starting immediately: "The fact that we started immediately communicated to schools that this was serious, that dual was coming."

However, when 2014–2015 began, many teachers and principals were frustrated by the rapid implementation of dual language. Cabrera and DS Durant sought advice from teachers, professors, and other stakeholders and ultimately agreed to create teacher committees and teacher roundtables around problematic issues. Committees developed materials and provided schools with guidance. One district administrator commented:

> The committees made this our program, not something from the outside…We created teacher committees to have conversations about different teacher needs. Teachers who had experience in dual were very helpful to these committees… They shared ideas and resources and helped to lower the frustration level… It also made the reform feel more authentic, like it wasn't just this top-down thing.

Despite this, committee members and facilitators reported how teachers came to meetings upset. A participant said, "There was tension in the roundtables. Teachers felt they weren't ready and they wanted training..." Cabrera recognized the value in giving teachers these opportunities, saying "They need to share their ideas and frustrations."

Cabrera also realized how some principals, especially in the first weeks of implementation, did not buy-in to the model or became passive resistors who did not publicly challenge dual language, but were slow to support it. DS Durant highlighted the importance of hiring and retraining principals. She also recognized some principals would not fit: "As we are replacing principals [due to retirement, transfer to other district, removal], we are replacing them with new blood that will be supportive...we have a process and by the time we pick the person, we make pretty darn sure that person is supportive of dual language." The recommendation was made that an "exemplar" dual language principal would facilitate monthly dual language professional development sessions with principals. While buy-in for dual language was slow, we found that the use of an exemplary principal as a professional development resource was a strategic move by Cabrera, as he understood how to use these well-placed advocates to promote reform and mitigate resistance.

6 Discussion and Conclusion

Few studies have examined the role of superintendents in implementing dual language models or how superintendents engage in social justice leadership. This study highlights the importance of leader consciousness toward equity issues in schools. As evidenced in our findings, Superintendent Cabrera's awareness of past injustices emotionally moved him, prompted him to identify and hire passionate administrators, and propelled him to use his position to promote dual language education despite competing district priorities. These findings are in line with descriptions of social justice leadership as a courageous practice that requires risk-taking and discomfort with complacency in light of injustice (Anderson, 2009).

Like other social justice leaders, Cabrera utilized his understanding of political networks to advocate for dual language education. Beyond framing dual language in ways that inspired others, Cabrera employed his situational awareness and knowledge of community power dynamics to build consensus around dual language. Before his tenure, dual language schools served predominately high-socioeconomic status communities whose parents advocated for their expansion. Rather than acquiesce to their demands, he engaged in advocacy to connect this powerful constituency to the broader cause of adopting dual language district-wide. Cabrera also acknowledged how vital the task force and grassroots efforts were to the adoption of dual language, noting that he could not have implemented such a policy on his own. While one can question if Cabrera's success has more to do with serendipity, it is clear that he recognized the political opportunity and took full advantage of the social capital available in the community.

Cabrera's situational awareness also allowed him to think critically about institutional problems, such as the structure of his central office and the existing human capital problems in EPISD. Like other social justice leaders in schools, Cabrera identified how longstanding arrangements maintained the status quo (Dantley & Tillman, 2010; Theoharis, 2007). As a consequence, Cabrera and Durant restructured the central office in a way that made the needs of emergent bilinguals a priority for all departments and divisions. Cabrera also recognized the sense of distrust that existed between the district, schools, and community. This awareness prompted Cabrera to be patient with principals and teachers, consider ways to build trust with families, and engage in conversations where educators can share their frustrations and ideas. At the same time, Cabrera sought ways to infuse the district with like-minded central office staff and principals who would support dual language education.

EPISD also confronted the technical challenge of a state-level bilingual education certification policy that threatened the adoption of dual language. Cabrera's situational awareness of this issue and his ability to engage in advocacy at the state level provided a positive solution. This finding is also essential for social justice leadership scholarship, which often emphasizes the importance of consciousness and recognition of injustices, but overlooks many of the structural and technical challenges to educational leadership that can cripple any equity-oriented reform before it gets off the ground (DeMatthews, 2016; DeMatthews & Mawhinney, 2014).

Finally, Cabrera recognized the importance of dialogue as evidenced by his recognition that change required communication through ongoing open forums. This advocacy work was not a function of typical power politics where interest groups and individuals battle for resources, but rather a process of social construction where the superintendent framed vital issues to cultivate a collective set of "interests" and "needs" that the district should address. Rather than utilize authoritarian approaches or mandates in the name of social justice, Cabrera and his deputy created forums and professional development opportunities where teachers and principals across the district could pose questions, share strategies, and problem-solve the unique challenges. In part, this was because Cabrera was able to think on multiple layers about how change could be slow and frustrating for a family, a classroom teacher, or a principal. Throughout the study, he continued to learn, reflect, and refine his approaches as well as his ongoing awareness that equity-oriented change was a bumpy road.

This study highlights the important role of the superintendent in supporting dual language education, identifies specific actions and values pertinent to social justice leadership at the district level, and distinguishes some of the central ways personal values, context, and continual learning can positively influence leadership. While EPISD provided a unique case for examining the superintendent's role in implementing dual language education in a particular context, the findings of this study highlight a general social justice imperative for other leaders. Either through personal experience or other means, superintendents should understand the lived experiences of their students and families, listen to their teachers and principals, identify political opportunities as they arise, and seek out social justice-oriented allies and networks within their communities. Superintendent Cabrera was an emergent bilingual and understood through personal experience what it meant to be marginalized, but he recognized that his desire for social justice was insufficient without community support and educator buy-in. He told a compelling story of injustice in a way that brought people together. Without such understandings and a dedication to listen and learn, superintendents will struggle to take full advantage of their pivotal position as district leaders and remain constrained in efforts to create more equitable schools by the politics, bureaucratic challenges, unequal power dynamics, and weight of the status quo.

References

Anderson, G. L. (2009). *Advocacy leadership: Toward a post-reform agenda in education*. New York, NY: Routledge.

Anderson, G. L., & Cohen, M. I. (2015). Redesigning the identities of teachers and leaders: A framework for studying new professionalism and educator resistance. *Education Policy Analysis Archives, 23*(85). https://doi.org/10.14507/epaa.v23.2086

Anderson, L. (2016, July 30). EPISD 5 years later: Fight for trust continues. *El Paso Times*. Retrieved from http://www.elpasotimes.com/longform/news/education/episd/2016/07/30/episd-5-years-later-fight-trust-continues/87618176/

Beard, K. S. (2012). Making the case for the outlier: Researcher reflections of an African-American female deputy superintendent who decided to close the achievement gap. *International Journal of Qualitative Studies in Education, 25*(1), 59–71. https://doi.org/10.1080/09518398.2011.647724

Benford, R. D., & Snow, D. A. (2000). Framing processes and social movements: An overview and assessment. *Annual Review of Sociology, 26*(1), 611–639. https://doi.org/10.1146/annurev.soc.26.1.611

Bird, J. J., Dunaway, D. M., Hancock, D. R., & Wang, C. (2013). The superintendent's leadership role in school improvement: Relationships between authenticity and best practices. *Leadership and Policy in Schools, 12*(1), 77–99. https://doi.org/10.1080/15700763.2013.766348

Blasé, J., & Anderson, G. (1995). *The micropolitics of educational leadership: From control to empowerment*. New York, NY: Teachers College Press.

Cheung, A. C., & Slavin, R. E. (2012). Effective reading programs for Spanish-dominant English language learners in the elementary grades: A synthesis of research. *Review of Educational Research, 82*(4), 351–395. https://doi.org/10.3102/0034654312465472

Collier, V. P., & Thomas, W. P. (2004). The astounding effectiveness of dual language education for all. *NABE Journal of Research and Practice, 2*(1), 1–20.

Cummins, J. (1981). Age on arrival and immigrant second language learning in Canada: A Reassessment1. *Applied Linguistics, 2*(2), 132–149.

Dantley, M. E., & Tillman, L. C. (2010). Social justice and moral transformative leadership. In C. Marshall & M. Oliva (Eds.), *Leadership for social justice* (2nd ed., pp. 19–34). Boston, MA: Allyn & Bacon.

DeMatthews, D. (2016). Social justice dilemmas: Evidence on the successes and shortcomings of three principals trying to make a difference. *International Journal of Leadership in Education*, 1–15. https://doi.org/10.1080/13603124.2016.1206972

DeMatthews, D., & Mawhinney, H. (2014). Social justice leadership and inclusion: Exploring challenges in an urban district struggling to address inequities. *Educational Administration Quarterly, 50*(5), 844–881. https://doi.org/10.1177/0013161X13514440

DeMatthews, D. E. (2018). *Community engaged leadership for social justice: A critical approach in urban schools*. New York, NY: Routledge.

DeMatthews, D. E., & Izquierdo, E. (2018). The role of principals in developing dual language education: Implications for social justice leadership and preparation. *Journal of Latinos and Education*. https://doi.org/10.1080/15348431.2017.1282365

DeMatthews, D. E., Izquierdo, E., & Knight, D. (2017). Righting past wrongs: A superintendent's social justice leadership for dual language education along the US-Mexico border. *Education Policy Analysis Archives, 25*(1), 1–28.

Elfers, A. M., & Stritikus, T. (2014). How school and district leaders support classroom teachers' work with English language learners. *Educational Administration Quarterly, 50*(2), 305–344. https://doi.org/10.1177/0013161X13492797

Fránquiz, M. E., Salazar, M., & DeNicolo, C. (2011). Challenging majoritarian tales: Portraits of bilingual teachers deconstructing deficit views of bilingual learners. *Bilingual Research Journal, 34*(3), 279–300. https://doi.org/10.1080/15235882.2011.625884

Freire, P. (2007). *Pedagogy of the oppressed*. New York, NY: Continuum.

Furman, G. (2012). Social justice leadership as praxis developing capacities through preparation programs. *Educational Administration Quarterly, 48*(2), 191–229.

García, E. E. (2005). *Teaching and learning in two languages: Bilingualism & schooling in the United States*. New York, NY: Teachers College Press.

Genesee, F., Lindholm-Leary, K., Saunders, W., & Christian, D. (2006). *Educating English language learners*. New York, NY: Cambridge University Press.

Good, M. E., Masewicz, S., & Vogel, L. (2010). Latino English language learners: Bridging achievement and cultural gaps between schools and families. *Journal of Latinos and Education, 9*(4), 321–339. https://doi.org/10.1080/15348431.2010.491048

Hakuta, K., Butler, Y. G., & Witt, D. (2000). *How long does it take English learners to attain proficiency?* (Policy Report 2000–1). Santa Barbara, CA: University of California Linguistic Minority Research Institute.

Huerta, T. M. (2011). Humanizing pedagogy: Beliefs and practices on the teaching of Latino children. *Bilingual Research Journal, 34*(1), 38–57. https://doi.org/10.1080/15235882.2011.568826

Iannaccone, L. (1991). Micropolitics of education: What and why. *Education and Urban Society, 23*(4), 465–471. https://doi.org/10.1177/0013124591023004008

Kreighbaum, A. (2013, June 20). Rep. Beto O'Rourke requests investigation of all EPISD. *El Paso Times*. Retrieved from http://www.elpasotimes.com/ci_23494556/rep-beto-orourke-requests-investigation-all-episd-schools?source=most_viewed

Lindholm-Leary, K., & Block, N. (2010). Achievement in predominantly low SES/Hispanic dual language schools. *International Journal of Bilingual Education and Bilingualism, 13*(1), 43–60. https://doi.org/10.1080/13670050902777546

Malen, B. (1994). The micropolitics of education: Mapping the multiple dimensions of power relations in school polities. *Journal of Education Policy, 9*(5), 147–167. https://doi.org/10.1080/0268093940090513

Mawhinney, H. B. (1999). Reappraisal: The problems and prospects of studying the micropolitics of leadership in reforming schools. *School Leadership & Management, 19*(2), 159–170. https://doi.org/10.1080/13632439969168

McLaughlin, B. (2013). *Second language acquisition in childhood: Volume 2: School-age children*. New York, NY: Psychology Press.

Menken, K. (2010). NCLB and English language learners: Challenges and consequences. *Theory Into Practice, 49*(2), 121–128. https://doi.org/10.1080/00405841003626619

Menken, K., & Kleyn, T. (2010). The long-term impact of subtractive schooling in the educational experiences of secondary English language learners. *International Journal of Bilingual Education and Bilingualism, 13*(4), 399–417.

Miles, M. B., & Huberman, A. M. (1994). *Qualitative data analysis: An expanded sourcebook*. Thousand Oaks, CA: Sage.

National Center for Educational Statistics. (2015). *Fast facts: English learners and NAEP*. Washington, DC. Author. Retrieved from: http://www.ncela.us/files/fast_facts/OELA_FastFacts_ELsandNAEP.pdf

Reyes, R., III. (2016). In a world of disposable students: The humanizing elements of border pedagogy in teacher education. *The High School Journal, 99*(4), 337–350. https://doi.org/10.1353/hsj.2016.0013

Ryan, J. (2016). Strategic activism, educational leadership and social justice. *International Journal of Leadership in Education, 19*(1), 87–100. https://doi.org/10.1080/13603124.2015.1096077

Schachter, J., & Gass, S. M. (2013). *Second language classroom research: Issues and opportunities*. New York, NY: Routledge.

Theoharis, G. (2007). Social justice educational leaders and resistance: Toward a theory of social justice leadership. *Educational Administration Quarterly, 43*(2), 221–258. https://doi.org/10.1177/0013161X06293717

Valenzuela, A. (2010). *Subtractive schooling: US-Mexican youth and the politics of caring*. Albany, NY: SUNY Press.

Waters, T., Marzano, R. J., & McNulty, B. (2003). *Balanced leadership*. Denver, CO: Mid- continent Research for Education and Learning.

Weaver & Tidwell. (2013, April 1). *Final report on investigation into alleged cheating scandal at El Paso Independent School District*. Retrieved October 17, 2015, from https://filemgr.episd.org/wl/?id=v&filename=Weaver%20Report%2020130401.pdf

Wiemelt, J., & Welton, A. (2015). Challenging the dominant narrative: Critical bilingual leadership (liderazgo) for emergent bilingual Latin@ students. *International Journal of Multicultural Education, 17*(1), 82. https://doi.org/10.18251/ijme.v17i1.877

Wiley, T. G., & Wright, W. E. (2004). Against the undertow: Language-minority education policy and politics in the "age of accountability". *Educational Policy, 18*(1), 142–168. https://doi.org/10.1177/0895904803260030

Leading Dual Language: Twenty Years of Innovation in a Borderland Elementary School

Elena Izquierdo, David E. DeMatthews, Estefania Balderas, and Becca Gregory

Abstract This chapter presents a qualitative case study of authentic and social justice leadership of one exemplary bilingual principal working along the U.S.-Mexico border. The principal at the center of this study nurtured, inspired, and motivated teachers and families to create innovative and inclusive school programs to meet the needs of all students, especially Mexican American ELLs. Two micro-cases are presented to examine the principal's role in founding a gifted and talented dual language program for ELLs and a merger with a low-performing school. The study's key findings highlight how the principal developed strategic relationships to advocate for the needs of Latinx students and families. This chapter draws attention to areas where authentic and advocacy-oriented approaches to leadership can mitigate resistance from dominant groups. Implications for future research and principal preparation are discussed at the conclusion of the chapter.

Keywords Dual language education · English Language learner · Latinx students · Social justice leadership · Principal · School leadership

Increasing neoliberal economic models of schooling have influenced current policies that view students as human capital investments for a "new global economy." Such models displace humanistic and democratic educational ideals that have been a cornerstone of public education, but also fail at closing achievement gaps (Apple,

---

This chapter has been adapted from a previously published article with permission from publisher: DeMatthews, D. E. & Izquierdo, E. (2017). Authentic and social justice leadership: A case study of an exemplary principal. Journal of School Leadership, 27(3), 333–360.

E. Izquierdo (✉) · E. Balderas · B. Gregory
Department of Teacher Education, University of Texas at El Paso, El Paso, TX, USA
e-mail: ielena@utep.edu; rebalderas@utep.edu

D. E. DeMatthews
Department of Educational Leadership and Policy, University of Texas at Austin, Austin, TX, USA
e-mail: ddematthews@austin.utexas.edu

© The Author(s) 2019
D. E. DeMatthews, E. Izquierdo (eds.), *Dual Language Education: Teaching and Leading in Two Languages*, Language Policy 18,
https://doi.org/10.1007/978-3-030-10831-1_11

2014; Carpenter, Diem & Young, 2014; Lipman, 2013). Nonetheless, these models place principals under intense pressure to lead to tests created by multinational corporations. In their efforts to lead, principals may consider themselves effective because they set expectations, provide adequate support, ensure compliance with bureaucratic mandates, and give subordinates autonomy when they meet expectations, but do not challenge the status quo (English, 1992; Pinton, 2015). These principals foster short-term incremental gains on standardized tests by helping to create well-trained student test takers, but fail to address longstanding injustices (exclusion of English language learners and students with disabilities, disproportionate suspension and dropout rates, among others) (Artiles, 2011; Valenzuela, 2010).

Authentic leadership and social justice leadership are useful constructs for examining leadership that extends beyond a narrow focus on testing and achievement gaps by recognizing and addressing other critical needs within schools and communities. Authentic leadership implies "a genuine kind of leadership—a hopeful, open-ended, visionary and creative response to social circumstances" (Begley, 2006, p. 570), while social justice leadership has become widely recognized as a powerful intervening force in creating inclusive, high-performing, and equitable schools where all students thrive socially, emotionally, and academically (Furman, 2012; Shields, 2010).

This chapter presents a qualitative case study that examines the leadership styles and actions one principal adopted to create a more inclusive and socially just school along the U.S.-Mexico border, especially for Mexican and Mexican American students classified as English language learners (ELLs). It also examines how this principal navigated a district stymied by a legacy of unjust policies and student marginalization, such as the segregation of ELLs in subtractive transitional English immersion models. And more recently, a district-wide cheating scandal that led to the "disappearance" of hundreds of Mexican and Mexican American ELLs dissuaded to leave school, forced to drop out, or inappropriately promoted or demoted to avoid testing. We believe a case study approach in this unfortunate educational context is rich for exploring how situations and events at a given time influence authentic and socially just leadership.

To begin, we briefly describe the impact of neoliberalism and its relationship to persistence educational injustices to provide a justification for merging authentic and social justice leadership. Then, we explore the nature and practices of authentic and social justice leadership. Following a description of our qualitative case study approach and selection criteria for the principal, we examine two micro-cases—one historical case focusing on the school's adoption of dual language and one recent case involving the school's merger with a low-performing school—to highlight the role of the principal and her evolving experiences and practices. Next, we present additional findings related to key leadership practices. We conclude with a call for research to explore the intersection of authentic and social justice leadership as well as implications for leadership preparation.

1 Setting the Stage

Cynicism has become an emerging theme in organizational life (Dean, Brandes, & Dharwadkar, 1998), especially in public schools where deficit views of educators are increasingly common and high-stakes accountability validates scientific management logics and the use of incentives and disincentives. Lipman (2013) argued that neoliberal educational policies have shaped an ideologically driven process where schools, "particularly 'low-performing' schools in communities of color, are saturated with a culture of competition and top-down accountability and disciplined by high stakes testing, the threat of being closed, and performance management practices" (p. 149). Fabricant and Fine (2015) contend that urban public schools are "underfinanced and pedagogically constrained, providing evermore degraded learning environments that lead students to early decisions of exit and dead-end jobs" (p. 24). Such policy constraints solidify inequities, produce negative unintended consequences (e.g., trust erosion, teaching to the test), and distract principals from addressing civic, humanistic, and social purposes of school (Anderson, 2009; Carpenter et al., 2014; Pinton, 2015). Pressures and demographic shifts of greater ethnic diversity have complicated school leadership, muddied the waters for identifying the best way to improve schools, and "tempt [principals] to veer towards inauthenticity" (Duignan, 2014, p. 158).

2 Authentic Leadership

In recent years, scholars have advanced numerous definitions of authentic leadership (see Gardner, Cogliser, Davis, & Dickens, 2011). Kernis and Goldman (2006) concluded on five central themes: (a) self-understanding and the ability to tolerate ambiguity, perceive events accurately, and not defensively distort undesirable aspects of self; (b) living fully in the moment, which entails being adaptive, flexible, and recognizing one is not a static entity; (c) trust of inner experiences to guide behaviors; (d) freedom and, despite circumstances, one has a stance that a choice exists; and (e) creative approaches toward living fueled by a strong trust in one's self, a willingness to adapt, and a refusal to fall back on restrictive behaviors or models of thinking. Authentic leadership approaches help to achieve positive organizational outcomes, which include increased follower and organizational self-esteem, friendliness, and performance (Grandey, Fiske, Mattila, Jansen, & Sideman, 2005).

Definitions of authentic leadership emphasize leaders' moral perspective guided by self-knowledge (Avolio et al., 2004; Gardner et al., 2011; Walumbwa, Avolio, Gardner, Wernsing, & Peterson, 2008). Ilies, Morgeson, and Nahrgang (2005) defined authentic leaders as those "deeply aware of their values and beliefs, they are self-confident, genuine, reliable and trustworthy, and they focus on building followers' strengths, broadening their thinking and creating a positive and engaging organizational context" (p. 374). Authentic leaders communicate intentionality, hope, optimism, and resiliency to leverage action (Avolio et al., 2004). Actions are purposeful, rooted in the creation of lasting relationships, and motivational to encourage professional growth and increased levels of performance. When challenges arise, authentic leaders engage in a "pattern of leader behavior that draws upon and promotes both positive psychological capacities and positive ethical climate" (Walumbwa et al., 2008, p. 94). This pattern consists of ongoing messaging of trust, genuineness, and self-confidence.

Authentic leadership is broadly associated with being "true to self" and acting in accordance to one's own beliefs. Authentic leaders have a well-developed self-concept, are clear about their values and convictions, have developed goals, and act in ways that are concordant with their self-concept (Shamir & Eilam, 2005). George (2000) argued authentic leaders desire to serve others and empower "people they lead to make a difference.... They are guided by qualities of the heart, by passion and compassion, as they are by qualities of the mind" (p. 12). Their desire to serve others guides them to address social injustices, build relationships that are aligned to democracy and inclusiveness, and empower marginalized communities. Moreover, authentic leadership encompasses a reflection on background, culture, context, and relationships with stakeholders (Begley, 2006; Wilson, 2014).

Authenticity has also been described as "relational in the sense of being culturally embedded and in representing shared values" (Wilson, 2014, p. 484). Authenticity must be socially constructed through ongoing interactions (Begley & Stefkovich, 2007; Woods, 2007). Authentic leaders have a concern for a balanced and fulfilled identity, maintain a degree of inner distance that allows them to maintain ethical values in the midst of immense pressures, recognize the importance of democratic engagement, build new connections and commitments to larger social goals, and recognize the way bureaucracies create rationalized boundaries that impact their identity, leadership, and taken for-granted assumptions about their students and school improvement processes (Woods, 2007).

Challenging school contexts, school district politics, and neoliberal education policies promoting distrust between teachers and administrators can complicate authenticity, create a cynical status quo, and produce ethical dilemmas that can impact individual and social constructions of authenticity (Cranston, Ehrich, & Kimber, 2006; Poliner Shapiro & Hassinger, 2007). Badaracco and Ellsworth (1989) argued authentic leaders find coherence in such contexts by reconciling their values and biases (general ways of thinking and predispositions) to guide decision making.

3 Authentic and Socially Just Leadership

Both authentic and social justice leaders recognize and embrace the complicated school-community context and respond by drawing from a sense of moral purpose to generate connections and foster positive cultures that inspire collective responsibility and action (DeMatthews, 2015; Theoharis, 2007; Wilson, 2014). Anderson (2009) suggested a multilevel approach to leadership authenticity that emphasized: (a) individual authenticity: living life in congruence to one's personal and professional values; (b) organizational authenticity: viewing human beings as ends rather than means; and (c) societal authenticity: finding congruence between society's cherished ideals and how individuals live out these ideals. Educational inequities can remain unchallenged when leaders have individual authenticity, but fail to deeply consider organizational and societal issues that shape schools, faculty, families, and students.

Social justice leadership enhances authentic leadership by emphasizing critical reflection and prioritizing democratic and inclusive leadership actions (Bogotch, 2002; DeMatthews & Mawhinney, 2014; DeMatthews, 2016a, 2016b; Furman, 2012; Horsford & Clark, 2015; Larson & Murtadha, 2002). From a social justice perspective, authenticity is not only about acting in accordance to a static set of personal and professional values or balancing individual, organizational, and societal authenticity, but identifying, understanding, and addressing injustices associated with racism, poverty, and segregation that are both persistent and evolving in schools and society. Theoharis (2007) defined social justice leadership in regard to how principals make issue of "race, class, gender, disability, sexual orientation, and other historically and currently marginalizing conditions" (p. 223). Dantley and Tillman (2010) described a social justice leader as one who "investigates and poses solutions for issues that generate and reproduce societal inequities" (p. 19). These leaders are problem-posing, "they find time to read widely, and have a well-developed social analysis… They are learners … constantly pushing their comfort zones. They create learning in their schools" (Anderson 2009, p. 14).

An emerging set of practices associated with social justice leadership is community-, district-, and school-oriented advocacy (DeMatthews, 2018; Furman, 2012; Khalifa, 2012; Watson & Bogotch, 2015). Ryan (2016) argued that given the persistence and potential resistance to addressing injustice, social justice leaders must be strategic and consider any likely opposition and how opposition will play out prior to taking action. Strategic action may be necessary because principals: (a) are subject to an ethical commitment to uphold federal, state, and district policies that produce or maintain injustice; (b) confront bureaucracies that slow innovation or yield misaligned policies; and (c) recognize how particular forms of justice work might be objectionable to powerful colleagues, violate cultural values, or be pitted against traditional community values about what is best for children (Berkovich, 2014; Capper & Young, 2014; Eyal, Berkovich, & Schwartz, 2011; Theoharis, 2007).

A vision focused on equitable schools, communities, and society is central to connecting authentic and social justice leadership, "because vision transcends political interests, testing the outer limits of the vested views that lock people into parochial perspectives, limit creativity, and prevent the emergence of new cultural and political realities" (Terry, 1993, p. 38).

4 Methodology

A qualitative case study methodology was used to examine the leadership actions of one principal. The case study took place between May 2014 and September 2015 and utilized in-depth interviews, observations, and document collection (Stake, 2010). At the center of this study is a bilingual female principal (Mrs. Lee) in a large urban school district. We sought to identify a principal with experience addressing multiple injustices within a school, at least 5 years of leadership experience, evidence of academic success and improvement, and evidence of creating a more inclusive school in regard to classroom diversity and parent engagement.

4.1 Data Collection and Analysis

Interviews and observational data were the primary data sources used to explore Mrs. Lee's leadership. District- and school-level documents were collected to provide additional information and verify principal interviews. All interviews were semi-structured and derived from our literature review to elicit information about the principal's values, authenticity, and actions. The principal was interviewed multiple times over the course of the school year. District administrators, an assistant principal, social workers, a librarian, ten current teachers, and two former teachers were also interviewed. Parents identified by the principal and teachers were interviewed to provide a parent perspective. Observations occurred in a variety of settings throughout the school year in order to collect data from different spaces. Observations lasted between 120 min and 180 min. Field notes were collected on how the principal engaged stakeholders and whether or not her actions and statements were reflective of one-on-one interviews.

4.2 Setting

Reveles ES is part of Border City Independent School District (BCISD) and located in a large urban area along the Texas/U.S.-Mexico border.[1] The district is large, urban, and serves a predominately Mexican American community. BCISD has a high student mobility rate and received a large influx of Mexican nationals after a significant increase in violence in Mexico. Superintendent turnover contributed to constant reform in the district while family and community trust was significantly harmed due to a cheating scandal. In 2014, with ongoing investigations pending, the new superintendent and school board determined to implement a citywide dual language program for all ELLs. Reveles ES is located approximately 3 miles from the

---

[1] All names used in this chapter are pseudonyms.

U.S.-Mexico border and enrolls 900 students in pre-K through fifth grade. The student population is mainly Hispanic (85% Hispanic, 12% White, 3% African American, Asian, and American Indian, 6% students with disabilities). Approximately 33% of students are ELLs, 49% are economically disadvantaged, and 54% meet the state's criteria for being considered "at-risk." In 2013, after the Texas Education Agency (TEA) distinguished Reveles ES for its excellence in the areas of Reading and English Language Arts, postsecondary readiness, and closing academic performance gaps, the school became a model school for the district, frequently hosting educational leaders from around the state, region, and nation.

5 Findings

The section begins with a description of Mrs. Lee and her beliefs about school leadership and social justice. Next, two micro-cases are presented to more closely understand Mrs. Lee's leadership actions establishing an innovative gifted and talented (GT) dual language program for ELLs and a school merger. Then, we present findings that reflect how Mrs. Lee's actions and values were reflective of authentic and social justice leadership.

6 Mrs. Lee

Mrs. Lee is a veteran principal with 17 years of leadership experience. Teachers, staff, and parents described her using many terms associated with authenticity and authentic leadership, such as "active," "passionate," engaging," "caring," "inspirational," "refreshing, "so real" and "down-to-earth." A former assistant principal from Reveles ES said, "She's action, she acts … she looks at the big picture, sees all the various components, thinks ahead, never makes a snap decision, thinks about everything carefully, thinks about teachers, students, parents. Very politically astute, very." A district administrator noted that Mrs. Lee was: "A team player, but also a leader with a vision and an agenda who knows how to get things done." Another community member added that Mrs. Lee is a "Savvy principal who is important to her community and to the city." Descriptions of Mrs. Lee's approach and leadership style suggest she is a confident, values-driven leader who is transparent, relationship-oriented, and capable of sending strong messages that affect her followers.

Prior to becoming the principal at Reveles ES, Mrs. Lee described how she developed a sense of awareness to injustice in schools and communities:

> I started my career in Southside schools and I saw firsthand how students were treated. Teachers would say, 'oh, don't worry about this one or that one' because they were ELL's [English language learners]. When you see that, and you see how students are isolated or sent to the back of classrooms because of the language they speak, I was angry …. As a teacher and assistant principal, I worked to make sure those students found success. We

worked with families and saw firsthand how those students could be successful and thrive ..... So I don't believe that you can just be idle or not push for change ..... We still need change.

Her early formative experiences formed a personal awareness of the deficit thinking effects on marginalized students. With the help of teachers and colleagues, Mrs. Lee recognized how Mexican and Mexican American ELLs were marginalized. She recalled how ELLs were segregated in separate classrooms or moved to the back of the classrooms, and also how curriculum did not reflect their culture and lived experiences. She said, "They were basically set up to fail, even besides the fact that teachers might hold a deficit view because, if they are in English immersion or in the back of a class and aren't getting supports they won't be successful." She added, "The curriculum must embrace student strengths, speaking Spanish is an asset, being from another culture is an asset. Diversity is an asset."

Mrs. Lee recognized a need to be transparent about her values and communicate her beliefs in ways that empowered teachers and community. Observations revealed the ways Mrs. Lee could refocus faculty around justice issues by encouraging teacher leadership and dialogue, and by avoiding opportunities to step in and fix problems. Her style was not to take control over conversations or evoke a top-down approach. We frequently observed her share an idea or question during professional learning communities (PLCs) or public forums and step back and let others engage in discussion.

A core component of Mrs. Lee's leadership was related to building relationships. We observed her in community meetings, school board meetings, and on bus duty each morning and afternoon talking with students and families. She cultivated relationships with the mayor, district leaders, neighbors of the school, families, and university faculty and administration. She noted, "It is important to be visible as a leader and for faculty to see that you are there for them." Mrs. Lee understood relationships and trust built motivation to increase organizational performance. She said:

> You can't just tell people what to do, how to do it, and expect perfect results. Teaching is a craft and it takes time to master that craft.... There is so much to learn and learning never stops. I'm still learning.... As a leader you have to trust your teachers. I trust they will do what's best for kids.

Teachers recognized the value of Mrs. Lee's trust and felt compelled to provide the best possible learning environment for students. For example, the school librarian said, "She just believes in us so much, we are forced to believe in ourselves. With all the things going on now in education, all the stress, she's so refreshing."

Parents also recognized Mrs. Lee's visibility and emphasis on relationships. A community leader said, "She's not just a principal at Reveles. She's a leader. If she says something, people listen. Her voice is important." A parent highlighted how Mrs. Lee's personality and leadership approach fostered trust and followership: "She listens to us. She always makes time for us, no matter how late. She views us like a partner." We consistently observed Mrs. Lee inviting community members into the school to participate in programs and activities. She was also observed being open and transparent about her school's ongoing struggles with acquiring resources and supporting families while offering support to other schools in need of assistance.

7 Micro-Case 1: Development and Maintenance of Dual Language Programs

In 1998, a fourth grade teacher asked Mrs. Lee if she could teach a GT section/class using a dual language approach. Mrs. Lee and the teacher talked to the district. BCISD denied the initial request but later agreed after additional requests to pilot a dual language GT program in early grades. Mrs. Lee recognized she did not know where to begin so she created an interdisciplinary team of teachers and parents to study dual language, develop a program and teaching materials, and prepare for the following school year. The group engaged in a yearlong study and found little evidence of GT dual language programs elsewhere. Mrs. Lee and the group were astounded to see that ELLs across the nation were not allowed into GT programs because of their language. While teachers began to develop curricula, identify curricular resources, and map out the two-way 50–50 dual language model, Mrs. Lee worked with the school district to identify native Spanish speaking ELLs who were eligible for GT based on the state's requirements. Reveles ES identified and enrolled 13 first graders, 16 second graders, and 16 third graders. Two years later, Mrs. Lee gathered student achievement data and petitioned the district to remove the program's pilot status and expand to all grades. Mrs. Lee stated, "We knew they could not say no to us because we had the data." The district agreed.

Soon after, parents and teachers asked Mrs. Lee to develop a general education dual language model. She reflected on the request, saying: "What about our kids who don't qualify for GT, because of a test? We believed in dual, so we wanted to bring it to all our kids." Mrs. Lee critiqued the state and district's policy of using a single assessment for eligibility in GT. She re-established a team of parents and teachers to develop the second dual language program that would address issues of diversity where all students would be eligible. More importantly, ELLs would no longer participate in the district's English immersion model she viewed as "subtractive" and "outdated." Mrs. Lee continued to fight to allow students who did not pass the state's GT exam into the program based on an independent evaluation by the school. Since she was unsuccessful repeatedly, the school developed a second dual language model, had all teachers trained in GT, and created an open admission policy for dual language. Reveles ES received numerous accolades as a result of both programs. The school's enrollment nearly doubled in 10 years. District administrators and community members attributed additional enrollment to the success of dual language. A parent said, "Families move here just to go to Reveles ES. They want into dual." Reveles ES would receive grants and funding from the prestigious Jacob V. Javits Gifted and Talented Students Education Program, the Ford Foundation, and other national, state, and regional organizations.

District administrators, teachers, and parents attributed the program's success to Mrs. Lee's leadership. Below are two representative quotes noting Mrs. Lee's role:

- "It's her vision, it's her hard work, it's her example we all follow."
- "Doing dual right is so difficult and time consuming and exhausting. Sometimes I ask myself, why did I sign up for this? But when Mrs. Lee talks, I am inspired. She motivates us…. She hired me. I don't want to let her down. I want to meet her expectations, which are endless by the way."

Mrs. Lee took little credit stating, "It wasn't my idea." She did, however, believe in the program and its alignment to address an important equity issue. She reflected on injustices she identified throughout her career: "I knew I had GT students there [who were ELLs], but they weren't labeled GT…. I thought to myself, some of these students are so bright…. This was an opportunity for them." When asked to describe her leadership role, she was humbled and claimed to play only a support role. She said: "I bartered, scrapped money together for the redesign of classrooms, materials, training for teachers and parents…. It hasn't stopped to this day, we still don't get all the things we need and we still tweak the recipe as needed."

8 Micro-Case 2: Merger with Low Performing School

The closing of several BCISD schools was suggested in 2014 after district consultants identified under-enrolled schools. The nearby Rio ES enrolled about 260 students although the total capacity was 700. Mrs. Lee recognized the opportunity to merge with Rio and to develop an early childhood center that would benefit both communities. She advocated for the merger with receptive district leaders. The chief academic officer also thought a merger would be an opportunity to expand access to a high-quality school to the Rio community. She said publicly: "Rio gives the District a unique opportunity to expand on a very popular and effective program like Reveles ES's dual language offerings while at the same time giving an underutilized facility a chance to remain a vital component of the community it serves." Rio ES parents were cautious about the proposed changes, but many recognized the opportunity to merge with a high-performing and innovative school. However, some Reveles ES parents and community members were angered.

Community meetings brought a variety of parent concerns, including local property values, transportation, and transparency. Mrs. Lee believed most parents' negative perspectives were tied to fear, self-interest, and prejudice. Student demographics at Rio ES (98% Hispanic, 92% economically disadvantaged, and 66% English language learners) were very different from Reveles ES. Rio students did not perform well on the Texas STAAR exam and were less likely to be on grade level. Rio was also closer to the border and had students commuting from Ciudad Juárez, Mexico. Reveles ES's parents raised concerns and spoke about the greater expense (buying homes in the Reveles area) to gain access to the school. Mrs. Lee recognized a need to challenge deficit perspectives and engaged key community stakeholders. During community town hall meetings, Mrs. Lee facilitated discussions, answered parent questions, and addressed concerns. Community meetings were often heated and contentious. Some Rio ES parents wanted to know if the merger would allow their favorite teachers to be retained. Some community members wondered how Mrs. Lee could manage the merger across two campuses. A local principal said: "Merging with a least effective language model, low expectations, inheriting faculty with a negative paradigm, that's a challenge.... They are low performing because of school quality, poor parent involvement.... This is risky." Mrs. Lee framed the merger as an opportunity:

> This is a way of bringing two communities together, sharing resources, and bringing what Reveles has to more students.... That's what people want, we are too crowded. This allows us to serve more students.... It's a win-win .... The naysayers, some have valid reasons, but a lot of the pushback is from parents who don't want to send their kids to Rio.

She added that some parents from her own school shared racist and deficit views of students. In response to those parents she said, "I think most of them will see how wrong they were, but if they can't, oh well. What's right is right.... If it's good enough for your kids, it should be good enough for everybody's." The merger highlights Mrs. Lee's willingness to take risks and the ways her values about dual language and success for all drive her leadership.

9 Merging Authentic and Social Justice Leadership

9.1 Framing Injustices as Possibilities

Mrs. Lee was able to frame injustices in ways that motivated teachers and families to work harder and develop more innovative programs. For example, Mrs. Lee focused teachers and parents on how to support struggling students, ELLs, or Spanish language learners, embracing more culturally relevant teaching practices, developing cross-curricular efforts or schoolwide initiatives to close achievement gaps, and adopting additional languages to the school's dual language program to make students more competitive for postsecondary opportunities (Mandarin Chinese). We observed her communicating passion, optimism, and a deep belief that the school community could "figure it out." Although teachers reported being physically and mentally tired from high expectations and workload, they appeared engaged, energetic, and working well beyond normal business hours. Mrs. Lee framed for teachers how their sacrifices were making a difference. She said, "To close gaps and make sure all of our kids are successful, it's hard work.... We have a lot of resources here and we've been at this for a while, and we still struggle but it's all worth it." These comments highlight how Mrs. Lee was able to continually improve school capacity.

Mrs. Lee conveyed a sense of urgency. From her perspective, leadership was about outlining perplexing issues so stakeholders could be aware, investigate problems, develop solutions, and act. Teachers adopted similar approaches, one teacher said to a group of teachers during a summer planning meeting, "Okay, so let's dig in deep and see how we can make next year better than the last." Later, this teacher would describe how Mrs. Lee kept her focused and motivated year round: "Sometimes, we can forget why we are here, especially when you are working hard. She can really refocus us on our students." Another teacher added that Reveles ES had a "culture where other teachers can put things back in perspective.... Everybody chips in, everybody sees all kids in the school as their own." These comments describe a culture of encouragement where teachers continually challenge themselves and each other to address student needs despite barriers or past failures.

Mrs. Lee's understanding of complex issues with the school and community allowed her both to recognize how change can make people feel uncomfortable and to frame her ideas and reforms in ways teachers would support: "When you try to make change, early on especially, you are going to have pushback." Mrs. Lee acted strategically to facilitate change. First, she believed transparency helped to build trust and she encouraged and welcomed a range of stakeholders to be involved. She also understood that sharing and dialogue "supports learning across the school." We observed numerous meetings where groups of faculty and/or stakeholders were invited and had opportunities to share their beliefs.

Second, Mrs. Lee encouraged teacher leadership and promoted collaborative inquiry. Mrs. Lee explained, "We need to do our homework, see what other people are doing and what we can learn from.... We also need to learn more about how we can improve ourselves." Sharing concerns and ideas was an important first step, but leaders needed to "problem-pose" to guide inquiry and identify solutions or new plans of action. A veteran teacher described the development of the GT dual language model:

> So, it [dual language] started with just one or two teachers who had an idea to do GT dual. They talked to Mrs. Lee and she said let's try to figure it out.... but the district said "no," in terms of support. Mrs. Lee didn't stop there. They started a team of parents and teachers, figured out some logistical issues, and tried again. Eventually, the district supported the model.... Now look at it.

This collaborative effort would eventually culminate in a nationally recognized GT dual language model. Consequently, Mrs. Lee would frame Reveles ES as an "innovative school" that knows how to "collaborate, solve problems, and find ways to get things done."

Finally, Mrs. Lee encouraged teacher inquiry and creativity, especially with unidentifiable solutions. For example, dual language teachers frequently shared how hard it was to find quality-teaching materials in English and Spanish. Mrs. Lee understood the challenge through talking to teachers and doing her own investigations. She encouraged a collaborative approach to creating materials together, sharing teaching strategies, and engaging in peer feedback. A fifth grade teacher added, "We are ready to get around challenges. She prepares us for that." Teachers shared that she was honest about being unable to fix particular problems. Her honesty resonated with teachers and fostered a culture that viewed problems as solvable through inquiry and collaborative effort.

9.2 Advocacy

Mrs. Lee advocated for social justice within her school, community, district, and state. She understood the principal's role as an advocate, but shared that her advocacy had been an evolving process. She said:

> My experience as a principal in the district has a lot to do with my ability to advocate for students and families....I've been here 17 years and I use the respect I have in the community as a way to advocate for the things I think are right.... And you know, when something isn't right or something isn't fair, I'm not just going to sit back. I'm going to speak my mind.

She recognized that sometimes the general public or policymakers could be unreasonable and that advocacy was required, but she thought a less experienced principal could not be as publicly opinioned or effective as an advocate. She responded:

> Part of being a good principal is understanding who the players are, building coalitions with parents or other principals, and being strategic about how you advocate. Just because you are right, doesn't mean people will agree with you.... The longer you work some place, the more you know people and build relationships. You start to understand who the key players are. I think young principals don't always get that.

Mrs. Lee's advocacy could be described as strategic, thoughtful, and understanding of complex situations. She found alliances and partnerships to deliver her message when situations were heated or controversial, just as they were with the merger of Reveles and Rio. She noted, "Finding the right people to deliver your message is important.... Not all problems can be solved head on. A good principal knows the people they can use to advocate for you." In other situations, she also noted that principals needed to be persistent, clear, and engaging parents and teachers to impact policy and practice. Mrs. Lee's comments highlighted how advocating for social justice may require a recognition of power dynamics and situations that do not favor strong principal leadership, but leadership from other stakeholders outside of the school or district. Thus, advocacy can also be about "planting the seed" in others (Ryan, 2016).

At the school level, Mrs. Lee used advocacy as a way of shaping school culture around the needs of students and families. She said, "I try to keep everyone focused on what's best for students and their families, but still being attentive to the teachers' needs and feelings." In PLCs, she would ask teachers to think deeply about the challenges of students and how the school can support families. One such issue was related to some families struggling with the dual language program because they could not help children with homework or provide extra support because they were not proficient in English or Spanish. Mrs. Lee helped them reframe and remember that "in order for students to succeed, parents needed to be supported too." Her framing of issues helped teachers problem solve and led to greater parent engagement, summer enrichment programs, after-school programs, and a "parent-partners" initiative (pairing of families from different language backgrounds). Mrs. Lee also knew, "The more you bring parents in and support them, the more they will do to support the school and the bilingualism and biculturalism."

Externally, Mrs. Lee served on the district's innovation task force, met with district leaders to discuss improvements and training ideas after the district's 2014 adoption of dual language for all ELLs, and was a mentor principal for new and area principals implementing dual language. She shared how she previously partnered with the BCISD superintendent, a local university professor, and the former mayor to advocate for changes to teacher certification requirements that would make dual language easier to implement across the state. She noted, "When you have a community that is engaged, it's a lot easier to make change.... It's not just about benefiting our kids here."

She also advocated across her district for principals and teachers. She shared with school board members the training needs for teachers and school leaders implementing dual language. We observed her posing questions, gathering information, and sharing information in ways that increased key leaders' understanding and action. She understood policymakers and leaders needed to witness success firsthand. Thus, provided key stakeholders with access to Reveles ES to see the benefits of dual language in action. She spoke publicly at school board meetings, and she co-presented at conferences with teachers.

10 Discussion

Mrs. Lee's leadership represented key aspects of authenticity, including her ability to increase the school's organizational outcomes, build teacher and parent followership, and develop confident teacher leaders working well beyond regular business hours to improve curricula and instruction. She revealed her "true self" to teachers, evidenced by comments about her being "so real" and "down-to-earth." These findings align with existing research describing how authenticity creates "meaningfulness of employees' lives" (Ilies et al., 2005, p. 374). Teachers emphasized that Mrs. Lee built strong relationships through encouragement and validation and described how her social justice orientation inspired faculty to work harder and toward social justice ends (e.g., closing achievement gaps, adopting cultural relevant teaching practices, engaging parents). Parents verified how she built meaningful relationships with the community and fostered a positive and welcoming school environment that she would tap as a source of knowledge and advocacy when needed. Clearly, Mrs. Lee was able to motivate others through her charisma and communication skills. High levels of achievement, closing achievement gaps, and effective dual language models are evidence of how authentic leadership practices can help to address the typical barriers to change and innovation in urban schools, including teacher cynicism, problematic accountability policies, and teacher burnout.

Mrs. Lee's leadership also represented key aspects of social justice leadership substantiated by observations of her ability to problem-pose educational injustices, advocate for district and state policies that support social justice causes, and mold school culture that emphasizes equitable access to innovative and culturally relevant programs (Furman, 2012). Yet, her ability to build meaningful relationships was not only about authenticity and authentic relationships. Mrs. Lee understood how relationships enabled the Reveles community to collectively identify, understand, and address racism, poverty, and segregation. Mrs. Lee extended the use of relationships for social justice purposes via parent advocacy. As the school's dual language models produced significantly improved academic outcomes, more parents wanted access to Reveles ES classrooms. Many savvy and so-called "effective" principals use their political capital to protect their schools and garner additional resources. Mrs. Lee actively sought a merger with a struggling school along the U.S.-Mexico border.

We can only speculate the rarity of a principal of a high-performing school advocating for a merger with a low-performing school serving a high proportion of students in poverty performing below grade level. Her willingness to take risks in the Texas accountability context further highlights her social justice orientation, especially when considering some parents who strongly disagreed with the merger. The merger serves as an example of how leading for social justice can be unsafe due to community resistance, which can problematize authentic leadership as being true to self or community. Mrs. Lee's individual convictions about what was socially just for students at Rio ES superseded a portion of her school community's wishes about the merger. She was able to safely engage in social justice leadership by deploying certain Reveles ES's parent-advocates, including white families from upper-middle-class homes that provided her with political cover. Her ingenious strategy represents a new arena for principal–parent engagement, a shift away from hegemonic patterns of top-down school–community relations (Abrams & Gibbs, 2002), and further highlighted Mrs. Lee's skill in building relationships and fostering a common vision. This finding is in line with previous research that suggests how under certain political conditions principals must be less forthright and more deceptive (Ryan, 2016).

Dual language emerged from Mrs. Lee's support of teachers seeking to improve access for ELLs and developed by a school–community partnership focused on ongoing improvement. At Reveles ES, school improvement consisted of organized teachers and families collaborating, inquiring, and developing a dual language curriculum for GT students, then a dual language curriculum for all students, and ultimately the ongoing refinement of culturally relevant teaching practices. This finding is aligned to previous research stressing how leaders must develop critical spaces for teacher reflection and professional growth for social justice pedagogy to take root. As Kose (2007) powerfully stated, principals should help teachers "continuously examine whether student learning is equitable for all student groups ... [and] foster a supportive, learning school culture that welcomes, affirms, and learns from student and community diversity" (p. 279). Mrs. Lee engaged in such work by facilitating discussions, posing critical questions, and providing teachers with motivation and opportunities to engage.

11 Conclusion

Mrs. Lee is an example of a principal who has refined her ability to effectively communicate enthusiasm and passion for social justice issues. She is also capable of navigating the politics of social justice reforms within a community and district. Her long-term commitment to the school community provided political capital to take risks, challenge the status quo, and support the district in advocacy at the state level. She also listened to others, engaged in collective inquiry, and remained reflective and transparent about her practice and shortcomings. Principals and assistant principals should understand that building community relationships and understanding how to navigate district and community politics takes time and ongoing effort. They must recruit teachers, parents, and leaders with experience working within communities to access parent networks for the purpose of advocacy and school improvement.

Principal preparation programs need to expose students to topics related to dual language education, authentic and social justice leadership practices, and the nuances of how effective principals lead and advocate within districts and communities. Programs should consider assigning students to observe and be mentored by veteran principals with authentic and social justice leadership characteristics so that students will have the opportunity to see the power of school–community partnerships, social justice pedagogy, and leadership techniques that inspire teachers and community to act on behalf of marginalized students.

References

Abrams, L. S., & Gibbs, J. T. (2002). Disrupting the logic of home-school relations parent involvement strategies and practices of inclusion and exclusion. *Urban Education, 37*(3), 384–407.

Anderson, G. L. (2009). *Advocacy leadership: Toward a post-reform agenda in education.* New York, NY: Routledge.

Apple, M. W. (2014). *Official knowledge: Democratic education in a conservative age.* New York, NY: Routledge.

Artiles, A. J. (2011). Toward an interdisciplinary understanding of educational equity and difference: The case of the racialization of ability. *Educational Researcher, 40*(9), 431–445.

Avolio, B. J., Gardner, W. L., Walumbwa, F. O., Luthans, F., & May, D. R. (2004). Unlocking the mask: A look at the process by which authentic leaders impact follower attitudes and behaviors. *Leadership Quarterly, 15*(6), 801–823.

Badaracco, J., & Ellsworth, R. R. (1989). *Leadership and the quest for integrity.* Boston, MA: Harvard Business Press.

Begley, P. T. (2006). Self-knowledge, capacity and sensitivity: Prerequisites to authentic leadership by school principals. *Journal of Educational Administration, 44*(6), 570–589.

Begley, P. T., & Stefkovich, J. (2007). Integrating values and ethics into post secondary teaching for leadership development: Principles, concepts, and strategies. *Journal of Educational Administration, 45*(4), 398–412.

Berkovich, I. (2014). A socio-ecological framework of social justice leadership in education. *Journal of Educational Administration, 52*(3), 282–309.

Bogotch, I. (2002). Educational leadership and social justice: Practice into theory. *Journal of School Leadership, 12,* 138–156.

Capper, C. A., & Young, M. D. (2014). Ironies and limitations of educational leadership for social justice: A call to social justice educators. *Theory Into Practice, 53*(2), 158–164.

Carpenter, B. W., Diem, S., & Young, M. D. (2014). The influence of values and policy vocabularies on understandings of leadership effectiveness. *International Journal of Qualitative Studies in Education, 27*(9), 1110–1133.

Cranston, N., Ehrich, L. C., & Kimber, M. (2006). Ethical dilemmas: the "bread and butter" of educational leaders' lives. *Journal of Educational Administration, 44*(2), 106–121.

Dantley, M. E., & Tillman, L. C. (2010). Social justice and moral transformative leadership. In C. Marshall & M. Oliva (Eds.), *Leadership for social justice* (2nd ed., pp. 19–34). Boston, MA: Allyn & Bacon.

Dean, J. W., Brandes, P., & Dharwadkar, R. (1998). Organizational cynicism. *Academy of Management Review, 23*(2), 341–352.

DeMatthews, D. E. (2015). Making sense of social justice leadership. A case study of a principal's experiences to create a more inclusive school. *Leadership and Policy in Schools, 14*(2), 139–166.

DeMatthews, D. E. (2016a). Competing priorities and challenges: Principal leadership for social justice along the US-Mexico border. *Teachers College Record, 118*(11).

DeMatthews, D. E. (2016b). Social justice dilemmas: Evidence on the successes and shortcomings of three principals trying to make a difference. *International Journal of Leadership in Education.* https://doi.org/10.1080/13603124.2016.1206972

DeMatthews, D. E. (2018). *Community engaged leadership for social justice.* New York, NY: Routledge.

DeMatthews, D. E., & Mawhinney, H. B. (2014). Social justice and inclusion: Exploring challenges in an urban district struggling to address inequities. *Educational Administration Quarterly, 50*(5), 844–881.

Duignan, P. (2014). Authenticity in educational leadership: History, ideal, reality. *Journal of Educational Administration, 52*(2), 152–172.

English, F. W. (1992). The principal and the prince: Machiavelli and school leadership. *NASSP Bulletin, 76*(10), 10–15.

Eyal, O., Berkovich, I., & Schwartz, T. (2011). Making the right choices: Ethical judgments among educational leaders. *Journal of Educational Administration, 49*(4), 396–413.

Fabricant, M., & Fine, M. (2015). *Changing politics of education: Privitization and the dispossessed lives left behind.* New York, NY: Routledge.

Furman, G. (2012). Social justice leadership as praxis: Developing capacities through preparation programs. *Educational Administration Quarterly, 48,* 191–229.

Gardner, W. L., Cogliser, C. C., Davis, K. M., & Dickens, M. P. (2011). Authentic leadership: A review of the literature and research agenda. *The Leadership Quarterly, 22*(6), 1120–1145.

George, J. M. (2000). Emotions and leadership: The role of emotional intelligence. *Human Relations, 53*(8), 1027–1055.

Grandey, A. A., Fisk, G. M., Mattila, A. S., Jansen, K. J., & Sideman, L. A. (2005). Is "service with a smile" enough? Authenticity of positive displays during service encounters. *Organizational Behavior and Human Decision Processes, 96*(1), 38–55.

Horsford, S. D., & Clark, C. (2015). Inclusive leadership and race. In G. Theoharis & M. Scanlan (Eds.), *Inclusive leadership for increasingly diverse schools* (pp. 58–81). New York, NY: Routledge.

Ilies, R., Morgeson, F. P., & Nahrgang, J. D. (2005). Authentic leadership and eudaemonic well-being: Understanding leader–follower outcomes. *Leadership Quarterly, 16*(3), 373–394.

Kernis, M. H., & Goldman, B. M. (2006). A multicomponent conceptualization of authenticity: Theory and research. *Advances in Experimental Social Psychology, 38*, 283–357.

Khalifa, M. (2012). A re-new-ed paradigm in successful urban school leadership principal as community leader. *Educational Administration Quarterly, 48*(3), 424–467.

Kose, B. W. (2007). Principal leadership for social justice: Uncovering the content of teacher professional development. *Journal of School Leadership, 17*(3), 276–312.

Larson, C., & Murtadha, K. (2002). Leadership for social justice. In J. Murphy (Ed.), *The educational leadership challenge: Redefining leadership for the 21st century* (pp. 134–161). Chicago, IL: University of Chicago Press.

Lipman, P. (2013). Economic crisis, accountability, and the state's coercive assault on public education in the USA. *Journal of Education Policy, 28*(5), 557–573.

Pinton, L. (2015). Fear and loathing neoliberalism: School leader responses to policy layers. *Journal of Educational Administration and History, 47*(2), 140–154.

Poliner Shapiro, J., & Hassinger, R. E. (2007). Using case studies of ethical dilemmas for the development of moral literacy: Towards educating for social justice. *Journal of Educational Administration, 45*(4), 451–470.

Ryan, J. (2016). Strategic activism, educational leadership and social justice. *International Journal of Leadership in Education, 19*(1), 87–100.

Shamir, B., & Eilam, G. (2005). "What's your story?" a life-stories approach to authentic leadership development. *The Leadership Quarterly, 16*, 295–417.

Shields, C. M. (2010). Transformative leadership: Working for equity in diverse contexts. *Educational Administration Quarterly, 46*(4), 558–589.

Stake, R. E. (2010). *Qualitative research: Studying how things work*. London, UK: The Guilford Press.

Terry, R. W. (1993). *Authentic leadership: Courage in action*. San Francisco, CA: Jossey-Bass.

Theoharis, G. (2007). Social justice educational leaders and resistance: Toward a theory of social justice leadership. *Educational Administration Quarterly, 43*(2), 221–258.

Valenzuela, A. (2010). *Subtractive schooling: US-Mexican youth and the politics of caring*. Albany, NY: SUNY Press.

Walumbwa, F. O., Avolio, B. J., Gardner, W. L., Wernsing, T. S., & Peterson, S. J. (2008). Authentic leadership: Development and validation of a theory-based measure. *Journal of Management, 34*(1), 89–126.

Watson, T. N., & Bogotch, I. (2015). Reframing parent involvement: What should urban school leaders do differently? *Leadership and Policy in Schools, 14*(3), 257–278.

Wilson, M. (2014). Critical reflection on authentic leadership and school leader development from a virtue ethical perspective. *Educational Review, 66*(4), 482–496.

Woods, P. A. (2007). Authenticity in the bureau-enterprise culture: The struggle for authentic meaning. *Educational Management Administration & Leadership, 35*(2), 295–320.

A School Leadership Framework for Dual Language

David E. DeMatthews, Elena Izquierdo, and Stephen Kotok

Abstract This chapter presents a social justice leadership framework for principals pursuing dual language education (DL) and focuses on schools serving Latinx communities. The purpose of this framework is to highlight the principal's role in creating more equitable schools for Latinx emergent bilinguals (EBs) and to foster a multi-dimensional social justice perspective that focuses on closing achievement gaps while equally valuing meaningful parent engagement and the rich cultural and linguistic assets of students and their community. We focus on the principal not because we are arguing for a model of heroic leadership that centers the principal as the dominant change agent, but because research on DL and EBs has primarily ignored this important position.

Keywords Dual language education · School leadership · Social justice leadership · Latinx students · Professional standards

---

This chapter has been adapted from a previous published article with permission from the publisher: DeMatthews and Izquierdo (2018).

D. E. DeMatthews (✉)
Department of Educational Leadership and Policy, University of Texas at Austin, Austin, TX, USA
e-mail: ddematthews@austin.utexas.edu

E. Izquierdo
Department of Teacher Education, University of Texas at El Paso, El Paso, TX, USA
e-mail: ielena@utep.edu

S. Kotok
Department of Administration and Instructional Leadership, St. John's University, New York, NY, USA
e-mail: kotoks@stjohns.edu

Numerous studies have documented how a deficit-thinking paradigm in public education has impacted Latinx emergent bilingual students (EBs),[1] especially from low-income immigrant communities (Valencia, 1997). Education language policies often reflect social and political perspectives related to race, class, and immigration status rather than on sound educational research. Schools and districts often fail to equitably distribute resources and learning opportunities or value Latinx immigrant communities' input, culture, history, or linguistic assets (Gándara & Contreras, 2009). Latinx EBs often perform poorly on standardized tests and are less likely to graduate, go to college, and gain access to professional jobs in comparison to white and English speaking peers (López & McEneaney, 2012). Unequal outcomes persist despite evidence that dual language education (DL), which builds on Latinx students' cultural and linguistic assets can close achievement gaps and improve other important student-related outcomes (Collier & Thomas, 2004). Critical scholars have made principled arguments about how false and subversive narratives describe the success of past generations immigrants learning English through full immersion while suggesting to Latinx EBs that their culture and language are neither valuable nor desirable (Wiley & Wright, 2004). These narratives are racist and contribute to broken teacher and leader preparation pipelines that fail to prepare educators to implement DL or even question the status quo of English immersion and subtractive programs.

Social justice-oriented principals who are knowledgeable about the needs of EBs can be influential because their organizational position allows them to serve as an instructional leader that shapes school culture, student expectations, budgets, hiring practices, parent engagement strategies, and service delivery models (DeMatthews & Izquierdo, 2016, 2018). While these principals may still confront deficit thinking and problematic state and district policies, a small body of research suggests particular leadership orientations, actions, and knowledge can contribute to the creation of DL schools that meet the academic, social, and emotional needs of Latinx EBs. This conceptual article presents a social justice leadership framework for principals pursuing DL and focuses on schools serving Latinx communities, although our recommendations are relevant to other communities. The purpose of this framework is to highlight the principal's role in creating more equitable schools for Latinx EBs and to foster a multi-dimensional social justice perspective that focuses on closing achievement gaps while equally valuing meaningful parent engagement and the rich cultural and linguistic assets of students and their community. We focus on the principal not because we are arguing for a model of heroic leadership that centers the principal as the dominant change agent, but because research on DL and EBs has primarily ignored this important position.

---

[1] We use the term emergent bilinguals rather than the term English Language Learners (ELLs) or Limited English Proficient (LEP). ELLs or LEP students are those students who speak a language other than English and are acquiring English in school. We prefer to use the term emergent bilinguals because we believe that when policymakers, educators, and researchers ignore bilingualism and its role in schooling, they perpetuate numerous inequities and discount the needs of children from linguistically diverse backgrounds.

1 Leadership and Dual Language

A small body of qualitative case study research highlights how a select group of principals promote DL despite challenges and resistance. In a case study of 90:10 DL elementary school, Alanís and Rodríguez (2008) found the principal had a strong grasp of DL and effective instruction practices that support EBs. The principal made an ongoing effort to remain current on DL research, state laws, and parent rights so she could advocate for DL with teachers and within the community. A teacher described her: "She knows everything, and it's amazing to me how I might pick up a book and read it today, well, she already knows it. She already read it" (p. 315). This principal also enlisted support from a local university to bolster the school's capacity and engaged in democratic leadership to promote teacher and parent engagement. A DL teacher said of the principal: "She expects a lot from us, and then I think that sort of turns around on us, and then we expect a lot from our parents and our kids, too" (p. 316). This principal encouraged teacher leadership and creativity and believed these aspects contributed to the sustainability of DL. Findings from this study highlight the importance of leadership to DL in general, but also the need for specific instructional and democratic leadership.

Theoharis and O'Toole (2011) explored the role of the efforts of two principals seeking to create more inclusive and effective schools for EBs. Each principal was critical of existing structures that segregated students, adopted new structures and staff responsibilities to promote inclusion, engaged in community building and professional development to change teacher expectations and build pedagogical competencies to provide high-quality instruction in two languages, and created systems of communication with families whose home language was not English. Each principal took different approaches, confronted different challenges, and had varying levels of preparedness to take on these challenges, but both were reflective and engaged in ongoing professional development and shared leadership with teachers and families. Theoharis and O'Toole also identified numerous challenges, including how teacher certification and state policy issues, vocal and disgruntled parents, deficit-oriented teachers and staff, and problematic or simplistic pedagogical approaches that do not support a positive school culture or reflect child-centered teaching practices.

Other studies examine the role of the principal as a social justice leader in response to the marginalization of EBs. Wiemelt and Welton (2015) conducted a qualitative case study of a DL school. The effective principal at the center of their study understood how deficit paradigms effected schools, students, and families. She said:

> Administrators always blame Latin@ youth and families for the dropout rate, but we never talk about why the dropout rate exists nor what we are doing early on to transform the opportunities for Latin@ youth. Other principals talk about the lack of English and Spanish for Latin@s and the lack of parental involvement but at the same time these principals are pushing for English-only programs in all of our schools even if we know research does not support this policy. (p. 90)

DL was successful because the principal understood research on DL, bilingualism, teachers and community roles, and acted. Wiemelt and Welton (2015) concluded "principals must challenge the subtractive system in which they work and transform the learning opportunities for students by leading their school communities forward with the goals of long-term bilingual programs such as dual language immersion" (p. 96).

In a study of six principals along the U.S./Texas-Mexico border, DeMatthews and Izquierdo (2016) highlighted the importance of leadership in challenging subtractive language programs and promoting additive DL models. The study identified five key leadership practices for DL: (a) laying foundations and valuing all stakeholders; (b) exploring diverse perspectives of language; (c) assessing the context of the school and community while planning; (d) recruiting and building capacity within the school and community; and (e) implementing a collective approach to monitoring, evaluating, and renewing DL. The principals had a range of experience with DL from 1 year to 18 years of experience but, they all recognized DL would always be challenging and require ongoing problem solving and reflection. A principal with 18 years of experience said: "Some problems are the same today as they were 17 years ago, some are new. We keep working and trying new things. We never stop learning" (p. 18). One important finding of the study was how principal leadership was insufficient for DL because teacher and community leadership was necessary to confront and address certain political and financial challenges.

Additional theoretical and prescriptive writings add nuance to challenges principals confront and skills needed to support EBs and families. Scanlan and López (2012) conducted a narrative synthesis consisting of 79 empirical articles between 2000 and 2010 to identify evidence that can guide school leadership for EBs. By reviewing research focused specifically on cultivating language proficiency, access to high-quality curricula, and sociocultural integration in schools, they found school leaders must be informed about how to organize a broad range of support services in a positive manner that is both inclusive, integrated into the core curriculum, and supports equitable access to all educational opportunities. They also highlight the importance of understandings funding and policy mechanisms that impact their schools. These findings align to previous research and detail how principals struggle to deal with policies, budgets, and instructional leadership in relation to the needs of EBs.

2 Dual Language Social Justice Leadership Framework

2.1 Operationalizing Social Justice for EBs

While near consensus can be reached about the significance of social justice in education, the concept is disputed and frequently used as an all-encompassing term for a teaching and school leadership. Rizvi (1998) argues that "the immediate difficulty one confronts when examining the idea of social justice is the fact that it does not have a single essential meaning – it is embedded within discourses that are historically constituted and that are sites of conflicting and divergent political endeavors" (p. 47). Meanwhile, shifting language policies put principals and teachers under scrutiny from multiple and potentially competing interest groups. Similarly, implementing DL raises socio-political tensions:

> When school language policies are put into action, they are linked with power and with social justice in a range of ways. Whenever schools set out to plan their response to the language problems they face, matters of language variety, race, culture, and class always affect the planning process, and an effective language policy process will always look critically at the impact of these and other aspects of human diversity. (Corson, 1999, p. 6)

If principals are to lead for social justice with DL, then it is critical to gain a complete understanding of what social justice means and requires. Thus, major facets of social justice (distributive, cultural, and associational) and tensions/challenges must be foregrounded.

Historically, social justice scholars have primarily considered issues of distributive justice, or how institutions like schools distribute fundamental rights or advantages (Rawls, 2009). In schools, distributive justice relates to the equitable distribution of resources and learning opportunities (DeMatthews, 2018). Yet, most scholars now argue for a plural conception that concerns the equitable distribution of rights and advantages and full recognition (cultural justice) of marginalized communities. Fraser's (1997) primary thesis is that marginalization is often two-dimensional and related both to inequitable distribution of rights and advantages and misrecognition or devaluing of particular cultural groups. Consider Mexican American EBs attending schools in low-income communities. Such schools are often underfunded, lack access to quality language acquisition models, do not value Spanish or Mexican culture in the same way English and Eurocentric culture are valued. Thus, social justice requires both distributive justice to ensure equitable access to resources and learning opportunities, but also cultural justice through curriculum, pedagogy, and a school that values diversity and the linguistic assets of students.

Although Fraser's dual focus also considers the importance of representation and shared decision-making, Gewirtz and Cribb (2002) extends her thesis by identifying a third facet of social justice: associational justice, or the ability of all groups to govern, participate, and make informed decisions that impact their lives. For historically marginalized families, such as Latinx immigrant communities, parents have not historically engaged in decisions that impact their children because of financial reasons, language barriers, perceptions of disrespect or devaluation, or due to English speaking parents' dominance in family-school activities (Howard, Sugarman, Christian, Lindholm-Leary, & Rogers, 2007). Associational justice is therefore related to cultural and distributive justice in that parents must have opportunities to learn about the school, be valued in decision-making processes, and be respected by school leaders and teachers.

Distributive, cultural, and associational justice can be contradictory when applied to practice (DeMatthews, 2018). For example, a principal might encourage shared decision-making with parents (associational justice) that generate a decision to limit funding or professional development for DL (distributive justice). This contradiction highlights the complexity of social justice leadership and how shifting circumstances impact leadership approaches. These contradictions raise the notion that "no single theory can guide this complex and messy work and that meanings of justice are inherently contingent and constantly reinvented" (Scanlan, 2013, p. 3). By understanding social justice as potentially contradictory, social justice leadership necessitates a deep understanding of context, shifting power dynamics, policies, and key players in schools and communities.

2.2 Social Justice Leadership and Dual Language

Social justice leadership has been defined in many ways, but reflects elements of distributive, cultural, and associational justice within schools and communities. Some scholars contend social justice leadership relates to specific school issues. For example, Theoharis (2007) defines social justice leadership as when "principals make issues of race, class, gender, disability, sexual orientation, and other historically and currently marginalizing conditions in the United States central to their advocacy, leadership practice, and vision" (p. 223). Marshall, Young, and Moll (2010) make a similar argument by describing social justice leadership as "a critical building block in the educational equity project" (p. 315). Principals leading for social justice schools engage teachers and families in creating more culturally relevant curriculum and pedagogy, value student assets and experiences, (Kose, 2007) and adopt shared governance practices that encourage teacher and parent leadership (Wasonga, 2010).

Other scholars claim social justice leadership must include a community focus. Khalifa (2012) rejects situating school leadership only within the school context. Instead, he argues principals must be community leaders that enlist marginalized and diffident parents, but also engage in leadership by "visiting a church, fighting for the rights of marginalized and abused children in the community, leading a rally against racism in schools, or going to homes on personal visits" (p. 461). Larson and Murtadha (2002) suggest the field could learn from leaders outside of education, like Dr. Martin Luther King Jr., Gloria Steinem, and Nelson Mandela and acknowledge the field's failure to deeply consider how leadership outside of schools "might enhance leadership theory and practice in education" (p. 150). Anderson (2009) reasons that principals must acknowledge schools are sites of struggle, advocate, and be:

> skilled at getting beneath high-sounding rhetoric to the devil in the details…they know that some causes [of inequities], such as inequitable policies may be beyond their immediate control, but they have a deep belief in the power of education to foster not just kids with high test scores, but also powerful and informed democratic citizens with influence over those very policies in the future (pp. 14–15).

DeMatthews (2018), Ryan (2016), and Siddle-Walker (2009) identify how outside of school issues perpetuate inside of school injustices and propose principals should engage in strategic activism behind the scenes to shape district and state policies, form community coalitions, and challenge deficit perspectives in the community.

A social justice leadership approach to DL necessitates thinking about school and community simultaneously across different policies, curriculum and pedagogical approaches, and family engagement strategies (Rodríguez & Alanís, 2011). To facilitate thinking about social justice leadership for DL, we pose four questions:

- How have schools and communities historically failed to distribute meaningful resources and opportunities to EB students?
- How have schools and communities historically failed to provide cultural recognition and value to EB students?
- How have schools and communities historically failed to provide teachers and culturally and linguistically diverse families with meaningful opportunities to engage in governance and shared decision-making?
- What are the potential challenges and tensions for social justice-minded principals when attempting to create DL schools that bring about distributive, cultural, and associational justice?

We explore each of these questions through a discussion of how principals should engage in *foregrounding and engaging*, *planning and implementing*, and *evaluating and sustaining* DL in Latinx immigrant communities.

Foregrounding and Engaging Principals must maintain a focus on distributive, cultural, and associational justice and recognize establishing DL can be a messy process. Rather than rush to implementation by individually drafting a plan or adopting a "canned or pre-packaged program," principals must understand DL cannot be forced onto families and teachers but must be developed iteratively through dialogue and an exploration of school community context and needs. As Frattura and Capper (2007) suggest, principals leading reforms like DL must be willing to accept that they do not have all the answers and play an active role facilitating dialogue grounded in school data, social justice values, and a commitment to personal and professional growth. Thus, principals must maintain a transformative perspective and sustain efforts over time despite resistance and short-term struggles challenges (Scanlan & López, 2012).

To promote associational justice, principals must actively engage all stakeholders in a needs assessment process that analyzes how resources and time are distributed, identifies all students and groups who are segregated, and reviews disaggregated student achievement and discipline data (Frattura & Capper, 2007). Principals must have an understanding of what is currently in place within their schools regarding: (a) curriculum, assessments, and teacher capacity (e.g., certification, experience, linguistic ability; (b) hiring practices and protocols; (c) service delivery models and intervention options; (d) school improvement team processes and teacher leadership; and (e) parent engagement approaches (DeMatthews & Izquierdo, 2016; López, González, & Fierro, 2006). While a systemic collection and analysis of data can be used to examine how schools distribute resources and opportunities to learn, it also provides a starting point for discussions about how cultural and linguistic diversity and families are valued. Information gleaned from these data will raise discussion questions about: (a) the ways students are labeled and placed in interventions and pullout programs; (b) whether or not curricula, teaching practices, and assessments are authentic, maximize the cultural and linguistic assets of the community, contribute to high levels of academic achievement for all students; and (c) if the school, teachers, and classrooms foster values of inclusion, bilingualism, multiculturalism.

While all schools and communities are different and an immediate shift toward DL may be apt, principals should not rush the process and instead utilize data to engage teachers and Latinx families in valuable discussions that (re)build trust (Nelson & Guerra, 2014). Principals, teachers, and families should consider the value of Spanish and other languages, how segregation impacts achievement and student well-being, the ways hiring practices support or limit the school's ability to meet the diverse needs of EBs, and whether or not curriculum, student discipline, and teaching practices reflect the same values and beliefs of families and the community (Heineke, Coleman, Ferrell, & Kersemeier, 2012). The results of such discussions may or may not lead to immediate buy-in for DL, but it will help to build trust, transparency, and advocacy that principals can capitalize on down the road. Principals should also be prepared to engage teachers and families with research findings and information about the benefits of bilingualism, inclusive schools, and DL. The outcomes of these actions should ultimately lead to a consensus around the school's strengths and weaknesses, a shared sense of responsibility for all students, an inclusive and transparent approach to decision-making, and a recognition that cultural and linguistic diversity is an asset that should be further developed through the adoption of DL (DeMatthews & Izquierdo, 2016; Nelson & Guerra, 2014). Additionally, this process of inquiry, reflection, and broad stakeholder engagement lays the groundwork for future collaborative efforts necessary to develop DL.

Planning and Implementing Implementing DL may require significant changes to the school's culture, budget and staffing model, service delivery model, master schedule, professional development and teacher evaluation practices, grading policies, and parent and community engagement strategies. The *foregrounding and engaging* process allows leaders to build intentional systems and processes to facilitate *planning and implementing* aligned to distributive, cultural, and associational justice. If the school has not previously adopted a school vision aligned to DL, this must occur before more technical planning. The vision should emphasize equitable resource distribution, curricula and teaching practices that are culturally and linguistically appropriate, and a shared decision-making process that values teachers and families. As stakeholders move forward and engage in collaborative inquiry and review research on DL, they will find that effective DL schools often have high levels of parent and teacher leadership (Theoharis & O'Toole, 2011), develop tailored systems of professional development (Howard et al., 2007), and provide research-based language instruction practices as well as a culturally relevant curriculum and approaches to teaching and learning (Samson & Collins, 2012). For teachers, professional development needs to include training and ongoing support in first and second language acquisition, teaching and learning through two languages across the curriculum, biliteracy, and strategies for appropriate student grouping and cooperative learning (Thomas & Collier, 2012). For example, they must understand contextual issues associated with translanguaging and how students move fluidly between academic and vernacular Spanish and English as well as how translanguaging allows students to make sense of academic content, their own language learning, and legitimizing their bicultural identities (García, 2009a, b). For parents, training and ongoing support must include the value and benefits of DL and bilingualism/biculturalism, how to support their children with homework and learning through two languages, and how to develop parent support networks (Kotok & DeMatthews, 2018; Miramontes, Nadeau, & Commins, 2011). Professional development and DL implementation plans as well as a timeline for the implementation should emphasize these important features.

After developing a professional development plan to increase the school's capacity for DL, principals must further engage stakeholders in considering how the school's budget, resources, service-delivery systems, and schedule can be revised to maximize resources. This process includes dismantling ESL pullout and other segregated programs that overload the school's resources and limit inclusivity (Frattura & Capper, 2007). This stage of planning may surface tensions and challenges, including a lack of appropriate curricular resources for DL, disgruntled teachers and parents who are fearful of change or do not believe in DL, the recognition that some parents may not be available or willing to participate in the school reform process, and potential staffing and state/district policy issues that may limit the changes a principal can make in a given year (Theoharis & O'Toole, 2011). This may be a point in time where principals and other stakeholders consider the pace of implementation and the time needed to develop DL, provide training, and build district, community, and school support. Depending on resistance and preparedness within the school and community, principals must consider how to build coalitions, engage in advocacy, develop partnerships with local organizations and businesses to enhance resources, and maintain steady improvement.

The *planning and implementation* process should continue to focus on refining the school's social justice vision. Part of the school's planning of DL implementation should have a family focus and include (a) developing a shared understanding between parents, teachers, and administrators about what was meant by parent involvement (Carreón, Drake, & Barton, 2005); (b) revised methods of communication with families and community organizations in multiple languages; (c) a schedule for parent events at the school and/or accessible parts of the community; (d) identification and training of parent liaisons to support families struggling with helping students with homework or understanding important aspects of bilingualism (López, Scribner, & Mahitivanichcha, 2001); and (e) a teacher-parent curriculum committee to review materials and further support diversity, culture, and multiculturalism (De Gaetano, 2007; Nelson & Guerra, 2014; Rodríguez & Alanís, 2011).

Evaluating and Sustaining Evaluating DL should be a collaborative and comprehensive process that is authentic and involves a broad range of stakeholders focused on more than just academic achievement in traditional subjects (e.g., reading, math) using standardized test scores. Evaluations should focus on: (a) the quality of the school as it relates to school culture and climate, overall support for bilingualism/biculturalism, productive relationships and collaborative inquiry, and the presence of teacher and parent leaders; (b) the quality of curricula as it relates to biliteracy, well-planned integration of language and academic content, curricula's relatedness to student interests and cultures, and the use of quality and varied curricular materials and assessments; (c) the quality of instruction as it relates to specific strategies of teaching in and through English and Spanish, the role of families and communities in classrooms, the use of varied student grouping strategies, and student-centered and inclusive lessons and activities; and (d) the degree to which all families and teachers feel connected to the school, knowledgeable about DL and biliteracy, engaged in decision making where appropriate, and supported by other parents and teachers (Howard et al., 2007).

Evaluations serve two primary purposes: to engage in continuous improvement of DL and to support advocacy for bilingualism and additional supports from the district and community. Evaluations should be shared with multiple audiences, such as teachers, families, school boards, superintendents, media, and other relevant constituencies and used as a tool to further advocate for the school overall, as well as for additional resources (Rodríguez & Alanís, 2011). Successes should be highlighted and used as a mechanism to further advocate for bilingualism and biculturalism while ongoing challenges should be used to make improvements and strategically advocate for additional resources and supports. Evaluations can also have a direct daily impact on the sustainability of DL because sharing information builds trust and transparency. Additionally, when principals are well-informed via evaluations and less formal review processes, they are better prepared to address and advocate for the needs of teachers, parents, and students through administrative decisions related to professional development topics, hiring practices, and resource procurement. Ultimately, *foregrounding and engaging*, *planning and implementing*, and *evaluating and sustaining* support a process of continuous improvement, reflection, advocacy, and school community engagement that can help to address many of the challenges of DL, such as shifting political perspectives on language models, budgets, changing student demographics, budget shortages, and turnover in district leadership (DeMatthews & Izquierdo, 2016).

3 Conclusions

The purpose of this article was to highlight the important role principals can play in addressing the unmet needs of Latinx EBs through DL. Drawing on theories of social justice emphasizing distributed, cultural, and associational justice, we proposed a process where principals can advocate for DL and work with teachers and Latinx immigrant communities to reconsider how resources and learning opportunities are equitably distributed, and how language and cultural identity can be an asset schools build upon. Since creating a DL school will be challenging and potentially take sustained effort, advocacy, and attention, we were purposeful in not being too specific or claiming our framework was a road map or recipe for leaders. DL is too complicated to be "pre-packaged." school.

Our framework focused on how school leaders infuse principles of social justice and what is often called "just good leadership,"(DeMatthews, Edwards, & Rincones, 2016; Theoharis, 2007) to engage stakeholders, collect and analyze a broad range of data, develop new systems that support inclusive and linguistically appropriate teaching practices, and maintain continuous reflection, evaluation, and improvement. We believe the framework is a first step and hopefully, a catalyst for further research, discussion, and critique. We believe additional research and theorizing is necessary to consider how principals can support Latinx immigrant communities in developing DL in their schools and examine principal preparation programs and coursework, assignments, and clinical experiences that can support the development of principals who are knowledgeable about bilingual education, DL, and the needs of EBs. Faculty in educational leadership at Hispanic-Serving Institutions must be at the forefront of such research and theorizing, although all scholars and researchers must consider the needs of Latinx EBs given demographic trends across the nation. Additional research is also needed to examine not only traditional school leaders like principals, but also the role of teacher, parent, and community leaders. Further understandings about the roles of such leaders will contribute to a social justice leadership framework that de-centers the principal and supports a more democratic and community-oriented approach to leadership.

Interdisciplinary collaboration is important to the field of educational leadership and the development of preparation and leadership standards. We proposed our framework close to the time the National Policy Board for Educational Administration (NPBEA, 2015) revised and approved new leadership standards with an increased focus on equity and social justice for diverse students and communities. While we acknowledge the improvements to the new standards, we recognize principals need specific skills and orientations related to language acquisition and the need of EBs and Latinx immigrant communities. In future iterations of standards, we hope more attention is paid to language acquisition and biliteracy. We invite criticism of our framework and hope scholars in educational leadership, teacher education, and bilingual education as well as education researchers interested in issues related to Latinx communities engage in discussions about the types and depths of knowledge and expertise principals need in terms of bilingual education and language acquisition, as well as the processes and approaches to transitioning schools from subtractive language models to additive language models. Additionally, we hope others will consider how principals support DL and bilingualism in schools that enroll students from multiple language backgrounds or in states with more restrictive language policies.

References

Alanís, I., & Rodríguez, M. A. (2008). Sustaining a dual language immersion program: Features of success. *Journal of Latinos and Education, 7*(4), 305–319.

Anderson, G. L. (2009). *Advocacy leadership: Toward a post-reform agenda in education*. New York, NY: Routledge.

Carreón, G. P., Drake, C., & Barton, A. C. (2005). The importance of presence: Immigrant parents' school engagement experiences. *American Educational Research Journal, 42*(3), 465–498.

Collier, V. P., & Thomas, W. P. (2004). The astounding effectiveness of dual language education for all. *NABE Journal of Research and Practice, 2*(1), 1–20.

Corson, D. (1999). *Language policy in schools. A resource for teachers and administrators*. Mahwah, NJ: Lawrence Erlbaum.

De Gaetano, Y. (2007). The role of culture in engaging Latino parents' involvement in school. *Urban Education, 42*(2), 145–162. https://doi.org/10.1177/0042085906296536

DeMatthews, D. E. (2018). *Community engaged leadership for social justice: A critical approach in urban schools*. New York, NY: Routledge.

DeMatthews, D. E., Edwards, D. B., & Rincones, R. (2016). Social justice leadership and community engagement: A successful case from Ciudad Juárez, Mexico. *Educational Administration Quarterly, 52*(5), 754–792.

DeMatthews, D. E., & Izquierdo, E. (2016). School leadership for Latina/o bilingual children: A social justice leadership approach. *The Educational Forum, 80*(3), 278–293.

DeMatthews, D. E., & Izquierdo, E. (2018). The role of principals in developing dual language education: Implications for social justice leadership and preparation. *Journal of Latinos and Education, 17*(1), 53–70.

Fraser, N. (1997). *Justice interruptus: Critical reflections on the "postsocialist" condition*. New York, NY: Routledge.

Frattura, E. M., & Capper, C. A. (2007). *Leading for social justice: Transforming schools for all learners*. Thousand Oaks, CA: Corwin.

Gándara, P. C., & Contreras, F. (2009). *The Latino education crisis: The consequences of failed social policies*. Cambridge, MA: Harvard University Press.

García, O. (2009a). *Bilingual education in the 21st century: A global perspective*. Malden, MA: Wiley-Blackwell.

García, O. (2009b). Emergent bilinguals and TESOL: What's in a name? *TESOL Quarterly, 43*(2), 322–326.

Gewirtz, S., & Cribb, A. (2002). Plural conceptions of social justice: Implications for policy sociology. *Journal of Education Policy, 17*(5), 499–509.

Heineke, A. J., Coleman, E., Ferrell, E., & Kersemeier, C. (2012). Opening doors for bilingual students: Recommendations for building linguistically responsive schools. *Improving Schools, 15*(2), 130–147.

Howard, E. R., Sugarman, J., Christian, D., Lindholm-Leary, K. J., & Rogers, D. (2007). *Guiding principles for dual language education* (2nd ed.). Washington, DC: Center for Applied Linguistics.

Khalifa, M. (2012). A re-new-ed paradigm in successful urban school leadership principal as community leader. *Educational Administration Quarterly, 48*(3), 424–467.

Kose, B. W. (2007). Principal leadership for social justice: Uncovering the content of teacher professional development. *Journal of School Leadership, 17*(3), 276.

Kotok, S., & DeMatthews, D. E. (2018). Challenging school segregation in the 21st century: How districts can leverage dual language education to increase school and classroom diversity. *The Clearing House: A Journal of Educational Strategies, Issues and Ideas, 91*(1), 1–6.

Larson, C. L., & Murtadha, K. (2002). Leadership for social justice. *Yearbook of the National Society for the Study of Education, 101*(1), 134–161.

López, F., & McEneaney, E. (2012). State implementation of language acquisition policies and reading achievement among Hispanic students. *Educational Policy, 26*(3), 418–464.

López, G. R., González, M. L., & Fierro, E. (2006). Educational leadership along the U.S.–México border: crossing borders/embracing hybridity/building bridges. In C. Marshall & M. Oliva (Eds.), *Leadership for social justice: Making revolutions in education* (pp. 64–84). Boston, MA: Pearson.

López, G. R., Scribner, J. D., & Mahitivanichcha, K. (2001). Redefining parental involvement: Lessons from high-performing migrant-impacted schools. *American Educational Research Journal, 38*(2), 253–288.

Marshall, C., Young, M. D., & Moll, L. (2010). The wider societal challenge: An afterword. In C. Marshall & M. Oliva (Eds.), *Leadership for social justice* (2nd ed., pp. 315–327). Boston, MA: Allyn & Bacon.

Miramontes, O. B., Nadeau, A., & Commins, N. L. (2011). *Restructuring schools for linguistic diversity: Linking decision making to effective programs*. New York, NY: Teachers College Press.

National Policy Board for Educational Administration. (2015). *Professional standards for educational leaders 2015*. Reston, VA: Author.

Nelson, S. W., & Guerra, P. L. (2014). Educator beliefs and cultural knowledge: Implications for school improvement efforts. *Educational Administration Quarterly, 50*(1), 67–95.

Rawls, J. (2009). *A theory of justice*. Cambridge, MA: Harvard University Press.

Rizvi, F. (1998). Some thoughts on contemporary theories of social justice. In B. Atweh, S. Kemmis, & P. Weeks (Eds.), *Action research in practice: Partnerships for social justice in education* (pp. 47–56). London, UK: Routledge.

Rodríguez, M. A., & Alanís, I. (2011). Negotiating linguistic and cultural identity: One borderlander's leadership initiative. *International Journal of Leadership in Education, 14*(1), 103–117. https://doi.org/10.1080/13603120903386951

Ryan, J. (2016). Strategic activism, educational leadership and social justice. *International Journal of Leadership in Education, 19*(1), 87–100.

Samson, J. F., & Collins, B. A. (2012). *Preparing all teachers to meet the needs of English language learners: Applying research to policy and practice for teacher effectiveness*. Washington, DC: Center for American Progress.

Scanlan, M. (2013). A learning architecture: How school leaders can design for learning social justice. *Educational Administration Quarterly, 49*(2), 348–391.

Scanlan, M., & López, F. (2012). ¡Vamos! How school leaders promote equity and excellence for bilingual students. *Educational Administration Quarterly, 48*(4), 583–625.

Siddle-Walker, V. (2009). *Hello professor: A Black principal and professional leadership in the segregated south*. Chapel Hill, NC: University of North Carolina Press.

Theoharis, G. (2007). Social justice educational leaders and resistance: Toward a theory of social justice leadership. *Educational Administration Quarterly, 43*(2), 221–258.

Theoharis, G., & O'Toole, J. (2011). Leading inclusive ELL social justice leadership for English language learners. *Educational Administration Quarterly, 47*(4), 646–688.

Thomas, W. P., & Collier, V. P. (2012). *Dual language education for a transformed world*. Albuquerque, NM: Fuente Press.

Valencia, R. (Ed.). (1997). *The evolution of deficit thinking: Educational thought and practice* (The Stanford series on education and public policy). London, UK: Falmer.

Wasonga, T. A. (2010). Leadership practices for social justice, democratic community, and learning: School principals' perspectives. *Journal of School Leadership, 19*, 200–224.

Wiemelt, J., & Welton, A. (2015). Challenging the dominant narrative: Critical bilingual leadership (liderazgo) for emergent bilingual Latin@ students. *International Journal of Multicultural Education, 17*(1), 82.

Wiley, T. G., & Wright, W. E. (2004). Against the undertow: Language-minority education policy and politics in the age of accountability. *Educational Policy, 18*(1), 142–168.

The Challenges of Recruiting and Retaining Dual Language Teachers

Elizabeth Howard and Angela M. López-Velásquez

Abstract Across the United States, the popularity of dual language education (DLE) has grown considerably over the past several decades, but finding qualified bilingual teachers to staff these programs is an ongoing issue for administrators. Using the *Guiding Principles for Dual Language Education* as a framework, this chapter addresses this urgent issue by exploring dual language teacher recruitment and retention through the experiences and recommendations of teachers and administrators in Connecticut. Findings address participants' perceptions of teacher recruitment and retention, staff selection, workplace climate, and staff evaluation. Cross-cutting themes include the value of shared responsibility and shared decision-making in addressing this complex issue, the need for creativity and flexibility to increase pathways to certification for dual language teachers, and the importance of positive working conditions.

Keywords Dual language · Teacher shortage · Teacher recruitment · Teacher retention · Teacher certification · Bilingual teachers · Alternative routes to certification · School-university partnerships · School climate

E. Howard (✉)
Department of Curriculum and Instruction, Neag School of Education, University of Connecticut, Storrs, CT, USA
e-mail: elizabeth.howard@uconn.edu

A. M. López-Velásquez
Department of Special Education, Southern Connecticut State University, New Haven, CT, USA
e-mail: lopezvelasa1@southernct.edu

© The Author(s) 2019
D. E. DeMatthews, E. Izquierdo (eds.), *Dual Language Education: Teaching and Leading in Two Languages*, Language Policy 18,
https://doi.org/10.1007/978-3-030-10831-1_13

1 Introduction

Across the United States, the popularity of dual language education (DLE) has grown considerably over the past several decades, with current estimates of as many as 2000 programs (Gross, 2016) and enrollments in some states of as high as 9% of the school population (Harris, 2015). Two-way immersion is one form of DLE in which students with varying levels of proficiency in the two languages of instruction are integrated for instruction with the goals of promoting academic achievement, bilingualism and biliteracy, and cross-cultural competence (Howard et al., 2018). In the state of Connecticut, as in Texas, two-way DLE is specifically referenced in the state education laws (Texas Code of Education, 2012). The Connecticut bilingual state statute requires that school districts provide bilingual education in any school with 20 or more English learners (ELs) who speak the same home language, and that in such cases, they "investigate the feasibility of establishing two-way language programs starting in kindergarten" (Connecticut State Department of Education). Despite the Connecticut bilingual education policy mandate, continued growth in the state's EL population (Connecticut State Department of Education, 2015), and ample evidence of the effectiveness of DLE for both ELs and native English speakers (Howard, Sugarman, & Christian, 2003; Lindholm-Leary, 2001; Steele et al., 2017; Thomas & Collier, 2012), there are only a handful of DLE programs in the state and the majority of students find themselves in mainstream classrooms where instruction is provided solely or primarily in English (Thomas, 2017).

One key reason for the limited availability of DLE programs in the state is the lack of qualified bilingual teachers, a problem that Connecticut shares with Texas despite the considerable differences between the two states. The bilingual education cross-endorsement in Connecticut requires initial certification in elementary education or a secondary subject area plus the completion of 18 graduate credits from a single university or through an alternative route to certification for teachers of English language learners (ARC-TELL), as well as demonstration of oral and written proficiency in both English and the other language of instruction (Connecticut State Department of Education, 2017). Bilingual education is consistently identified as a subject shortage area in Connecticut, and the future looks even more challenging as close to half of existing bilingual teachers will be eligible to retire within the next 5 years (Connecticut State Department of Education, 2015). Connecticut's dilemma is representative of similar problems in Texas and across the nation, and the shortage of teachers who are qualified to teach bilingual learners is compromising the learning of these students and placing a cap on the continued expansion of DLE programs (Ballantyne, Sanderman, & Levy, 2008; Kennedy, 2013; Lachance, 2017; National Academies, 2017). This chapter addresses this urgent issue by exploring DLE teacher recruitment and retention through the experiences and recommendations of teachers and administrators in Connecticut.

2 Framing the Issue

The *Guiding Principles for Dual Language Education* (Howard et al., 2018), and in particular, the four key points of the recruitment and retention principle within the *professional development and staff quality* strand, serve as the framework for this study. The first key point speaks to the importance of considering program goals when developing a plan for teacher recruitment and retention. This requires a commitment to hiring processes that are centered on program goals and carried out by individuals with expertise in dual language; cultivating a variety of approaches to recruiting teachers, including within district grow-your-own programs, university partnerships, and international outreach; providing professional support to new and veteran teachers; and offering financial incentives to recruit and retain qualified teachers (Claycomb & Hawley, 2000; Kennedy, 2013; National Academies, 2017).

A related issue is the importance of ensuring that new staff have the necessary credentials, knowledge of content and instructional strategies, language proficiency, and commitment to program goals to work effectively in a DLE program (Ballantyne et al., 2008; Gándara, Maxwell-Jolly, & Driscoll, 2005; Hamayan, Genesee, & Cloud, 2013; National Academies, 2017). Making sure that teachers have sufficient proficiency in the partner language to provide high-level academic content instruction through that language (in the case of partner language teachers) or at least understand and support the students who are dominant in that language (in the case of the English teachers) is of particular importance (Aquino-Sterling & Rodríguez-Valls, 2016; Lachance, 2017), as is the knowledge and disposition to create culturally sustaining pedagogies that promote equity and social justice (Alfaro & Hernandez, 2016).

Another key aspect of recruitment and retention is a positive workplace climate that communicates the value of all members and provides them with needed supports, such as adequate planning time, necessary supplies, relevant professional development, and professional respect and autonomy. Teachers who experience positive school climate and thus feel empowered in their work tend to experience greater job satisfaction and are more likely to remain in their position (Atchinstein, Ogawa, Sexton, & Freitas 2010; Claycomb & Hawley, 2000; Ingersoll & May, 2011; Johnson, 2006). Finally, it is important that administrators in DLE programs have both sufficient knowledge of and commitment to DLE, and that they use appropriate metrics that are aligned with program goals, so that staff evaluations are both fair and informative and serve to advance program goals (DeMatthews & Izquierdo, 2017; Menken, 2017; National Academies, 2017; Scanlan & López, 2012).

3 Methods

3.1 Context and Participants

We invited the seven existing DLE programs in the state at the time of data collection to participate in the study and received permission to carry out the study in six of those programs. The six programs were located throughout the state in four districts as well as one inter-district magnet operated by a regional educational service center. All programs followed a 50/50 model and provided instruction in English and Spanish (not surprising given that 72% of ELs in Connecticut are Spanish-speakers (Connecticut State Department of Education, 2015)), enrolling students with varying proficiency in English and/or Spanish. At all six schools, we collected questionnaire data from all classroom teachers and carried out interviews with the administrative leader(s) of each program. Our final sample consisted of 93 DLE teachers across the six schools, as well as seven administrators or program leaders (four principals, one lead teacher, and two district-level directors of bilingual/ESL education) representing all of the sites.

3.2 Measures and Data Collection

We developed and administered a teacher questionnaire that solicited teachers' recommendations for recruitment and retention, using existing questionnaires from our previous work (Howard & Loeb, 1998; Levine, Howard, & Moss, 2014) as a point of departure. The development phase of the survey included external review and content validity assessment by four experts in the field. With help from the program administrators, we anonymously administered the final questionnaire to all practicing DLE teachers in the six participating DLE programs, typically during whole-staff faculty meetings. We collected the completed questionnaires when we visited the schools to interview the administrators. Response rates for each question ranged from 92% to 100%. We also carried out semi-structured interviews (Patton, 2015) with DLE program leaders in the five districts to gather their perspectives on key topics included in the questionnaire. The interviews included questions about the administrators' experiences with their DLE program, the professional development opportunities available to the teachers, strategies for teacher recruitment and retention, and needed supports for teachers.

3.3 Data Analysis

We conducted qualitative analysis of the open-ended teacher questionnaire responses, starting with the four key points of the first guiding principle for *staff quality and professional development* as primary codes, and looking to the data for emergent secondary codes. We created a table to record the responses and then read through the responses, noticing patterns and grouping responses by emergent coding labels. As we progressed through the analysis, we used the constant comparative method (Glaser & Strauss, 1999) to check the teachers' responses against the existing codes and reach consensus on new codes as they were needed. We then used these codes to analyze the administrators' interview data, seeking to find connections between their responses and those of the teachers. We repeatedly read through the interview data and again applied the constant comparative method to relate administrators' statements to the teachers' responses, thus allowing for a deeper analysis of the issues raised by the teachers through the questionnaires.

4 Findings

4.1 Teacher Recruitment and Retention Plan

To address recruitment, participants recommended university partnerships, grow-your-own initiatives, outside recruiting, and financial incentives. Their ideas highlight the importance of forming partnerships between DLE schools and university-based teacher education programs that will expose preservice teachers to the benefits of bilingualism and multiculturalism and encourage them to pursue careers in DLE. Specific suggestions included requiring preservice teachers "to visit a dual language school or do a few hours of observation," "inviting DLE teachers into the university for guest lectures," and "holding information sessions during teacher fairs at universities." One teacher suggested moving the pipeline back further into K12 education through grow-your-own programs based in DLE programs – "'Home grow' our current youth that speak the minority language to be successful college graduates with academic proficiency in the minority language – do so by improving current DLE programs." Finally, some teachers offered ideas for outside recruitment of "qualified, experienced teachers from other districts," from other states, or from Puerto Rico. Administrators echoed these suggestions (although one did reference a 'no-poaching' agreement among bilingual directors across districts in the state), but their responses also spoke to the frustrations they experience in recruiting teachers. One administrator commented,

"If there is a dual language network, we need to be posting in that dual language network that will go out all over Connecticut, all over to other New England states, anywhere, so we can get the word out in a much broader manner. Because it's really difficult. District office has said to me in the past, 'Let's grow the program." And I keep saying, 'Put the brakes on. If I can't staff the program, we can't grow it.'

In speaking to the challenge of recruiting qualified DLE teachers, another administrator recommended that the state provide funding incentives for bilingual teachers, noting that it would be highly unlikely that a teacher from another state would be compelled to move to Connecticut with its high cost of living without sufficient compensation. In the administrator's words,

...the state should give districts that have mandated bilingual education programs a stipend to recruit bilingual teachers. Because why would somebody from Texas come over here? ... Why should somebody come to a state that is more expensive?

Perhaps not surprisingly, a number of teachers conveyed the same idea, saying that extra pay would be incentivizing and appropriate given the additional demands placed on DLE teachers, and would help not only with recruitment but also with retention. In the words of one teacher who suggested financial incentives, "Dual language teachers have a greater load of work compared to regular teachers. Teachers who are in the program leave because they say it is too much."

Beyond financial incentives, participants referenced the importance of professional support for new and veteran teachers as an important aspect of retention. Suggestions included mentoring of new teachers by experienced DLE teachers, in-service professional development focused specifically on DLE topics, on-site collaboration with team members, visits to other DLE programs in the region, and participation in regional and national conferences. Overall, the suggestions focused on two key ideas: (1) professional development content related specifically to DLE; and (2) professional development formats that promote professional exchanges with other DLE teachers within and beyond the school. In the words of one participant, DLE teachers need opportunities to "explore and discuss strategies, methods, and techniques in the classrooms."

4.2 Staff Selection

While there is agreement about the importance of bilingual certification in ensuring teacher quality, there is also frustration that current requirements may tie administrators' hands and make it more difficult to find teachers, particularly those who are representative of the communities they serve. One administrator noted:

Bilingual certified teachers are a huge shortage. And I'm losing one of my best teachers because she doesn't have certification. She's a great teacher, she's a fluent speaker, she's a native speaker, but I can't keep her in the program [...] That's really the biggest challenge.

Efforts to increase the pool of Spanish teachers have included hiring teachers from Spanish-speaking countries, but in many cases, these teachers have experienced difficulties in meeting certification requirements, sometimes due to challenges in getting credit for courses, degrees, or credentials from those countries, and sometimes due to insufficient English language proficiency. Teachers suggested that "the Department of Education should be more flexible with the requirements/credentials with the teachers that come from Hispanic countries and who need some support with the English language... It would be helpful for Hispanic teachers from other countries to get help getting certified to teach the Spanish component."

Because the state requires a bilingual cross-endorsement on top of initial certification, a common pathway is for teachers to get a durational short-term area permit (DSAP), which enables them to teach in bilingual classrooms for up to 3 years while they pursue the cross-endorsement, either through university coursework or through ARC-TELL, which is administered through a regional educational service center. In the words of one administrator:

> Recruitment is very difficult. The person that we recruited, he actually came in as an elementary certified teacher, speaking Spanish with no [bilingual] certification, but he's a native Spanish teacher. So he had to DSAP through the state. And that's pretty much everybody that we had in the last few years. Everybody had to DSAP.

One issue administrators noted with the DSAP route is that new teachers have to spend considerable time and money to pursue the cross-endorsement while they are simultaneously adjusting to their new work responsibilities and possibly paying off student loans from their pre-service preparation.

A final suggestion involves streamlining the certification process by incorporating it into preservice teacher education, enabling teachers to take relevant coursework and also gain bilingual teaching experience through clinical placements in DLE programs. Teachers suggested that the state and institutions of higher education work together to 'create dual language certification and make it available at most/all of state colleges, and promote this certification within the colleges,' 'have [dual language] certification programs that are in undergrad,' or 'offer a dual language strand in university prep programs." Administrators echoed this advice, suggesting either that universities find ways to fit in the additional required coursework for the bilingual cross-endorsement within the preservice program or that the state allow for integrated programs that enable students to pursue bilingual versions of initial certification. In the words of one participant, "You should be able to do it, you know, both at the same time, not having to graduate and then NOW, go get a bilingual [cross-endorsement], it doesn't make sense like that. Like if you are already bilingual, it would make sense to do a bilingual math, a bilingual social studies, bilingual English, or bilingual science, at the same time. It would make sense."

4.3 Positive Workplace Climate

Teachers had a lot to say about workplace climate and the changes that would promote a more positive working environment for them. Teachers stressed the need to "have the teachers feel validated and valued in the work that is required," and also requested "consensus in the school that this [dual language] is important." They indicated a number of administrative supports that the district could provide to convey this importance and support the work of DLE teachers, including ensuring that school administrators and specialists are trained to work in DLE programs. One teacher commented on the importance of "administrators who have had training [in dual language]," and another noted that "support staff (i.e., reading teachers, math support) need to be supportive of the dual language programs they provide services for." Other teachers called for instructional supports such as "additional classroom support" and "smaller class sizes." The call for smaller class sizes reflects not only the heightened challenge of teaching large classes that any teacher faces, but also the burden DLE teachers in particular face due to the need to teach, monitor, and assess two groups of students. In the words of one teacher, "as much as I LOVE dual language, we have double the students that 'regular' teachers have, and it is a lot more work – I think people avoid it for that reason." Other suggestions for dealing with the additional workload of two groups include providing teachers with "more assistance" and "more time and money," and also reducing bureaucratic tasks. As one teacher emphatically stated, "Don't wear them out so much with paperwork and let them do the job they were hired to do – teach!"

A large number of teachers called for more professional development that addresses their needs, such as promoting oral language and literacy development in both languages. Participants also addressed the need to differentiate PD for certain topics, such as language-specific literacy development. Similarly, one teacher noted that "Spanish teachers have a greater ability to make cross-linguistic connections. English [teachers] could benefit from more PD on Spanish language." Many administrators echoed the need for ongoing professional development and the challenges of district-sponsored PD that is not designed with DLE in mind, but they also showed resourcefulness and a commitment to "redefine what they [central office] are giving us so it matches what we do." In some cases, school-level administrators were able to help teachers think about required modifications to content for DLE, and in other cases, it was possible for the schools to plan in-house PD, often with practicing teachers as presenters. This approach resonated with teachers, who emphasized that they would like to see PD formats that enable them to learn with and from DLE teachers within and across programs, such as peer mentoring, collaboration with teaching partners and grade-level teams, visits to other classrooms and programs, regional and national conferences, and university coursework.

The calls for professional development tailored specifically to the needs of the Spanish teachers speak to a general call for greater equity related to the Spanish component of DLE programs. One teacher requested that the school "increase the status of the minority language in the school and community." One possible mechanism for doing this suggested by several teachers is to "offer more training and materials in Spanish." As a teacher elaborated, "Often the Spanish component is left out because materials and training is directed towards the English component. Materials and training should be equal. Spanish components are often left to translate and have extra burdens put on them!" Many teachers also spoke to equity concerns related to state assessment policies, commenting that the state needs to understand the different trajectories of bilingual learners when looking at English-only test results, or calling for the state to use bilingual assessments and/or assessments in both English and Spanish to "show a state priority for improving DLE programs." One teacher commented: "The state needs to take into consideration that students are doing more work with two languages, but are being measured against their mainstream peers on English-only assessments. Should the expectations be the same?"

4.4 Staff Evaluation

As noted in the previous section, a number of teachers commented about the pressure they feel for their students and themselves when being held to monolingual assessment expectations, stressing that this is not a fair evaluation metric for either students or teachers. One teacher expressed this clearly by saying that the "state should understand that students need time to learn two languages and that teachers need more time to meet the standard set by the state." Teachers also commented on the need for administrators to be knowledgeable about dual language, "so they have an understanding of our program/children and an awareness of how they will learn/ obstacles they may face before obtaining both languages," and so that they can "skillfully support building staff and parents and their children."

5 Discussion and Conclusion

5.1 Shared Responsibility and Shared Problem-Solving

One clear theme emerging from the findings and echoed in the literature is the complexity of the bilingual teacher shortage and the resulting need for multi-faceted responses that involve a variety of stakeholders (Gándara et al., 2005; Lachance, 2017, National Academies, 2017). One potential mechanism for this would be strengthened legislation that goes beyond the current recommendation that districts explore the feasibility of DLE and provides a funded mandate that the state department of education support high-quality implementation of such programs, as has been accomplished in Utah (Roberts, Leite, & Wade, 2017). A second approach involves convening stakeholders from across the state to create consensus about

DLE programs and practices, particularly with regard to teacher support (Gándara et al., 2005). Connecticut is already making efforts in this area, through Higher Education Advocates for Language Learners (HEALL), which began as a group of university faculty with interests in the education of bilingual learners from institutions across the state, and has expanded to include representatives from the state department of education and relevant professional organizations. The group meets biannually to share information about state initiatives related to the education of bilingual learners and consider ways to strengthen preK-16 practices. Finally, there is also a need for shared responsibility within schools, such that principals as well as all teachers and staff are familiar with DLE goals and instructional approaches, and see the work as part of a larger social justice mission (DeMatthews & Izquierdo, 2017; Howard & Loeb, 1998; Menken, 2017; National Academies, 2017; Scanlan & López, 2012).

5.2 Creativity and Flexibility to Increase Pathways for Certification

A major factor in the bilingual teacher shortage in Connecticut is the challenge of bilingual certification and the resulting reality that many incoming DLE teachers are hired with provisional certifications, thus needing to acquire appropriate skills and knowledge on the job. While there is consensus among the participants and the literature that bilingual certification is essential for teacher efficacy (Gándara et al., 2005; Lindholm-Leary, 2001), there is also a belief that creative and flexible approaches are needed to increase pathways for certification, particularly for underrepresented groups. These approaches cluster within the three main categories of university-based programs, grow-your-own approaches, and streamlined certification for out-of-state candidates. All of these approaches would be made more viable with financial support as well as advocacy related to licensing exams, which disproportionately screen out teachers of color (Ingersoll & May, 2011).

Within university-based preservice programs, it would be helpful to create integrated pathways for initial certification in elementary or secondary education together with the bilingual cross-endorsement, so that preservice candidates could fulfill the requirements for both at the same time and enter bilingual classrooms fully prepared. With renewed calls for universities to prepare all preservice teachers to work with bilingual learners (National Academies, 2017), this type of integrated program could enrich offerings for all teachers while also leading to the specialized preparation of bilingual teachers in a more efficient and cost-effective way.

A related idea is to increase the grow-your-own programs throughout the state, particularly those targeting paraprofessionals and tutors working in the building, who not only have relevant professional experience, but also frequently live in the school neighborhoods and share linguistic and cultural backgrounds with many of the students. These programs have been found to not only promote greater diversity of the teacher workforce, but also to enhance teacher retention (National Academies, 2017).

Finally, facilitating teaching opportunities for external candidates, including bilingually certified teachers from other states and Puerto Rico as well as international teacher exchanges, would also enhance the state's bilingual teacher pool. Given the national shortage of bilingual educators, perhaps it would make sense to think of national accreditation that would be recognized across states. Thinking globally, hiring temporary international teachers through exchange programs has the potential to convey considerable cultural and linguistic benefits (Roberts et al., 2017), but it is important to keep in mind the additional need for training and support that these teachers have (Lachance, 2017).

5.3 Create Positive Working Conditions

A final recommendation emerging from participants' responses and supported by the literature is the need for schools to create positive working conditions to retain bilingual teachers (Howard & Sugarman, 2007; Ingersoll & May, 2011; Johnson, 2006; National Academies, 2017). One way to promote positive working conditions is through valuing multicultural/multilingual capital, which can include looking to teachers of color for their insights, including families and communities in decision-making, choosing culturally sustaining instructional materials and pedagogies, providing sufficient professional development and instructional materials related to partner language instruction, and offering incentives to teachers with bilingual certification (Alfaro & Hernandez, 2016; Atchinstein et al., 2010; Claycomb & Hawley, 2000; Ingersoll & May, 2011; National Academies, 2017). A second factor is the need to align work responsibilities with program goals and consider the additional demands of DLE teaching when configuring class sizes, assigning additional duties, and determining assessment plans and expectations (Howard & Loeb, 1998). A final suggestion for improving work climate is to provide mentoring to new teachers and offer sustained relevant professional development of desired content in collaborative formats such as visits to other programs and teacher-led conferences (Ballantyne et al., 2008; Gándara et al., 2005; Howard & Loeb, 1998; National Academies, 2017). This type of sustained, meaningful professional development will not only improve workplace climate, but will also lead to improved instruction and student outcomes.

The challenge of the bilingual teacher shortage is clearly a vexing problem in Connecticut, in Texas, and across the country. However, there are still a number of steps that can be taken to work towards better recruitment and retention, as noted by the participating teachers and administrators in this study and reinforced by the existing literature. In particular, creating an environment of collaboration and shared responsibility, forging new and flexible pathways for bilingual certification, and enhancing the working conditions of bilingual teachers are all factors that are likely to improve recruitment and retention efforts. Given the ongoing growth of bilingual learners as well as the increasing demand for DLE, it is essential that efforts be made to consider and implement these approaches.

References

Alfaro, C., & Hernandez, A. M. (2016, March). *Ideology, pedagogy, access and equity: A critical examination.* Multilingual Educator, CABE Conference Edition, 8–11. Retrieved online http://www.gocabe.org/wp-content/uploads/2016/03/ME2016.pdf .

Aquino-Sterling, C. R., & Rodríguez-Valls, F. (2016). Developing teaching-specific Spanish competencies in bilingual teacher education: Toward a culturally, linguistically, and professionally relevant approach. *Multicultural Perspectives, 18*(2), 73–81. https://doi.org/10.1080/1521096 0.2016.1152894

Atchinstein, B., Ogawa, R. T., Sexton, D., & Freitas, C. (2010). Retaining teachers of color: A pressing problem and a promising strategy for "hard to staff" schools. *Review of Educational Research, 80*(1), 71–107.

Ballantyne, K. G., Sanderman, A. R., & Levy, J. (2008). *Educating English language learners: Building teacher capacity.* Washington, DC: National Clearinghouse for English Language Acquisition. Retrieved from http://www.ncela.us/files/uploads/3/EducatingELLsBuildingTeacherCapacityVol1.pdf

Claycomb, C., & Hawley, W. D. (2000). *Recruiting and retaining effective teachers for urban schools: Developing a strategic plan for action.* Washington, DC: National Partnership for Excellence and Accountability in Teaching.

Connecticut State Department of Education. (2015). *Data bulletin: Connecticut's English learners (grades K-12), school year 2014–15.* Retrieved from www.sde.ct.gov/sde/lib/sde/pdf/.../el_databulletin_aug2015.pdf

Connecticut State Department of Education. Bilingual education statute: Section 10-17e-j, inclusive, of the Connecticut General Statutes. Retrieved from https://portal.ct.gov/SDE/English-Learners/Bilingual-Education/Regulations.

DeMatthews, D. E. & Izquierdo, E. (2017). The importance of principals supporting dual language education: A social justice leadership framework. *Journal of Latinos and Education*, published online, 1–18.

Gándara, P., Maxwell-Jolly, J., & Driscoll, A. (2005). *Listening to teachers of English language learners: A survey of California teachers' challenges, experiences, and professional development needs.* Berkeley, CA: Joint Publications, University of California Linguistic Minority Research Institute, UC Berkeley.

Glaser, B. G., & Strauss, A. L. (1999). *The discovery of grounded theory: Strategies for qualitative research.* New York: Aldine de Gruyter.

Gross, N. (2016). *Dual language programs on the rise across the U.S.* Blog: Latino Ed Beat. Educator Writers Association. Downloaded http://www.ewa.org/blog-latino-ed-beat/dual-language-programs-rise-across-us

Hamayan, E., Genesee, F., & Cloud, N. (2013). *Dual language instruction: From A to Z.* Portsmouth, NH: Heinemann.

Harris, E. A. (2015, October 8). Dual language programs are on the rise, even for native English speakers. *New York Times.* Retrieved online: https://www.nytimes.com/2015/10/09/nyregion/dual-language-programs-are-on-the-rise-even-for-native-english-speakers.html?mcubz=1

Howard, E. R., Lindholm-Leary, K. J., Rogers, D., Olague, N., Medina, J., Kennedy, B., … Christian, D. (2018). *Guiding principles for dual language education* (3rd ed.). Washington, DC: Center for Applied Linguistics.

Howard, E. R. & Loeb, M. I. (1998). *In their own words: Two-way immersion teachers talk about their professional experiences (Eric digest edo-fl-98-14).* Retrieved from http://www.cal.org/resources/digest/intheirownwords.html

Howard, E. R., & Sugarman, J. (2007). *Realizing the vision of two-way immersion: Fostering effective programs and classrooms.* Washington, DC/McHenry, IL: Center for Applied Linguistics and Delta Systems, Co.

Howard, E. R., Sugarman, J., & Christian, D. (2003). *Trends in two-way immersion education: A review of the research* (Report no. 63). Baltimore, MD: Center for Research on the Education of Students Placed At Risk.

Ingersoll, R. M., & May, H. (2011). *Recruitment, retention and the minority teacher shortage.* Consortium for Policy Research in Education. CPRE Research Report #RR-69.

Johnson, S. M. (2006). *The workplace matters: Teacher quality, retention, and effectiveness.* Washington, DC: National Education Association.

Kennedy, B. (2013). *A qualitative case study of the bilingual teacher shortage in one Texas school district* (Doctoral dissertation). Available from ProQuest Dissertations and Theses database. (UMI No. 3606445).

Lachance, J. (2017). A case study of dual language program administrators: The teachers we need. *NCPEA International Journal of Educational Leadership Preparation, 12*(1), 1–18.

Levine, T. H., Howard, E. R., & Moss, D. M. (Eds.). (2014). *Preparing classroom teachers to succeed with second language learners: Lessons from a faculty learning community.* New York, NY: Routledge.

Lindholm-Leary, K. J. (2001). *Dual-language education.* Avon, UK: Multilingual Matters.

Menken, K. (2017). *Leadership in dual language bilingual education.* Washington, DC: National Dual Language Research Forum.

National Academies of Sciences, Engineering, and Medicine. (2017). *Promoting the educational success of children and youth learning English: Promising futures.* Washington, DC: The National Academies Press. https://doi.org/10.17226/24677

Patton, M. Q. (2015). *Qualitative research and evaluation methods* (4th ed.). Thousand Oaks, CA: Sage.

Roberts, G., Leite, J., & Wade, O. (2017). Monolingualism is the illiteracy of the 21st century. *Hispania, 100*(5), 116–118.

Scanlan, M., & López, F. (2012). ¡Vamos! How school leaders promote equity and excellence for bilingual students. *Educational Administration Quarterly, 48*(4), 583–625.

Steele, J. L., Slater, R. O., Zamaro, G., Miller, T., Li, J., Burkhauser, S., & Bacon, M. (2017). Effects of dual language programs on student achievement: Evidence from lottery data. *American Educational Research Journal, 54*(1), 282S–306S.

Texas Education Code (2012). Chapter 89. Adaptations for special populations. TexReg 3822.

Thomas, J. R. (2017). *English learners: Struggling Connecticut schools ignore a proven path.* Retrieved from https://ctmirror.org/2017/05/22/english-learners-struggling-ct-schools-ignore-a-proven-path/

Thomas, W. P., & Collier, V. P. (2012). *Dual language education for a transformed world.* Albuquerque, NM: Fuente Press.

Implications for the Future

Elena Izquierdo and David E. DeMatthews

Abstract This chapter concludes the book and provides a summary and analysis of the chapters as well as implications for pursuing dual language education. The authors call the readers to recognize that dual language education is a social justice-oriented reform movement grounded in research that can powerfully impact students, educators, families, and communities.

Keywords Dual language education · Social justice · Latinx students · School leadership · District leadership

In this book, contributors described the challenges confronting Latinx students from immigrant families and communities. Legal and historical perspectives revealed how Latinx students have been placed in underfunded schools with Eurocentric, monolingual English curriculum. Many of these schools lack qualified and prepared teachers and administrators. In some instances, the harmful effects of high-stakes accountability and racist ideologies have led to the pushout of Latinx students. This complex and unfortunate history has damaged relationships between public schools and Latinx immigrant communities, families, and students. However, despite these problematic realities, public schools can be transformative and have a significant impact on students and communities. The contributors of this book deeply believe in dual language education not only because it is cognitively rigorous or because bilingualism can place students at an economic advantage as they matriculate and move into the workforce, but also because dual language education is about social justice and creating a more equitable society.

E. Izquierdo
Department of Teacher Education, University of Texas at El Paso, El Paso, TX, USA
e-mail: ielena@utep.edu

D. E. DeMatthews (✉)
Department of Educational Leadership and Policy, University of Texas at Austin, Austin, TX, USA
e-mail: ddematthews@austin.utexas.edu

© The Author(s) 2019
D. E. DeMatthews, E. Izquierdo (eds.), *Dual Language Education: Teaching and Leading in Two Languages*, Language Policy 18, https://doi.org/10.1007/978-3-030-10831-1_14

Creating schools that value the cultural and linguistic diversity of all students cannot be done solely through the efforts of a dedicated teacher or administrator. Instead, as we have shown, dual language requires a new conceptualization about the role of public schools, school districts, school leaders, teachers, and parents. Routines, assumptions, and taken-for-granted assumptions about language, culture, literacy, family and community involvement must shift. Moreover, principals, teachers, and other staff need to not only make this shift, but also develop the skills and competencies necessary to making dual language a reality. Districts can provide tailored and meaningful professional development that is aligned to teacher feedback and best practices described in the literature. Principals, assistant principals, instructional coaches, teacher leaders, and other school-level leaders can create the systems, processes, and school-based policies to provide teachers with the resources, time, and support necessary to making dual language education a reality. Together, districts and school leaders can help transform teaching and learning. To do so, they must turn their attention to the needs of teachers and students.

1 Final Words on Dual Language Education

In the U.S., dual language education is a reform movement grounded in research. Researchers have consistently documented the success of dual language education as the most effective model of bilingual education for English language learners (ELLs) (Lindholm-Leary, 2001; Lindholm-Leary & Block, 2010; Thomas & Collier, 2012). Smaller scale individual and multi-case studies of dual language education implementation have also documented improvements in test scores, parent engagement, and teacher professional learning (Alanís & Rodriguez, 2008; DeMatthews & Izquierdo, 2017, 2018; Freeman, 1996). However, dual language education is not just about students learning a second language. Dual language education is about a paradigm shift in how students are educated and how they experience school. This paradigm shift extends beyond simply learning the Spanish and English languages to learning critical thinking skills in two languages. Dual language education focuses on biliteracy, high academic achievement through two languages, and the advancement of socio-cultural competence. Dual language education, as we view it and as it has been described throughout this book, emphasizes cultural and linguistic diversity. Educators recognize the cultural and linguistic assets students bring to school. School leaders recognize that they must reorganize their schools and their priorities to value their students' assets. When cultural and linguistic diversity are viewed as assets rather than testing liabilities, school leaders and teachers have the power to cultivate positive lifelong attitudes for all languages and cultures within their students. They impact the school climate in powerful ways. We believe that by improving school climate, dual language education can also improve test scores and other traditionally measured indicators of student success, because inclusive and positive classroom and school culture are central to both teacher and student learning (Kraft, Marinell, & Yee, 2016).

Many districts in Texas and across the nation are making the switch from a transitional model of bilingual education to a dual language education model. Amid tough financial times, dual language can be a budget neutral type of change because it creates inclusive classrooms and eliminates small-segregated units with low student-teacher ratios. Moreover, districts already have the bilingual teachers in place and logistically, they are able to change programs from a transitional model to a dual language model. Despite some of the administrative and logistical benefits to dual language education, shifting to dual language education also requires a significant, long-term and critical commitment to foundational transformations that need to happen in the philosophy, knowledges, and skills possessed by teachers and administrators.

Teaching can be divided into four domains: (1) planning and preparation; (2) classroom environment; (3) instruction; and (4) professional responsibilities (Danielson, 2007). Within each of these domains are competencies that promote effective teaching practices. Competencies are the skills and knowledge that enable a teacher to be successful. With traditional teaching competencies in mind, what additional competencies does a dual language teacher need? The answers to this question inform the practices of teachers going from a transitional classroom to a dual language classroom.

Dual language education competencies require a paradigm shift in how both English and the partner language (i.e. Spanish) are valued and viewed. Both languages must be viewed as equally important and as resources for each other. Teachers must also possess the knowledge and skills to systematically bridge and align lessons between both languages (Language 1 (L1) and Language 2 (L2)). Dual language teachers must also be able to:

- Incorporate and integrate speaking, listening, reading and writing in all activities;
- Make bi-directional, cross-linguistic connections;
- Practice holistic biliteracy assessment;
- Monitor progress of biliteracy and academic achievement through both L1/L2; electing quality texts in L1/L2 to include authentic texts, trans-adapted texts and translated texts;
- Cultivate positive identity formation; incorporating social justice into the curriculum;
- Prepare students to live and work together in a diverse world.

As districts and school leaders move into dual language education, they need to consider these competencies to support their teachers through professional development. Both novice and experienced teachers can benefit from ongoing professional development focused on these important dual language education competencies. While these competencies are important, districts and school leaders must also recognize that they must recruit and retain teachers that will be able to adopt a cultural shift in how they view language in the classroom. Recruitment of dual language teachers should include proactively seeking out teachers who already demonstrated awareness and skill in dual language competencies.

For districts that have taken dual language education to scale, such as the El Paso Independent School District, it becomes even more important to use these competencies to evaluate the consistency and continuity across the district. These competencies are the fundamental qualities and features that will contribute to school and overall school district performance. Districts can work with teacher and leader preparation programs to ensure their pipelines are producing educators who are prepared to perform in dual language schools.

2 Now Is the Time for Dual Language Education

The demographics of public schools in the U.S. continue to change as the nation becomes more racially, culturally, and linguistically diverse. At the same time, many states, districts, and schools continue to struggle in their efforts to close racial achievement gaps and provide meaningful learning opportunities for Latinx immigrant students and other racially and culturally diverse students. Racism and racist discourses remain in society and find their ways into public schools. All students suffer when racism and other forms of prejudice are not rooted out of schools and society.

Throughout this book, contributors underscored the benefits of valuing student diversity. They spoke to the multiple ways researchers, educators, and activists have come to believe that dual language education offers one way to close achievement gaps and improve the lives of students. Now is the time for dual language education. The timing is not necessarily perfect. The Great Recession (2007–2012) was a period of economic decline that seriously impacted federal and state funding of public education. Many states, districts, and schools are still recovering. The politics of local school boards, high superintendent turnover rates, and a diversity of political perspectives about language complicate adopting dual language education. Unequal power dynamics between different racial groups and parents of differing financial means might complicate dual language education and cause conflict in communities in the short-term. Of course, teachers and principals have enough new programs, policies, and curricula to implement. Dual language education would require a significant investment of time and energy, which can be draining for busy teachers. Implementation of dual language education will surely be difficult, time consuming, and may even create a short-term dip in test scores before students and schools see the full benefits. Despite these challenges, the time to implement dual language education for all students is now, because Latinx students cannot afford to lose their language and heritage and all students cannot afford to be educated in a country that does not value bilingualism and biculturalism.

For those who have taken the time to read this book and fully consider the experiences of Latinx students and the benefits of dual language education, we ask that you take the next step in making dual language education a reality. If you are a researcher, engage with the existing literature in bilingual education and develop research that can inform best practices for Latinx students and immigrant communities. If you are a district or school-leader, critically consider your curriculum and ask if you are fully preparing your students to meet the assorted needs of the surrounding community as well as a rapidly changing and more diverse world. If you are a teacher, ask if you are valuing your students' unique assets and building on them through instruction. Most importantly, consider dual language education as a way to foster a more inclusive, inquiry-oriented, and socially just school. There will be challenges, but there will also be great rewards. We believe dual language education is the way of the future and we invite you to advance a bilingual, biliterate, and bicultural agenda.

References

Alanís, I., & Rodriguez, M. A. (2008). Sustaining a dual language immersion program: Features of success. *Journal of Latinos and Education, 7*(4), 305–319.

Danielson, C. (2007). *Enhancing professional practice: A framework for teaching.* Alexandria, VA: ASCD.

DeMatthews, D. E., & Izquierdo, E. (2017). Authentic and social justice leadership: A case study of an exemplary principal. *Journal of School Leadership, 27*(3), 333–360.

DeMatthews, D. E., & Izquierdo, E. (2018). Supporting Mexican American immigrant students on the border. A case study of culturally responsive leadership in a dual language elementary school. *Urban Education.* https://doi.org/10.1177/0042085918756715

Freeman, R. D. (1996). Dual-language planning at oyster bilingual school: "Its much more than language". *TESOL Quarterly, 30*(3), 557–582.

Kraft, M. A., Marinell, W. H., & Shen-Wei Yee, D. (2016). School organizational contexts, teacher turnover, and student achievement: Evidence from panel data. *American Educational Research Journal, 53*(5), 1411–1449.

Lindholm-Leary, K., & Block, N. (2010). Achievement in predominantly low SES/Hispanic dual language schools. *International Journal of Bilingual Education and Bilingualism, 13*(1), 43–60.

Lindholm-Leary, K. J. (2001). *Dual language education.* Clevedon, UK: Multilingual Matters.

Thomas, W. P., & Collier, V. P. (2012). *Dual language education for a transformed world.* Albuquerque, NM: Dual Language Education of New Mexico/Fuente Press.